WORKING WITH NEWS IN PRINT

William L. Rivers
STANFORD UNIVERSITY

Marion Lewenstein
STANFORD UNIVERSITY

The Poynter Institute For Media Studies

HARPER & ROW, PUBLISHERS, New York
Cambridge, Philadelphia, San Francisco,
London, Mexico City, São Paulo, Sydney

Sponsoring Editor: Phillip Leininger
Project Editor: Rita Williams
Designer: Dawn Stanley/Madalyn Hart
Production: Marion Palen/Delia Tedoff
Compositor: ComCom Division of Haddon Craftsmen, Inc.
Printer and Binder: R.R. Donnelley & Sons Company
Art Studio: Jay's Publishers Services, Inc.

WORKING WITH NEWS IN PRINT: Practices in Writing and Reporting

Copyright © 1984 by William L. Rivers and Marion Lewenstein

All rights reserved. Printed in the United States of America. No part of this book may be used or reproduced in any manner whatsoever without written permission, except in the case of brief quotations embodied in critical articles and reviews. For information address Harper & Row, Publishers, Inc., 10 East 53d Street, New York, NY 10022.

Library of Congress Cataloging in Publication Data

Rivers, William L.
    Working with news in print.

    1. Journalism. I. Lewenstein, Marion, 1927–
II. Title.
PN4775.R47   1984   070   83-13004
ISBN 0-06-045423-7

Contents

Preface v

Chapter 1
NEWSPAPER STYLE AND FORMAT 1

Chapter 2
NEWSPAPER FORM AND SENTENCE STRUCTURE 18

Chapter 3
WHAT MAKES NEWS? 41

Chapter 4
NEWSPAPER LEADS 52

Chapter 5
CONTINUING THE NEWS STORY 66

Chapter 6
INTERVIEWING AND OBSERVING 83

Chapter 7
CREATING COLOR IN NEWS STORIES 94

Chapter 8
FEATURE STORIES 108

Chapter 9
COMPLETING THE NEWS 121

Chapter 10
SPEECHES, MEETINGS, AND NEWS CONFERENCES 131

Chapter 11
STORIES FROM ANNOUNCEMENTS 146

Chapter 12
REWRITES AND PRESS RELEASES 155

Chapter 13
CRIME AND ACCIDENTS 177

Chapter 14
REPORTS AND NUMBERS 190

Chapter 15
THE NEWSPAPER-MAGAZINE OF THE FUTURE 201

Appendix A
AP STYLEBOOK (ABBREVIATED) 219

Appendix B
GLOSSARY OF NEWSPAPER TERMS 242

Preface

We have written *Working with News In Print* for the student with little prior experience who seeks real world practice in writing and reporting for the print media. We have sought to be particularly attentive to the impact of changing styles within the print media while covering the relevant on-the-job fundamentals in the carefully sequenced text and exercises.

Note especially the number of exercises. Students completing all of them successfully should emerge capable of coping with a beginning reporting job. The exercises are equally appropriate for use in a classroom or for use as take-home assignments to simulate or supplement journalistic experience. They cover a wide range of journalistic skills—writing, gathering information, interpreting and using numbers accurately, assessing news, organizing news, and meeting the ethical responsibilities of news reporting and writing. Simple, direct instructions precede each exercise and provide students with a quick review before they prepare their assignment. The exercises present increasingly difficult problems and tactics, and progress to writing story "brights" and magazine-style features. We include quick reviews of spelling and usage, an abbreviated Associated Press Stylebook, and a glossary of newspaper terms in an appendix.

Because this is primarily a workbook, the chapter material before the exercises is sometimes rather short. Teachers with wide experience may wish to use this text to supplement their own lessons. This workbook may also be used to accompany Rivers's *News in Print: Writing and Reporting,* or any other reporting and writing text.

While we have drawn upon our own field experience, we wish to thank particularly Mark Stephens and Rusty Todd, both of whom have contributed many of the exercises. John Austin, Don Dodson, John Durham, Linda Peterson, Diana Tillinghast, Jay Thorwaldson, and Charles Whitney have also contributed some of the exercises. We would also like to thank our many colleagues who reviewed this book during its developmental stages.

WILLIAM L. RIVERS
MARION LEWENSTEIN

Chapter 1

Newspaper Style and Format

Before starting to write news stories, you should understand what happens to the copy you produce. You gather facts, impressions, ideas, and write. What happens then? Someone edits. What do they do?

Because you should proofread and mark the stories you write just as the editor does, you should learn the commonly used editing marks and news story format from the beginning. In class, of course, your instructor may pose as a copy editor—and is likely to make even further marks. If you learn copy editing marks now, you will save the almost endless time ordinarily expended on explaining what the marks mean.

First, in simplified form, here is the news story format:

Leave a margin of about 1 inch

Marianne Smith   -2-
Carter Speech (repeat slug on each page)

  Use only one side of each page. Check each fact you write, and be especially careful about your grammar and spelling. Start all pages except the first just below the slug.

  At the end of the story, use -30- or the mark, #, and circle it.)

-30-

3 NEWSPAPER STYLE AND FORMAT

You will also need to use these copy editing marks:

Paragraph indent

Run it in

with connecting line

Join words: week end

Insert a *single* word or phrase

Insert mising letter

Take out onne letter

Transpose elements two

Transpose wto letters

Make this Lower Case

Capitalize dallas

Abbreviate street

Spell out abbrev.

Make twelve figures

Separate twowords

Join let ters in word

Write in period

Insert comma

Take out some word

Don't make this correction (stet)

Mark centering like this

4 NEWSPAPER STYLE AND FORMAT

```
Do not obliterate
  copy; mark it out with
  a thin line so it can
  be compared with
  editing
```

Chapter 1 Exercises

Become accustomed to reading these "remember" notes before doing the exercises in each chapter. They highlight the important points covered in each section.

Remember:

1. The task of an editor is all-important. That is why we begin this first chapter by noting the importance of learning editing symbols and format.
2. Memorize the format of news stories so you can focus on the story rather than thinking about the form of typing.
3. Memorize the copy editing marks. Knowing what the symbols mean can save you many minutes of worrying about them.

Exercise 1.1

Read carefully the following story. As you can see, it illustrates some of the material you have learned from the preceding pages. Also, read the abbreviated AP-UPI Stylebook (Appendix A) before writing your first story.

⟦The Roxbury Construction (Company) has been awarded the   1

largest building contract ever granted a minority firm in   2

federal school construction history.   3

⟦The contract for $1,575,500 was announced *Monday* ~~yesterday~~ by the   4

~~US~~ *U.S.* Department of Health, Education and Welfare and the Small   5

Business Administration. It will finance an addition to the   6

(Fort) Devens elementary school.   7

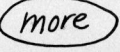

5   EXERCISE 1.1

¶ The building project will begin around November 1st. Its completion is set for Sept. of next year.

¶ The contract to the Roxbury firm was granted through a special SBA program which allows government agencies to negotiate contracts with firms owned by minority persons and other disadvantaged businessmen.

¶ Marshall Parker, associate administrator of the SBA in Washington, D.C., said the program is intended "to use government procurement to get minorities and other disadvantaged into the economic mainstream."

The program, known as the 8-A "set aside" effort, was created 3 years ago, said Parker. Since then, more than 2000 contracts valued at almost $100 million have been signed with minority firms across the country.

The New England region, the smallest in the country, "barely did $1 million worth" of business through the program last year, according to Parker. "By June 30 we expect to hit the $6.5 millon level," he said.

Contracts worth that have gone to eighty minority firms throughout New England.

Most were granted to provide services at military operations.

line 1   abbreviate word *company*
line 3   capitalize word *federal*

6 NEWSPAPER STYLE AND FORMAT

line 4	this sentence should be indented for a new paragraph Substitute the proper day of week for word *yesterday*
line 5	insert periods in *US*
line 7	abbreviate word *Fort* capitalize words *elementary school*
line 8	*November* should be abbreviated
line 9	change word *first* to arabic number 1 spell out *Sept.*
line 14	spell out *assoc.* Should read *associate*
line 15	insert D.C. after *Washington*
line 17	quote marks go outside the period
line 18	insert quote marks after word *aside*. Should read *set aside*
line 19	change *said Parker* to *Parker said;* change *3* to *three*
line 20	insert comma in *2000* change *$100,000,000* to *$100 million*
lines 22–28	complete these instructions as though you were the author

Exercise 1.2 *Edit this story using the conventional copy editing symbols. Do not attempt to rearrange or rewrite the story. Then check the changes in the list of corrections following the story.*

The first of twofire fighters have been hired in   1

Palo Alto as a result of a circuit court decision which   2

requires depts. to hire from a statewide civil service list.   3

William A. Hughes, 21, 1204 Roosevelt Rd., and Stephen   4

P. Choate of Brewster have been hired. Choate is a Stanford Student.   5

Hughes is a newcomer to P. A. He grew up in   6

xxxxxxx Dallas, Texas, and finds the move to this area not an   7

easy transition.

Choate is a senior in Electrical Engineering at Stanford.   9

He has worked summers as a Life Guard at Virginia Beach,   10

near Norfolk, Virginia. His step father is Police Chief in   11

7 EXERCISE 1.2

Brewster. Choate's wife, Nancy, is a Key Punch operator with   12

Pacific Telephone co. here.   13

    The city had expected to appeal the Court's decision,   14

but last week Robert Orr, the city's legal Adviser, and   15

members of city council decided against appeal. Orr said the   16

City will hire 4 more firefighters within the next thirty days.   17

    We'll abide by the courts decision" Orr said monday.   18

line 1	make *fire fighter* one word
	separate words *two* and *fire*
line 2	words *circuit court* should be capitalized
line 3	spell out *depts.*
	state wide should be hyphenated
	capitalize words *civil service*
line 4	insert word *of* after 21 and before 1204
	word *Rd.* should be spelled out
line 5	lower case *s* in word *student*
line 6	spell out *Palo Alto*
line 7	use your copy pencil to further obliterate the x'd out material at beginning of line
	Texas should be abbreviated
	put opening quote mark before the word *not*
line 8	put closing quote mark after word *transition*
line 9	lowercase *Electrical Engineering*
line 10	lowercase *Life Guard*
line 11	*Virginia* should be abbreviated
	step father should be closed up
	lowercase *Police Chief*
line 12	lower case *Key Punch*
line 13	capitalize *co*
line 14	lower case *Court's*
line 15	lower case *Adviser*
line 17	arabic figure *4* should be spelled out
	thirty should be an arabic figure
line 18	put opening quote mark before word *We'll*
	word *courts* should read *court's:* Insert apostrophe
	insert comma after word *decision*
	capitalize word *monday*

8   NEWSPAPER STYLE AND FORMAT

— place an end mark at the bottom of the copy
— mark all paragraphs

Exercise 1.3   *Indicate which of the following words or phrases should be capitalized.*

1. secretary of state ted brown
2. ted brown, secretary of state
3. ambassador henry cabot lodge
4. henry cabot lodge, ambassador
5. david williams, defense attorney
6. defense attorney david williams
7. republic of korea
8. u.s. senate
9. ohio legislature
10. legislature
11. house ways and means committee
12. subcommittee of the ohio house
13. the legislature adopted the strip mining bill.
14. ohio real estate commission
15. the commission's chairman recently resigned.
16. air force
17. hurricane zelda
18. good friday, black history week, lent, passover
19. middle west
20. rain is expected in western ohio.
21. democratic party
22. do you identify with a major political party?
23. england has a democratic form of government.
24. caucasian, white, negro, black
25. franklin county courthouse.
26. boeing 707 jet

EXERCISE 1.3

27. peace rose
28. paris green
29. koran
30. devil and hell

Write the abbreviations for the following words or phrases. Note that some words cannot be abbreviated.

1. Eastern Daylight Time
2. absent without official leave
3. Brown & Company, Incorporated
4. versus
5. Georgia
6. Kansas
7. Kentucky
8. Louisiana
9. Maryland
10. Missouri
11. Montana
12. Nebraska
13. North Carolina
14. Oklahoma
15. Oregon
16. Pennsylvania
17. Texas
18. Vermont
19. Virginia
20. West Virginia
21. Alaska
22. Maine
23. Utah
24. Iowa
25. Idaho
26. Alaska
27. Lieutenant Governor John Brown
28. Professor Paul V. Peterson
29. State Senator Ted Gray
30. Governor John J. Gilligan
31. association
32. treasurer
33. Christmas
34. port
35. detective
36. October 1971
37. October 12, 1971
38. Mount Everest
39. Mount Vernon
40. Chief Warrant Officer (Army)
41. Sergeant First Class (Army)
42. Private First Class (Army)
43. Airman 1st Class (Air Force)
44. Commander (Navy, Coast Guard)

10 NEWSPAPER STYLE AND FORMAT

Indicate which of the following words or phrases should be abbreviated.

1. Fred lives at Sixteen East Seventy-second Street in Columbus, Ohio.
2. Darwin lives on Fifth Avenue in New York.
3. Suzanne lives at Ten Hickory Place Northwest in Ann Arbor, Michigan.
4. United States Junior Chamber of Commerce.
5. United Nations World Health Organization.
6. The Japanese Emperor visited the United States.

Punctuate the following sentences.

1. A delegation from Montgomery Ala met with the governors press secretary.
2. John is taking chemistry psychology English and math this quarter
3. The Ohio Bombshell the favorite easily won the fifth race.
4. Holton Joseph Wolcott Jr
5. Elected were the following John J. Delino president David Bett vice president Samuel Kanto secretary and Dale Darwen treasurer

How would you write the following?

1. 3,300,000 dollars
2. 330,000 dollars
3. 3,330,000 dollars
4. Lenore, six months old
5. Lassie, is 4 years old
6. seventeen mile trip

Mark the following true or false.

_____ A rule of thumb is not to abbreviate any state having six or fewer letters, except Texas.

_____ A long title should precede a person's name.

_____ News stories should never identify anyone by race.

_____ Days of the week should be abbreviated.

EXERCISE 1.4

_____ The titles of books, plays, hymns, poems, and songs should be capitalized and put in quotes.

_____ Lowercase abbreviations usually need periods.

_____ Abbreviate March, April, May, June, and July only in tabular or financial material.

_____ The names of organizations, firms, agencies, groups, etc., should be spelled out on first mention.

_____ Newspaper usage has, in most cases, eliminated the comma before *and* and *or* in a series.

Exercise 1.4

Correct the following sentences.

1. Mr. Thomas Shaw will speak at a Lions Club meeting Thursday afternoon at 4:00 P.M.

2. Captain Thomas Cunningham of Monroe, North Carolina, was stationed in Viet Nam for 3 years.

3. Four men robbed the nine year-old boy of ten dollars yesterday at 5:00 P.M.

4. According to Dr. Derek Bok, President of Harvard University, the auditorium will accomodate about 10 thousand persons.

5. About 20 percent of the murders committed in Kansas City are done with knives, according to Capt. Harry Snipes, Chief of the City's detectives.

6. Executive Vice President of the Bank of America George Jones said he had "no argument with the decision".

7. A bus, ten automobiles, and two trucks were involved in the collision.

8. Mrs. Elizabeth Smith, widow of the late Mr. David P. Smith, is an employee of the bank.

9. Senator Strom Thurmond (D.- S. C.) spoke to the group on Mar. 22, 1980.

10. Defense Attorney John Abelson lives at 2121 Middlefield Rd., Minneapolis.

11. Lawmen from 21 states will convene a three-day conference Friday in Ft. Worth, Texas.

12 NEWSPAPER STYLE AND FORMAT

Exercise 1.5

There are no more than two errors in any item below, and there may be less than two. Correct them.

1. Six atheletes set new records at the state high school track meet in Los Angeles.

2. Defense Attorney Gavin Bates met briefly with Dist. Atty. William Stilwell Monday. The meeting concerned disclosure of evidence for the forthcoming Welby trial.

3. The controversy surrounding the placement of a U.S. electronic surveillance unit on the Sinai Penninsula continues in Congress.

4. Winston tastes good, like a cigaret should.

5. The member ship is comprised of representatives from labor, political, religious, and business groups. In a meeting Friday, members were unable to reach a concensus on the busing issue, and presiding officer Agnes Blanchard said no statement would be released.

6. Mrs. Mildred Waites, widow of the late Dr. John Waites, suffered a second tragedy late Wednesday. Her nine-year-old daughter Phoebe drowned in the Pacific near Santa Cruz.

7. Brig. Gen. Walter Porter is to be the keynote speaker of the first annual convention of the Little Lads' Marching Club. The convention begins at 8 tonight.

8. Chief of Police, Jack Bailey, said 34 persons were injured in the derailment. The accident ocurred when a railway employe failed to throw a switch.

9. Mildred Douglas, assistant vice president for sales, absconded with almost $3 million in negotiable checks, according to police reports.

10. Volume on the New York Stock exchange was down, with less than 13 million shares traded.

11. "The principle component in the new system," Addams said, "is a CDC 6600 computer, which increases our ability to process data by 100 per cent".

12. Leypoldt, who said he found the incident "profoundly embarassing," left the meeting early, he later apologized to Wilson and Browning.

13. The kidnaping of Miss Falacci, the attractive red-headed daughter of Rome Industrialist Bruno Falacci, was Italy's 65th reported abduction this year.

14. None of those present were able to give details of the explosion, which completely destroyed the house. However, Jerry Lynn, a Berkeley pharmacist, said he saw a brilliant light and heard a noice "like a clap of thunder."

15. Caton said that although the F.B.I. reports showed some improvement in the rate of increase in violent crimes, the data are misleading.

16. Charles Dillon (Casey) Stengel, died late Monday after a serious illness recently diagnosed as cancer. Stengel, 85, was a major league baseball manager for 25 years.

17. The Phillippines is predominately a Catholic nation with a small Muslim population. The people here seem to enjoy Ali's antics, but they seem to respect Frazier more.

18. The boy told the reporter, almost in tears, "you should have seen it.

Exercise 1.6

There are 20 errors in this story; edit to indicate them. Pay attention to the meaning of words.

A Hollywood actor died and an Army private was arrested for robbery after a freak auto accident in Gainesville yesterday.

Pablo O'Brien, 27, a 1972 alumna of Princeton who reached the epitome of his career with an oscar nomination last year, died after suddenly collapsing shortly after a pickup sheered off the left front of his convertible at El Camino Real and Embarcadero streets.

Gainesville police arrested the other driver, Neil Olafson, 21, of Ft. Ord, for the Thursday theft of $20,000 in jewelry from the empty Jeffrey Seaton estate. The Seatons are vacationing in Europe.

Detective David Shidaka said the Olafson vehicle was crossing the intersection, eastbound on University Avenue, when the left front tire blew out. Olafson attempted to try and eliminate the accident but his pickup careened into the southbound lane and collided with the O'Brien car. O'Brien had stopped as the light turned red.

Shidaka said O'Brien appeared uninjured at first but fell prostate just after police arrived. The trooper of more than 20 movies began hemorrhaging and minutes later was pronounced dead at the scene.

Olafson was arrested after police spotted a 24-caret diamond ring and four pedants on the truck seat. They matched the description of the missing jewelry.

Alachua County Superior Court Judge James Sterling refused to accept the private's guilty plea Thursday.

Although the present incumbent is known for handing down stiff sentences to people who flaunt the law, he instead ordered that a qualified expert conduct a psychiatric examination.

Services for the cowboy star will be at 10 a.m. in St. James Church in Gainesville. Internment will follow.

Exercise 1.7

Edit the following stories. It is not necessary to make substantial changes except in cases of redundancies.

STORY 1

The nine-year-old boy was riding his ten-speed bycicle near Eighty-seventh St. and Saint Andrews Rd. at 10:00 a.m. on Tuesday, Sept. 16

15 EXERCISE 1.7

An ordinary street scene, it seemed-except that the boy was not in school and he "Had a bulge in his pocket". The bulge turned out to be a loaded 32-caliber, nickle platedpistil with a two inch barrel.

Along with the gun, two police offiers of the Los Angeles Police Department (L.A.P.D.) 77th division confiscated a set of Japanese-made handcuffs, 35 dollars in cash, and two 38-cal. bulllets.

The pistol was only one of 29 guns taken into custody that day by the LAPD's seventeen patrol divisions throughout the city of nearly three million persons.

STORY 2

Waldport, Oregon—Autoroities are instigating reports that about twenty persons have sold their property, and left the area since a meeting last month with a man who claimed to represent beings from outer space.

Sherriff's detective Ron Sutton said Sunday the had recieved reports about a man who sold his $5000 fishing boat for $5.00 and of a new van that was given away.

"one hippie is said to have given away his guiatar" Sutton said, "to him, that meant every thing.

About three hundred persons attended the meeting September 14 at a motel in this coastal hamlet of 800.

The Manager of the Bayshore Inn, George Thompson siad he was paid fifty dollars for the use of the meeting room, but knew little about the renter.

16 NEWSPAPER STYLE AND FORMAT

STORY 3

COPENHAGEN (AP)—More than 500 paratroops and other special units lead by SS Captain Otto Skorzeny were ready in 1942 to fly from a German airfield in Poland in order to kidnap Societ Dictator Josef Stalin from the dremlin, a Danish newspaper said Sunday.

Fifteen planes were to land the troops inside the walls of the Kremlin in the blitz kidnapping oerpation, the newspaper "Berlingske Tidende" reported.

STORY 4

BUENOS AIRES (AP)—A band of Leftist Argentine guerrilas raided a provincial army garrisson Sunday and were then evacuated by comrads in a highjacked jet liner, according to Government sources.

The Army said that at least fifteen guerrilas, and eleven security officers were killed.

Security sources and the official Telam news agency said that more than fifty Montomero guerrilas attaccted an infantary garrisson in Formosa, a small provisncial capitol 575 mi. North of here.

They were baeten back by soldiers and police in bloody fighting.

Exercise 1.8

Make all the necessary copy editor's marks. When you notice redundant or useless words, eliminate them.

The function of the copyeditor is critikal not creative. In no Circomstances should he totally rewrite a story completely. If it cannot be saved except by being rewritten, that work should bedone by a rewrite man or by the man who wrote the original story.

17   EXERCISE 1.8

The desk man must cope with the material that is give him and make the mostof that material by recasting, striking out superfluous words, substituting active or colorful words for dead ones, expressing a word in a phrase and by variou s other similar means. The finished product should concise forceful, complete. This should be the copy editors aim with every story, note mearly the impo tant ones. A great story virt ally tells itself; it is the bief ones That most often are allowed to slip b y with only a few strokes of the pencil to indicate, that they have been read. Any story can be improved even though the editing consis of transposing a word, shifting a puncaution mark, substituting a concrea word for a general, or an an10-Saxon verb for a Latin. Leaving unaltered 1 word that should be changed is not a trivial matter. The care ful copyeditor leaves nothing at all to chance. his object is not only to correct errors, but also to improve.

Reporters profess to regard the copyeditor as a multilater of good copy. Actually, the aimm of the copydesk is to perserve as far as possiblethe words of the reporter, if they express what desires he to convey, and to retain the spirit imparted by him, if it is proper.

The desk man should recognize and retain the merrits of a story gi to him to edit, the reporter should realise that the copy editor often saves him from g grave mistakes and generally improves his work in many

Chapter 2 Newspaper Form and Sentence Structure

Although newspapers are changing with the times, one basic element will remain for many years. It is illustrated below:

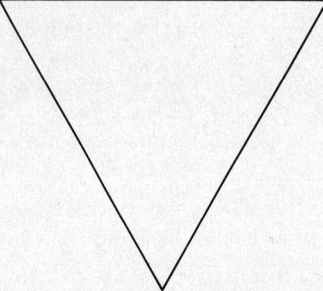

The Inverted Pyramid

    The illustration is useful because of the analogy: The base of the pyramid is the broadest and strongest, and so it is with the news story. Use first the most important facts you can find. In the succeeding sentences use the next most important facts, then the next most important, and so on. By the time you reach the end of the story, you should be writing the least important details.

    Why do it this way? First, think of the readers. Very few—if any—read the entire newspaper, and perhaps less than half of your readers have the time or the inclination to read all of your story. Remember, you are competing with other reporters who are also writing stories. Together, you and the other reporters are supplying the newspaper with dozens of stories. A reader may ask what he should read. If you can state the most important fact first—and compellingly—you will have a chance to capture many readers.

Second, think of the copy editors. Each story must compete with hundreds of others. If the story itself is important, almost every word of it may be used. However, on a busy news day, your story may be cut from the bottom by the copy editor. In such a case, if your story runs 15 paragraphs, it may be printed in, say, 3 paragraphs. Your story is complete—provided you take care in fashioning the beginning of the story.

In the next chapter, you will learn how to write the first few paragraphs of straight news stories. In the succeeding chapters, you will find other story forms. For the rest of this chapter, focus on simplicity, conciseness, and drama.

Simplicity and Conciseness

In thinking how to write for a newspaper, you should know what the late Ernest Hemingway—who began as a reporter for the *Kansas City Star*—said: "The first and most important thing of all, at least for writers today, is to strip language clean, to lay it bare down to the bone." Although he left the *Star* to become a short story writer and novelist—and became a Nobel Prize laureate—he continued preaching that writing style. Simplicity. You should always strive to use language simply.

Words and Phrases

How? First, think of the words you're using. Are you writing "the city of Minneapolis"? Why "the city of"? "Minneapolis" says the same and saves three words. Are you writing "the sum of $10"? Why not write "$10"? Again, you save three words. Also, consider the words in the left column below, then the words in the right column. The left and right say the same thing.

past history	history
an oblong shape	oblong
completely decapitated	decapitated
canary bird	canary
collie dog	collie
start off	start
invited guests	guests
the year of 1967	1967
old adage	adage
entirely unique	unique
old traditions of the past	traditions
lift up	lift
in a dying condition	dying
future plans	plans

20 NEWSPAPER FORM AND SENTENCE STRUCTURE

the hour of noon	noon
Easter Sunday	Easter
first of all	first
consensus of opinion	consensus
none at all	none
two twins	twins
complete monopoly	monopoly
winter months	winter
new recruit	recruit
present incumbent	incumbent
in the meantime	meanwhile
close proximity	proximity
large-sized	large
made out of iron	iron
reported to the effect that	reported
actual fact	fact
finished up	finished
seem to be	seem
the subject of charity	charity

Plain language is central in good writing. When you are choosing simple terms that reflect a clear image, make that image as specific as you can. Don't settle for *house* when you mean *cottage,* or *bungalow,* or *mansion,* or *shack.* Don't use *businessman* when you mean *salesman,* or *bank officer,* or *shopkeeper,* or *promoter,* or *tycoon.* Don't write *idea* when you mean *insight, argument, decision,* or *deduction.*

When you are writing a news story, you may reach for words that sound like good substitutes for *say* or *said.* If you have a sense of language, you may become tired of quoting someone, and then tacking on the same tired words. So you may vary attribution, choosing *mention* or *declare* or *assert.* You may be right, but carefully study the following list of the synonyms of *say* and their meanings:

say	express in words
remark	express casually
mention	express in pausing
comment	express with interpretation
declare	express in a formal or public way
state	express clearly and definitely
aver	express with confidence
maintain	express with conviction
assert	express boldly on the basis of personal authority or conviction
allege	assert without proof

21 SIMPLICITY AND CONCISENESS

affirm	declare as true
charge	accuse formally
claim	demand as right
explain	make plain something not known or clearly understood
relate	give account of something experienced
report	give a public account
announce	declare for the first time
reveal	uncover as if drawing away a veil
disclose	make known what has been secret or private
divulge	disclose an impropriety or surprising fact
point out	refer to an undisputed fact

Sentences In writing, think of the following sentences written by a reporter:

> Educators throughout the state will keep close tabs on a unique experiment as six northern California counties try to establish a joint vocational school district.
> One of the aims of the ambitious venture, which will offer vocational programs that are not currently available at the high schools the students now attend, will be to act as a deterrent to the dropout problem besetting schools in the area.

Do those seem like good sentences? Perhaps. But if you pay close attention to what the reporter is saying, you can say exactly the same thing in these words:

> California educators will keep close tabs as six northern California counties try to establish a joint vocational district.
> One of the aims of the venture, which will offer vocational programs unavailable at the high schools the students attend, will be a deterrent to the dropout problem.

If you choose the latter, you save 20 words. Is that a remarkable feat? It certainly is. Think of the readers this way: They may be in a hurry and don't have time to read as many words as the first example contains. Also, it could be that the longer the sentence, the less likely the readers will understand.

You should also think of what Theodore Bernstein, the former assistant managing editor of the *New York Times,* wrote in a critique about the august *Times:*

> If in a single night each of 40 copy editors saved only a line in each of, say, 10 stories, the total savings would be almost two columns. Is that piddling? The idea here is not to destroy the writer's style, but rather to be alert to word-saving locutions.

Think of word-saving locutions in reading the following sentence written by a student:

> Throwing modesty aside, he claims to be the world's greatest musician.

The instructor deleted the first three words, reasoning that the rest of the sentence makes it clear that the musician threw modesty aside. The student argued that, because the sentences immediately before and after the edited sentence were short and in a subject-verb, subject-verb pattern, the deletion destroyed the balance of the passage. One cheer for the student. But only one cheer. Sentences must be balanced with substance, not ballast. You should take a hard lesson from that: Balance passages by using different sentence structure, not sentences carrying dead words.

What should you do with the following sentence?

> The past experiences of future prospects for employment in Jacksonville were brought out in interviews that were conducted throughout the entire day of June 12 in the year of 1979.

In contrast, that sentence should be written:

> The experiences of the prospects for employment in Jacksonville were related in interviews conducted on June 12, 1979.

Also be careful in using adjectives. Voltaire, a great writer, said: "An adjective is the enemy of the noun." Although Voltaire exaggerated his point, it's basically true if you're a beginning writer. A professional reporter wrote this sentence, trying to describe how a rich man protected the wealth of his company:

> An elaborate and payrolled watchdog system was set to safeguard his interests, should any ambitiously piratical executive attempt a personal seduction of organizational assets.

This is a bad sentence for many reasons, especially because the reader must work to determine exactly what it means. The most obvious flaw is that the sentence is drunk with adjectives. The force of each is reduced because the reader must give his attention first to one adjective, then to another. The nouns are almost submerged by their enemies.

In most cases, the adjective is the enemy of the noun. If you must use an adjective, search for the right one—usually *only* one. The major message is simple: Be concise. Sir Ernest Gowers, author of *Plain Words,* makes the point this way:

23 SIMPLICITY AND CONCISENESS

Use no more words than are necessary to express your meanings, for if you use more you are likely to obscure it and to tire your reader. In particular, do not use superfluous adjectives. (*Source:* Sir Ernest Gowers, *Plain Words.* London: Her Majesty's Stationery Office, p. 13)

Stories

The student who wrote the news story in the right column for his college paper objected to the edited version, with its many deleted words:

EDITED VERSION	ORIGINAL VERSION
Time is running out for the world. Our technological advances may destroy us, warned Barbara Ward.	The world is at a time this year where time is running out. The world cannot long stand the problems caused by its technological advances, predicted Barbara Ward.
Miss Ward, the 56-year-old English economist, author of the widely known book *The Lopsided World,* spoke before a capacity crowd in the Art Auditorium Friday on "A World Out of Balance."	Barbara Ward, the 56-year-old English-born economist and author of the well-known book *The Lopsided World,* spoke before a packed Art Auditorium Friday on the subject "A World Out of Balance."
Technological advances are causing a widening gulf between the "developed" nations and the "developing" nations. Persons she deemed "wasteful, filthy, and unconcerned" are overloading the environment.	Society's technological advances of late are causing the imbalance in two main areas: It is (1) causing a widening gulf between the "developed" nations and the "developing nations." (2) causing an overloading of the world's environment by persons she deemed as "wasteful, filthy, and unconcerned."
Miss Ward said that the developed nations try to get everything for "us," and later think of "them." The unconcerned have. . . .	In respect to problem (1) Barbara Ward said that the thought of the developed nations is get everything for "us," and afterward think about "them." The unconcerned have. . . .

The student argued that the editing ruined the balance and rhythm of his sentences. The editor countered that although a straight news story should provide a reasonably balanced and rhythmic collection of sentences, its first purpose is to give information. Instead of expecting news stories to provide the pleasant reading experience they expect from feature stories, most readers seek facts from straight news. Moreover, the editor argued, even in a judgment of balance and rhythm, the edited version was better. Although the sentence structure of the original is a bit more varied, variation is achieved at the cost of useless and awkward repetitions.

The editor was right. Although repetition can occasionally be used to good effect, using "time" twice in the first sentence is graceless, and "the world" is used at the beginning of each of the first two sentences to no purpose.

Note that in the second paragraph of the original version the writer says that Barbara Ward spoke "on the subject." To write that she spoke "on" says the same thing in two less words. Using two extra words is not a crime, of course, but a writer who does not know to delete such phrases is quite likely to do what this one did: use so many unneeded words in the next paragraph ("Society's," "of late," "causing . . . causing . . . causing," and others) that the reader must work to gather information.

Overwriting Sentences

Don't be so concerned with avoiding sentence fragments that you overwrite sentences. Here is an example of a hopelessly convoluted, yet grammatical, sentence from Lewis Carroll's *Alice's Adventures in Wonderland:*

> "I quite agree with you," said the Duchess, "and the moral of that is—'Be what you seem to be'—or if you'd like to put it more simply—'Never imagine yourself not to be otherwise than what it might appear to others that what you were or might have been was not otherwise than what you had been would have appeared to them to be otherwise.'"
> "I think I should understand that better," Alice said very politely, "if I had it written down; but I can't quite follow it as you say it."

Alice was wrong. If the duchess had written down her sentence, Alice would have vainly puzzled over the meaning for hours.

Run-on sentences like the duchess's result from punctuating two sentences as though they were one. Here is a *fused sentence,* which is one of the two kinds of run-on sentences:

> She placed the television set in her bedroom she watched it every night from January to March.

Read that sentence aloud. As you can hear, there's a full stop after *bedroom,* which means that a period should have been used.

The second kind of run-on sentence is the *comma splice:*

> The president spoke at length, later he said he regretted speaking so long.

In this case, the writer is attempting to have a comma join two sentences. But with a bit of rewriting the writer could have had:

1. A comma: Although the president spoke at length, he said later that he regretted speaking so long.
2. A period: The president spoke at length. Later he regretted speaking so long.
3. A semicolon: The president spoke at length; however, later he regretted speaking so long.

Dangling Modifiers

To understand dangling modifiers, read the following sentence:

Having little reason, the questions had to be guesswork.

As you can judge, the sentence seems to say that the questions had little reason. The sentence structure is faulty because the phrase *having little reason* has no word to modify. Now read the problem sentence after correction:

Having little reason, she was led to guess at the proper questions.

Here is another example of a dangling modifier:

A rock concert is a bad place to be, when unsettled in mind.

This sentence seems to say that the rock concert is unsettled in mind. After revising the sentence, it reads:

A rock concert is a bad place to be when one is unsettled in mind.

Misplaced Modifiers

You should always keep the modifier and the word modified together to prevent the reader's confusion. For example, read the following sentence:

A 10-page statement has been received that the Jacksonville port harbor has been polluted by the Jacksonville Port Harbor Commission.

The writer meant "by the Jacksonville Port Harbor Commission" to modify "received," not "polluted." The writer should have written the sentence this way:

A 10-page statement declaring that the Jacksonville harbor has been polluted has been received by the Jacksonville Port Harbor Commission.

Faulty Parallelism

Elements of the same rank in a sentence should be expressed in parallel structure. For example, read the following sentence:

She likes to walk, to run, and swimming.

This sentence is not parallel. It can be corrected this way:

She likes *to walk, to run,* and *to swim.*

The italicized words give each verb in the sentence a similar form.
Read the following sentence:

Last night Bob talked of his vacation and what he planned to do.

This sentence is not parallel. The problem sentence can be corrected in this way:

Last night Bob talked of his vacation and his plans.

Vague References

Pronouns occur in our speech more frequently than any other words except articles and conjunctions (*a, the, and, but,* and so forth) and forms of the verbs *to be* and *to have.* We use pronouns so lavishly in order to avoid the monotonous repetition of the same noun in a series of related sentences. The pronouns also offer the convenience of a kind of shorthand, in which a "they," for example, can be substituted for a whole string of names or objects, or in which an "it" can express an action or process that originally required several words for its description.

The primary problem with pronouns is their tendency toward *vague reference.* Pronouns often are used in ways which do not make a clear reference to an antecedent noun (*antecedent* means "going before"). The following sentences include examples of pronouns that leave some uncertainty as to the particular antecedent nouns they refer to:

Unclear   John wrote to Bill every day when he was on vacation. (Who was on vacation, John or Bill?)
Clear   When John was on vacation, he wrote to Bill every day.

Unclear   After hearing Gail's ideas and Janet's proposals, Marianne liked hers better. (Marianne liked "hers" better. Who is "hers," Gail's or Janet's?)

Clear   Marianne agreed with Gail after hearing Janet's proposals.

This problem with vague pronoun references results from the writer's carelessness or ignorance, both in the initial composition of sentences and in the review and revision of the early drafts of a story. The following list of the most common kinds of pronoun reference errors and their remedies will help you to recognize and to correct similar mistakes in your own writing.

1. **Avoid remote reference.** Place pronouns as close as possible to their antecedents. If proximity of noun and pronoun is not possible or does not resolve the ambiguity, repeat the antecedent, devise a suitable synonym, or simply recast the problem sentences.

Unclear   Bill was angry, and his employer reprimanded him. That was why he quit his job.

Clear   Bill quit his job because his employer reprimanded him for being angry.

2. **Avoid using a pronoun which would refer to either of two possible antecedents.** Place only one antecedent before a pronoun, or recast the sentence to eliminate the pronoun, or to make the reference unmistakable.

Unclear   While my sister and my mother were sailing, she fell in the lake.

Clear   While my sister and my mother were sailing, my mother fell in the lake.

3. **Avoid reference to an antecedent in the possessive case.** To remedy this problem, recast the sentence and eliminate the possessive.

Unclear   John reached for the dog's leash, but it ran away.

Clear   The dog ran away after John reached for its leash.

4. **Avoid the use of *it, this, that, which,* and *such* in reference to the general idea of a whole clause, sentence, or paragraph.** To ensure clarity and precision of meaning, make each of your pronouns refer to a *specific* word rather than to a general thought or an implied word or idea. In the case of *this, that,* and *such,* combine these pronouns with a noun that will describe or summarize the antecedent idea.

Unclear Len received a failing grade, which frightens him.
Clear   Receiving a failing grade frightens Len.

5. **Avoid the awkward use of the indefinite *it*.** Recast the sentence to remove the unnecessary and confusing pronoun.

Unclear In the spring, I worked on a river boat, but in the winter it froze over.
Clear   I worked on a river boat in the spring, but in the winter the river froze over.

6. **Avoid using the pronoun *it* and the expletive *it* in the same sentence.** One or the other of the *its* should be eliminated from the sentence.

Unclear Trying to find it elsewhere is as fatal as pulling up a tree from its roots.
Clear   Trying to find food elsewhere is as fatal as pulling up a tree from its roots.

Active and Passive Voice

Passive voice is the omission or subordination of the actor in a sentence.

PASSIVE	ACTIVE
It is thought by Bill Jameson that another official must be placed in control of the military by the president.	Bill Jameson thinks the president must place another official in control of the military.
Even though Redwood Hall is heavily populated by students, study of the structure is seldom done.	The many students going through Redwood Hall seldom study its structure.

Often, the word *by* is a kind of signal that a sentence is passive ("It is thought by Bill Jameson"); in any case, the *by* is always implied ("study of the structure is seldom done"—by whom? *by students*).

When you're fashioning a sentence and writing about an action, think this way: Should I stress the actor—the "doer"—or should I feature the action? Like the author of the following sentence, you may decide to write in a *passive voice:* "The unpretentious monarchs of Scandinavia and the Low Countries are respectfully accepted by their sober subjects." In this case, the writer decided that the action was more important than the actors.

However, in most cases, rely on the *active voice.* For example, in an essay in which you're featuring what you did, you should write a sentence this way: "I cheered the team but doubted the quarterback's decisions." If you had drifted into a passive voice, the sentence would have read: "The team was cheered by me, but the quarterback's decisions were doubted." As you can see, using the passive makes the sentence colorless, lengthy, and ambiguous. If you decided to add "by me" at the end of the sentence to make certain the readers would understand that you doubted the quarterback's decisions, the sentence would be longer.

An active transitive verb has a direct object:

Jack owns a typewriter. (*Jack* is the subject; *owns* is the verb; and *typewriter* is the object.)

Intransitive verbs don't take objects:

The building collapsed.

Agreement

Agreement between subject and verb in number and person frustrates some college writers—including at least a few who are writing dissertations. Lack of agreement between subject and verb can result from carelessness, but often writers use a plural subject with a singular verb or a singular subject with a plural verb. You should memorize the following rules:

1. When two or more subjects are connected by the conjunction *and*, you should use a plural verb:

An introvert and an extravert *are* nearly always enemies.

You should use a singular verb, however, when two parts of a compound subject refer to a single person or thing:

His friend and lover *is* very patient.
"Publish or perish" *is* the rule—unless you can also teach.

2. Don't let words before or between the subject and the verb mislead you. First, find your sentence's subject, then make its predicate agree:

The last two innings of the game *were* dull. (Although *game* is the nearest noun, it isn't the subject. The subject is *innings*.)

The *bulk* of the gorillas *surprises* me. (*Bulk* is the subject).

Singular subjects followed by words such as *accompanied by, with,* and *as well as* take singular verbs. Even though the intervening words or phrases may suggest plural meaning, they aren't part of the subject:

The singer, accompanied by a pianist, *was* delirious about the applause.

The *shortstop,* with his friends, *was* there all day.

3. When two or more subjects are presented as alternatives with the use of *but, or,* or *nor,* the verb should be singular:

Either Bill *or* Jack *is* to be at the stadium by 1 P.M.

Neither Mary *nor* Shirley *is* to be in class.

Not ability, *but* hard work *is* prized.

4. In most cases singular pronouns take singular verbs:

Everyone ate *his* hot dog.

Nobody *was* there.

It *is* time to go.

The verb used with *none, any, either,* and *neither,* however, depends on whether you intend singular or plural meaning for the pronoun.

Neither was there on time (neither *these players* nor *those players*); or,

Neither were there on time (neither *this player* nor *that player*).

When you are using a collective noun, use a singular verb to indicate the group is acting as a single unit:

The team *is* winning.

The committee *is* indecisive.

The government *is* in turmoil.

The congregation *is* here.

If individual members in a collective noun are acting separately, use a plural verb:

31   DRAMA

>The congregation *aren't* able to decide because so many of them change their minds.
>
>The team *are* coming in, one by one.
>
>The class *are* going on field trips to the zoo and the dairy. (Some class members will go to the zoo, others to the dairy.)

Drama

When you are plotting your story and thinking about the angle to take, consider drama potential. Readers respond to drama, although they may not always realize it.

For example, are you reading a story on the worst and longest cold spell in Chicago history? If so, almost automatically you'll prefer to read the story starting with a snowplow driver running amuck, driving his plow over snowbound cars in frustration due to prolonged winter storms.

What about the two children and their dog lost in a swamp? One child falls into a bog; the other runs with the dog to find help. Although help is found, the boy cannot find his way back through the swamp to his friend. The dog, however, leads the rescuers straight to the bog. The parents of both children are overjoyed at the happy outcome. What's the angle for you? The dramatic rescue by the dog, of course.

Whether the story you write is serious or lighthearted, drama spices news accounts. Search for the dramatic theme. Use it.

Chapter 2 Exercises

Remember:

Observe these guidelines:

1. A sentence that causes you to stumble, if only slightly, will make your readers stumble harder. Rewrite it.

2. A sentence will not be clear to readers if you must read it more than once in order to understand what you've said. Rewrite it.

3. A sentence that you've begun with *In other words,* or *That is,* or *That is to say,* probably follows a sentence that should be rewritten. Rewrite it.

4. Limit the number of ideas expressed in each sentence.

5. Strip your sentences of superfluous words.

32   NEWSPAPER FORM AND SENTENCE STRUCTURE

Exercise 2.1   *Rewrite each sentence below to correct dangling and misplaced modifiers. Make a checkmark next to any sentence not needing revision.*

1. While thinking about the coming day, the moon slowly faded.
2. Having taken her seat, we began to ask her some questions.
3. The actor nearly entertained me for two hours.
4. Sally said in the morning she would leave.
5. The house was advertised on the radio which is fifty years years old and in deplorable condition.
6. At the age of 5, his father put him in the first grade.
7. The dog was stopped before the dog food was eaten by his owner.
8. We bought groceries in White Plains at a large grocery store which cost $30.
9. When talking about writing, the instructor pointed out my ability in creative writing.
10. The cook gave chocolate cookies to me with peanuts in them.

Exercise 2.2   *Rewrite each sentence below to correct faulty parallelism. Checkmark any sentence not needing revision.*

1. The actions she plans to do: to try and succeed.
2. An acquaintance told him that his visit would be later but to be ready to start on Tuesday.
3. The outside of our building was wooden, brick, and stone.
4. The book has no opinions against to either the Socialists or to the Communists on that issue.
5. The vacationer stocked the lake with trout, bream, and bass were added by an owner going away on business.
6. Either he will buy the suit tomorrow morning or the following day.

Exercise 2.3 *Tighten the following sentences, by eliminating words, using shorter words, and trimming repetitive words.*

1. Bob tipped the scales at 200 pounds.
2. John was found in a dying condition at the side of the road.
3. She placed the letter in the mails.
4. He lifted up the glass.
5. It happened all of a sudden.
6. He made his escape through the window.
7. The present incumbent is Senator Cranston.
8. He will join the firm in the capacity of general manager.
9. She made a trip to Jacksonville by airplane.
10. He made the statement that. . . .
11. The members of the board voted to close the schools.
12. The walls are 48 inches in thickness.
13. He denied that he had placed the aforementioned letter in the mail.
14. They spent the winter months in the state of Arizona.
15. The play was under the direction of Bill Jones.
16. On two occasions Rob's injured knee kept him from participating in the game.
17. Chris who committed the murder was never found.
18. Podunk University has never won a victory over Nevada.
19. She went to New York to visit her son John who is convalescing from an operation for appendicitis and a daughter.
20. Jane obtained her divorce from Jack Harlan in 1968.

Exercise 2.4 *Shorten the following sentences. Where a specific noun or verb will do the work of several words, use it. Be suspicious of long words, general words, and empty words. What is the main action in the sentence? Is it expressed by the verb alone? Cut words that merely repeat what has been said.*

1. Sporadic dissatisfaction was found in business circles over the tax changes but general agreement as to their fairness.
2. Widespread anxiety exists throughout the medical profession over the possibility of a reduction in salaries in order to keep down taxes.
3. A recommendation for the purchase of a linotype machine was made by Dr. Naton.
4. The Rev. Eustace Alford in an address to the members of the Kiwanis Club made the statement that juvenile delinquency was increasing.
5. Garland appeared before the committee and said that he had never been offered a bribe.
6. Upon investigation, police found footprints leading from the little building in the rear of the house.
7. Three shots were fired, the first by Greenfield at the policeman and the second and third by the policeman at Greenfield who had started to run away.
8. He was shot as he raised his hand to brush away a mosquito as he lay on the ground to wait for a squirrel to appear three miles north of here.
9. Mrs. Brennan passed away shortly after she had prepared dinner as a result of a heart attack.
10. F. T. Pennyfeather died of an illness caused by hardening of the arteries in the family residence late Thursday.

Exercise 2.5

Reduce the following story as much as you can, and be careful that what you write says exactly what the story attempts to say.

U. S. Senator Jack Austin, who spoke to a joint session of local civic organizations here on Tuesday night, in summing up the work of the current session of Congress, pointed to the improvement of foreign relations as one of the bright spots in the picture. This, he said, was the result of cooperative action between the president and the Democratic leadership in Congress, and it came despite prophecies of doom emulating in some quarters during the political campaign last fall.

Acting in cooperation with the president, Democratic leadership stood fast with the Peace Through Strength policy, thus warning China that the people of the United States would take quick action to stop further red aggression

35 EXERCISE 2.6

in Asia. Since last January, the picture has continued to brighten, and today the danger of immediate war appears remote. It was not so last January, Senator Austin said.

The Senator is on a statewide tour, pointing out the accomplishments of the current Congress, but he is also looking over the vast development in Kansas while he is in the state. The major part of his Tuesday night talk was devoted to the development of Kansas.

Exercise 2.6 *Edit and tighten the following story. Eliminate needless words. Take care to look for errors in style.*

BURKBURNETT, Texas—Burkburnett voters are expected to trek off to the poles in large numbers Saturday and will decide the immediate fate of cable television in Burkburnett.

If absencee voting is any indication of what can be expected this Saturday it'll probably be one of the largest elections ever to be held in Burkburnett.

By noon Tuesday almost sixty persons had cast absentee ballots for Saturday's cable television ordinance referendum election. That figure is about double what is normally cast during the absentee period.

The special election will be held in kthe Burkburnett Community Center, located at the corner of Kramer and Davey Dr. Polls will be open from seven A.M. until 7 P.M.

The proposition on the ballot will be whether or not to approve ordinance #354 granting to TV Cable of Burk the right to construct and operate a cable television system within Burkburnett, subject to the provisions and conditions set forth in the franchise ordinance.

36 NEWSPAPER FORM AND SENTENCE STRUCTURE

A vote FOR will show voters' approval of the franchise ordinance as it has been written.

If the FOR's carry the election, TV Cable of Burkburnett could proceed with the construction of a cable television system for Burkburnett. Representatives of that company report that some residents would receive cable television in as little as 60 days that the entire system would be completed within six months.

If those who oppose the ordinance are in the majority, then the whole cable television issue is thrown back to the Burkburnett City Council for what ever action they desire to take.

If franchise ordinance #354 fails in Saturday's election, any affirmative action by the Burkburnett city council torwad a cable television system in Burkburnett would have to be written in another franchise ordinance. That ordinance would then have to be approved on three separate monthly meetings by the council. Following that third and final reading, local citizens would again have a 30 day period in which to draw petitions which would force the council to call for a referendum election on the franchise ordinance.

Exercise 2.7

This story has been rearranged. Put the paragraphs back into the proper order. Then edit the piece. Remember: the most important graph first, then the rest in descending order of importance.

Sheriff's deputies today were releasing few details of the shooting and refused to speculate on a motive, although drugs reportedly were involved.

37 EXERCISE 2.8

Several semi-automatic weapons were confiscated and three men were in custody today as authorities tried to find a motivation for a shooting that left two men dead and three others wounded in Santa Rosa.

The only one of the woundid too be identifeid immediately was Charles Scurini, apparently a brother to the deadman.

One man, found dead at the scene in a lowermiddle class neighborhood just outside Santa Rosa, was identified as Gino Scurini, 22, of Sebastepol.

A second man, who, died later at Santa Rosa community hospital, could not be immediately identified. But invistigators said they believed his first name was Jeremiah, that he was from Portland, Ore. or Salem and that he was in his early 20s.

Authorities said they went to the scene about a mile nroth of Santa Rosa at about four thirty in the after noon yesterday after they received a call that shots were being fried.

Booked for investigation of murder and being held in county jail were Eddie McGRaw, 30, of Las Gatos, John R. Wells, 22, of San Jose, and Mitchell Gustafson, 18, of Santa Rosa.

The three men were taken into custody "during the incident or shortly thereafter in the vicinity, said deputy sheriff Larry Sheets.

Exercise 2.8 *This story covers a speech by a Sierra Club official. The author failed to provide the attribution necessary to inform the reader that all the information came from the speech. Edit to provide attribution. Remember: Resist the temptation to use anything but a simple "said." Also edit for other errors.*

Environmental "housekeeping" may actually benefit businesses, Mike McCloskey, executive director of the Sierra Bluc, said Thursday at Stanford University.

In a speech entitled "Business and the Environment: Reluctant Bedfellows," McCloskey told students at the Graduate School of Business that "businesses with a sense of social responsibility and good leadership are not being held back" by the conservation controls proposed by the Sierra Blub, an environmentalist organization.

As a result of some of the Sierra Club programs, harbor seals live once more in San Francisco Bay, and oxident levels are declining in airsheds. Since McCloskey became executive director in 1969, membership in the club has increased from 70 to 180 thousand members.

The antagonistic relationship between community businesses and environmentalists is due to a misperception of the purpose of the Sierra Club. Like businesses, they are seeking constructive growth and progress, but not where only a few gain. Ninety percent of all developments proceed without interference.

"The Sierra Blub motto is not blind opposition to progress, but opposition to blind progress," McCloskey said. "It is not impossible for businesses to live with the environmentalists."

The environmentalists have complemented businesses by creating new industries such as those that manufacture service control equipment.

EXERCISE 2.8

Last year $34 billion was spend on preventing environmental pollution. By 1985, that total could rise to $500 billion. McCloskey estimated that with over one million employes employed, unemployment is decreased by one-half of one percent.

Furthermore, industries are discovering that they can market some of their by-products instead of disposing them.

An attractive environmentl surrounding a business has added psychological benefits as well as medical ones. McCloskey said, "Most of these programs produce a healther, happier work force." He also pointed out that 60 percent of cancer is thought to be environmentally induced and worth about $18 billion in economic losses, not to mention human suffering.

The investments that businesses spend on environmental controls is less than six percent of their total investments. Only two percent of the firms studied in a 1977 report postponed other investments to use the capital for conservation purposes.

Naturally, the businesses pass the costs on to the consumer. But the U.S. consuper price index rose less than one percent last year due to mony spent on conservation controls. Further,more, this is a one-time cost increase because the investment only has to be made once.

The costs for consdrvation are relative, too. Without the rapid pace our country is consuming its natural resources, more people are chacing after scarcer resources and settling for worse low grade substitutes, which cost the consumer more anyway. Considering the benefits derived from energy conservation controls, McCloskey feels that "the public is getting more for its money."

Environmentalism is here to stay. Many businesses are just accepting it and finding new ways to adapt their industries to keep within conservation control guidelines. McCloskey concluded that businesses will "never find a morerewarding task."

Chapter 3
What Makes News?

In 1978, the respected Harris poll asked people what kind of news they read—local, national, or international—most frequently. Seventy-four percent of the people interviewed put local news first by far.

Although it may not be surprising to learn that local news comes first, you should try to think about what the local news is. After all, if you become a reporter, you will almost certainly be reporting local news. Even if you eventually become a Washington correspondent or a foreign correspondent, knowing what local news is will give you a good grasp on news.

Think of news this way: A reader chooses news expecting a reward, and it can come in two kinds. The first is called *immediate reward*. The second, *delayed reward*.

The immediate reward comes as news of crime and corruption, accidents and disasters, sports and recreation, social events, and human interest. This kind of news pays its reward at once. Readers can enjoy a vicarious experience without any of the dangers or stresses involved. They can shiver luxuriously at a murder, shake their heads sympathetically and safely at a hurricane, identify with the winning team or with the guest at a reception, and laugh understandingly at a warm little story of children or dogs.

The delayed reward, of course, pays its rewards later. Readers may have to endure unpleasantness or annoyance. For example, they may read of an unpleasant foreign situation, the mounting national debt, inflation, the falling market, scarce housing, cancer, and epidemics. When readers choose delayed reward news, they jerk into the world of surrounding reality. When they choose immediate reward news, there is a retreat from the world of threatening reality.

In order to understand news, you should read the following five paragraphs about a young man who began just as you did—in the classroom—and eventually worked in all the major media.

He went to work as a reporter for the campus newspaper during his freshman year in college. His newspaper reading proved valuable, but he had to become accustomed to aiming at a limited audience; the campus paper was concerned almost solely with the college community. Important events occurring beyond the boundaries of the campus were not reported unless they involved students or faculty members.

In his junior year, our reporter began to work for the campus radio station, helping to write and broadcast a daily 15-minute news program. He continued as a part-time reporter for the campus paper, thinking that the jobs were similar. He soon learned, however, that there were distinct differences. He gathered news from the same sources, but the radio station was designed to serve the city as well as the university community. It did not attempt to compete with the city stations in presenting local and world news, but the news of the university community was presented in a broader context. For him it was an entirely new dimension; the news presented in shorter, simpler, sketchier form. Most of the radio news stories ran less than half as long as the newspaper stories. Because they were written to be listened to, they were simplified in scope and language.

Later, he became a reporter for a daily newspaper in a university city of 200,000. Now the audience was much larger and much more diverse. Because relatively few of the paper's readers were on the campus, university news was much less important. Only a minority of the subscribers had been to college; a poll disclosed that only 9 percent of the city's residents knew the name of the president of the university. A sharply worded speech by the Dean of the College of Arts and Sciences—front page fare for the college paper—was relegated to page 22 of the downtown daily. The university was only one element in a very large world.

Like many another young newspaper reporter, he devoted much of his spare time to writing articles for national magazines. It was hard; only the most unusual places, events, and personalities in the entire state could command national attention. Eventually, he became a staff writer for a national magazine and began to think exclusively of addressing large groups of people who had interests, but not geography, in common. The scope was much the same when he began to write scripts for television programs: News was judged in broad terms, for he was addressing a national audience—and reaching only a few of the university-city newspaper readers he had written for years earlier. Moreover, he found that words in television are synchronized with—and sacrificed to—pictures; the visual element was dominant.

The broad concept of news remained the same throughout these experiences; interest and timeliness were standards throughout. But emphatic changes were dictated by changing audiences.

Whatever the changes in audiences and writing practices, some stories are simply more compelling than others. Those stories have these elements.

Conflict: A fight, verbal or physical, captures more interest than does tranquillity.

Proximity: A local election is more likely to interest local residents than an election in a city hundreds of miles away; a tornado that hits a nearby town excites more local attention than one that strikes in the next state.

Prominence: When the governor of New York and John Jones arrive in Rochester on the same day, the governor makes news and Jones does not; Paul Newman's views on acting are more newsworthy than those of the man who has the lead in a Little Theatre production.

Unusualness: A woman is elected mayor for the first time in the city's history; state newspapers, which traditionally pay little attention to the city's mayoralty elections, carry the story.

Human Interest: A Boy Scout hitchhikes 900 miles to attend the annual Scout Jamboree; a man is involved in a quirky incident in which he stops a fight between husband and wife.

Consequence: When something happens that is of consequence—such as when the state governor announces his campaign for president of the United States—the newspapers consider it news.

Sex: The sexual involvement of prominent figures has become news. For example, when former Vice-President Nelson Rockefeller died in 1979, news stories extended over several days. Information gradually came out that his heart attack came on a night when he was in an apartment with an attractive 25-year-old woman.

News is the timely report of events, facts, and opinions that interest a significant number of people. The key words are "timely" and "interest a significant number." It is not enough that a report be only timely; if it does not interest at least a large minority of its potential audience, it is not news. Similarly, information that is only interesting cannot be considered news. It must have some element of timeliness. In unusual cases, "hot news" can be derived from old and cold events. A historian's discovery that the fate of a 1900 polar expedition was different than what was reported in 1900 is news. The *Washington Post* put a news story about an American Revolutionary War plan on its front page. Historians discovered a letter revealing that the War's leaders devised a potential counterattack, using camouflaged warships, on British cities. The letter was nearly 200 years old, but its discovery in a collection of Revolutionary War papers provided new information.

The late poet A. E. Housman said that he could not define poetry any more than a terrier could define a rat, but that the terrier certainly knew a rat when he saw one. Just as a poet knows a poem when he sees one, you too can recognize news if you can do the following exercises accurately.

Chapter 3 Exercises

Remember:

In making your choices in the following exercises:

1. Keep in mind: immediate reward/delayed reward; timeliness/significant number

2. Think of your audience: In what context do they need the news?

3. Consider: Conflict
              Proximity
              Prominence
              Unusualness
              Human Interest
              Consequence
              Sex

Exercise 3.1

Consider the following pairs of events and decide which one the editor should give the most detailed coverage and the most prominent position in his paper. Be prepared to defend your choice at the next class meeting.

1. a. Local soldier wins Silver Star in battle.
   b. Soldier from nearby city wins Congressional Medal of Honor in battle.

2. a. City commission passes ordinance limiting height of new apartment construction to 4 stories.
   b. County commission decides to build 1.5 miles of new rural roads.

3. a. Heavy rains cause $150,000 in damage to local streets.
   b. Flood drowns 2,000 in Bombay.

4. a. Governor of New York announces candidacy for president.
   b. Governor of Delaware charges fraud in Delaware senatorial election.

5. a. The local university football team receives a Bluebonnet Bowl bid.
   b. The local baseball team loses the pennant after leading the league all season.

6. a. Baccardi, a local acrobat, is killed falling from a tightrope.
   b. Childers, a local acrobat, is killed falling from the roof of his home.

7. a. Two Iranian cabinet members are accused of grafting $550,000.
   b. Local tax collector is accused of a $5,000 shortage.

8. a. Local city council increases the tax rate.
   b. State legislature is expected to cut income taxes by 5 percent.

9. a. Faulty electric wiring causes $6,000 damage to local warehouse.
   b. A $30,000 home is burned to the ground.

10. a. Customer in grocery store hits manager, causing the manager to be hospitalized.
    b. An irate employee smashes both the plate glass windows in the local bakery.

Exercise 3.2

In the spaces below the following leads, write which of these is the most important: conflict, proximity, prominence, unusualness, human interest, consequence, or sex. Some of these examples may contain a combination of these elements. If so, list all applicable.

1. Thieves broke into the home of city council member John Todd last night and stole $3500 worth of clothing and jewelry.

46   WHAT MAKES NEWS?

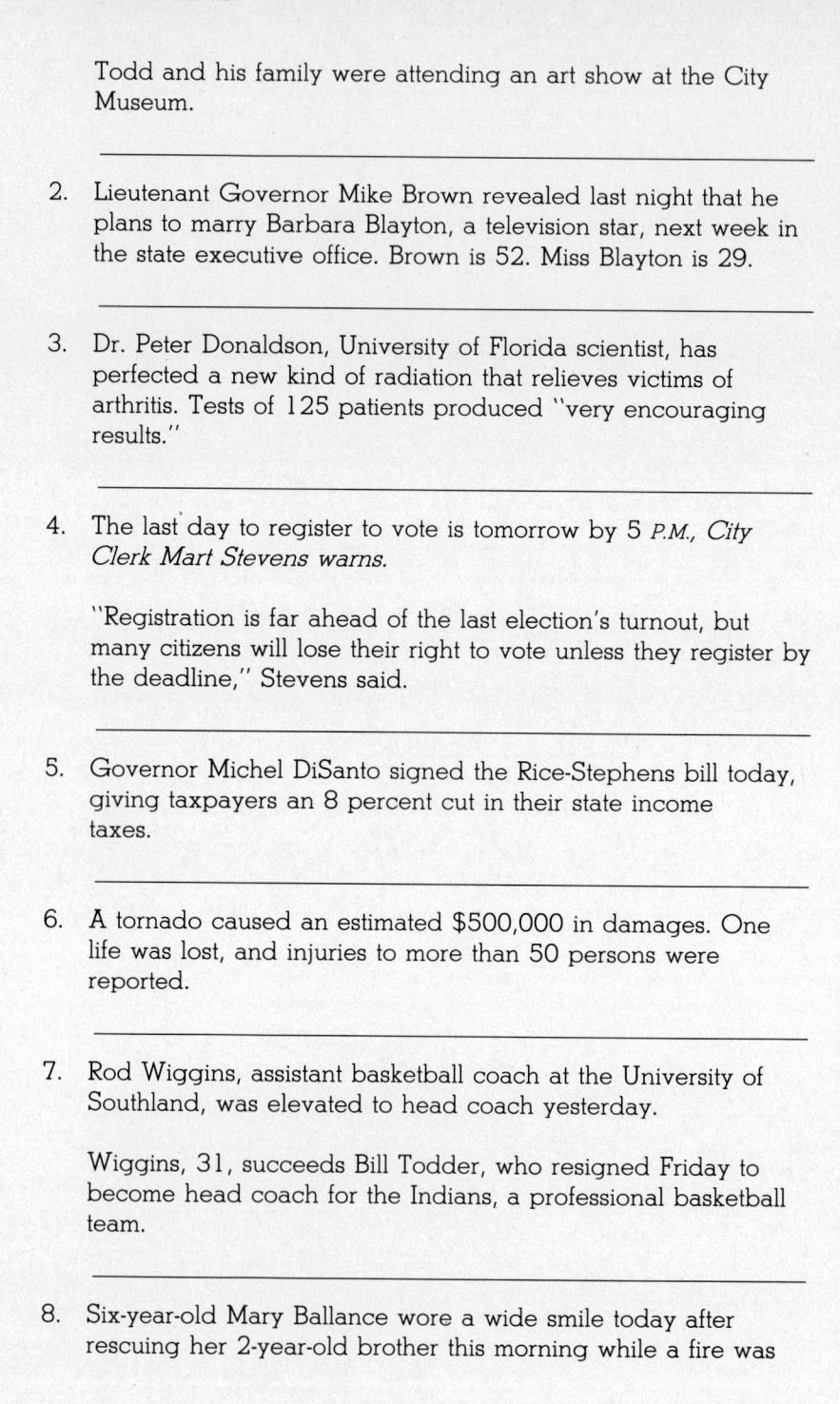

Todd and his family were attending an art show at the City Museum.

2. Lieutenant Governor Mike Brown revealed last night that he plans to marry Barbara Blayton, a television star, next week in the state executive office. Brown is 52. Miss Blayton is 29.

3. Dr. Peter Donaldson, University of Florida scientist, has perfected a new kind of radiation that relieves victims of arthritis. Tests of 125 patients produced "very encouraging results."

4. The last day to register to vote is tomorrow by 5 *P.M., City Clerk Mart Stevens warns.*

"Registration is far ahead of the last election's turnout, but many citizens will lose their right to vote unless they register by the deadline," Stevens said.

5. Governor Michel DiSanto signed the Rice-Stephens bill today, giving taxpayers an 8 percent cut in their state income taxes.

6. A tornado caused an estimated $500,000 in damages. One life was lost, and injuries to more than 50 persons were reported.

7. Rod Wiggins, assistant basketball coach at the University of Southland, was elevated to head coach yesterday.

Wiggins, 31, succeeds Bill Todder, who resigned Friday to become head coach for the Indians, a professional basketball team.

8. Six-year-old Mary Ballance wore a wide smile today after rescuing her 2-year-old brother this morning while a fire was

destroying their home. Their parents were at work when the fire broke out at 8:30.

_____

9. A high school coed charged that the principal, Ron Hightower, tried to fondle her instead of punishing her for skipping classes.

_____

10. Detective Robert Joneston was fired yesterday by Chief Bill Downer. He was accused of taking graft.

_____

Exercise 3.3

Evaluate the events below by writing "Yes" beside those that might be published in a large metropolitan daily and "No" beside those that should not be published in a large metropolitan daily. In the second case, decide "Yes" or "No" about the same story in the case of a small-town daily.

1. Local resident wins $50,000 libel suit against your paper.
 Metropolitan _____
 Small-town _____

2. Governor of the state, a local resident, elopes with his secretary.
 Metropolitan _____
 Small-town _____

3. Local shopkeeper elopes with a woman who works for him.
 Metropolitan _____
 Small-town _____

4. New, small shop will be opened tomorrow.
 Metropolitan _____
 Small-town _____

5. Eight local residents are fined $25 each for gambling.
 Metropolitan _____
 Small-town _____

6. City clerk reports that the number of building permits issued last month are the same as the previous month.
 Metropolitan _____
 Small-town _____

48 WHAT MAKES NEWS?

7. City clerk reports that the number of
   building permits issued last month
   established a record high.   Metropolitan _____
                                         Small-town   _____

8. Roofing company worker and wife
   celebrate their twenty-fifth anniversary. Metropolitan _____
                                              Small-town   _____

9. Mayor and wife celebrate their
   twenty-fifth anniversary.   Metropolitan _____
                                         Small-town   _____

10. Pioneering resident to observe his
    eighty-ninth birthday tomorrow.   Metropolitan _____
                                         Small-town   _____

Exercise 3.4

As news editor it is your job to decide what goes on page 1 and what goes inside. From the following list choose 6 stories for page 1. Then choose 14 more to go in the first section of the paper. Write "page 1" or "first section" in right column. Those you do not choose will go into other sections of the paper. For this exercise, assume you are an editor for Minneapolis's daily paper.

A squally weather front drenched the Bay Area, then swept toward the Sierra to add to the snowpack. _____

An emergent conservative coalition is designing a revolt to limit both taxes and spending. _____

Angry, wet San Francisco airline passengers found themselves slowed down by demolition at the airport. _____

Anwar Sadat reportedly offered to have Egypt take over as the police of the Middle East. _____

President Reagan said the strife in Iran and Indochina would not lead to any revision of U.S. foreign policy. _____

Chinese war planes were reported attacking deep inside Vietnam as fighting continued on the ground. _____

EXERCISE 3.4

Nominations for the Academy Awards had *The Deer Hunter* and *Heaven Can Wait* leading the way. _____

Dr. Alfred Rider withdrew his plan for a $6 million hotel near the University of California. _____

The season's latest storm left a 1000-mile snowscape along the mid-Atlantic coast. _____

Mardi Gras was canceled as 18 groups decided not to march in New Orleans because of the police strike. _____

Last week's "mystery" Lee Marvin witness testified he made love to Michelle Marvin more than 50 times. _____

The GOP leader of the state senate proposed tax cuts that could save taxpayers $7 billion over 5 years. _____

An environmental group called for more efficient energy use. _____

A pollster found Americans far more ready to take stands against prejudice than is commonly assumed. _____

George Meany said he was thinking of retiring and will be thinking of it for years. _____

Senator Kennedy said failure to ratify the U.S.-Soviet arms treaty would invite nuclear disaster. _____

The summer job program designed to give disadvantaged youths experience was condemned by the General Accounting Office. _____

The delay in installing a new General Services Administration inspector general is hampering the probe of wrongdoing. _____

Members of the Shah's retinue hijacked his jet in Morocco and flew it to Iran. _____

Tehran radio says oil exports may resume. _____

The philosophy of Italy's Red Brigades is examined by a former *Newsweek* correspondent. _____

French decaffeinated coffee roasted can taste almost like the real thing. _____

Usually outspoken, Mme. Chiang Kai-shek is living in mysterious seclusion in her Long Island estate. _____

Lauren Bacall's long-lost father said references to him in the star's autobiography aren't true. _____

An invasion of cowbirds into the Sierra has federal foresters worried about the songbird population. _____

The Warriors beat the Los Angeles Lakers last night. _____

The Oakland Stompers are playing in Edmonton tonight. _____

Mission High School upset Balboa High School last night. _____

Bay area weather calls for partly cloudy and chance for showers. _____

Exercise 3.5

For this exercise assume you are a wire editor *or* telegraph editor. *It is your job to keep track of what is coming into your paper over the news wires. Choose 2 stories from the following list for page 1. Then choose 7 more which will go into a* wire page *on the inside of the paper. For this exercise, assume you are working for the* Arkansas Gazette.

BANGKOK—China's drive halts 6 miles inside Vietnam.

MOSCOW—The Kremlin gives Vietnam strong moral support.

A big snowstorm has hit the South.

BAL HARBOUR, Florida—President Reagan is expected to be roundly criticized at an AFL-CIO gathering here.

NEW ORLEANS—The police strike continues as Mardi Gras nears.

ATLANTA—Venereal disease is making many women sterile, says Center for Disease Control.

KITTERY, Maine—Radiation suspected in deaths of shipyard workers near here.

MEMPHIS—Antique store owner is held for moonshining.

51   EXERCISE 3.5

NEW YORK—A man wanted for 22 bank robberies has been arrested.

WALLA WALLA, Washington—Local citizens have raised nearly $30,000 to mend local girl's heart.

BOSTON—Coast Guard suspends its search for helicopter crewman missing at sea.

WASHINGTON, D.C.—The Agriculture Department announces grants to New Mexico and Indians.

WASHINGTON, D.C.—Mrs. Mamie Eisenhower is in the hospital in Washington. Officials will not reveal why.

WASHINGTON, D.C.—A survey by a business lobby says confidence in the economy is way down.

WASHINGTON, D.C.—The president has invited all 50 governors to a White House conference on inflation.

ANKARA, Turkey—Turkey and the United States are negotiating a new extradition treaty.

ORBASSANO, Italy—A terrorist group claims responsibility for a firebombing here.

TORONTO, Canada—A Picasso painting was stolen from a gallery here.

TURIN, Italy—In spite of economic problems, Italy is biggest importer of champagne for third year in row.

Chapter 4 Newspaper Leads

Structuring and Writing Leads

The lead (sometimes known as *lede*) is the first sentence, or the first two or three sentences, you read in a news story. A lead gives the reader enough facts to quickly grasp what happened.

Before you write your lead sentence or sentences, analyze what really happened. Choose the most significant information the reader needs to know—then put that first.

Some editors consider only the first sentence the lead; others, the first or second paragraphs. Either way, you have only 5 or 6 typewritten lines to grab your reader's attention. Your story will be competing with 7 to 10 other stories on the same page. So you have to act fast in recording the events.

You have several possibilities. You can tell the readers:

something new

something important to them

something amusing

something unexpected, perhaps startling

something that stirs emotions

Once you catch your reader's attention, you proceed to flesh out the story with additional information, but the lead controls and sets the tone for continuing the news story.

Once you have a well thought out lead, the rest of the story will virtually write itself. The lead captures the main idea; the supporting ideas play follow the leader in descending order.

Let us analyze a lead. Compare Lead 1 and Lead 2:

1

A controversial Memphis city ordinance proposed by the city staff would require businesses to contribute "in-lieu payments" of either money or land into the city's low cost housing fund and this would place an unfair burden on the city's major industry, The Ace Co., Frank Koch, that firm's vice-president said at the Memphis City Council meeting last night.

2

The Ace Co., Memphis' biggest business, will wind up paying almost all of a new penalty housing fee if the city enacts it, Frank Koch, company vice-president protested at last night's Memphis City Council meeting.

The first lead contains too much information. It backs into the "unfair burden" on Ace Company; it includes the descriptions "controversial" and "unfair."

The second lead implies both: Koch's remarks make the matter controversial, and the unfairness, mentioned specifically later in the story, is implicit in the idea that one firm will be paying almost all of a new tax. And the words "ordinance" and "in-lieu payments" are translated into simpler language: "penalty housing fee."

Which lead tells what's *really* going on? Which says it most quickly and clearly?

Sample lead 2 tells you immediately what the news is. You can expect to learn more details as you proceed. If you lived in Memphis, that straightforward lead would capture your interest at once. What is this about a local big business taking over some of your tax burden, you would wonder? You would read on.

This typical lead plunges the reader right into the biggest news angle, highlighting what *really* is taking place.

This simple, hard news lead has been around a long time; it is sometimes labeled a formula lead because it summarizes the key action. But it does the job, getting information across quickly.

The straight factual opening, highlighting the most important piece of news, is easy for the reader to take in. And the reporter can write it in a hurry when deadlines are pressing.

The Five Ws and One H

Six basic questions were answered by lead 2. Answers to these are basic to all journalism stories, and are known as the five Ws and one H.

> WHAT happened? A proposed housing fee is protested.
> —The reader learns the proposal exists.
>
> WHO says so? The Ace Company vice-president, Frank Koch.
> —If the readers live in Memphis, they know it is the biggest firm in town.
>
> WHERE did it happen? Memphis City Council meeting.
> —The readers live there; they are interested.
>
> WHEN did it happen?
> —Last night, so it's probably still news to the reader.
>
> WHY is The Ace Company protesting? Because the company will pay almost all of a new housing fee.
> —Readers may be sympathetic or unsympathetic to the company, but they care because it is the biggest employer around.
>
> HOW did The Ace Company protest?
> —By having its vice-president speak up at a public meeting.

Our lead answered the most important elements of the story. It provided answers to the five Ws and one H. The main news was highlighted. But was it quick and easy to read? Not especially.

Use the information in lead 1 to rewrite the lead into 2 or 3 shorter sentences. See if it is easier to follow the action. (Time yourself: unless instructed otherwise, take no more than 5 minutes.)

Perhaps you wrote something like:

> Under a new proposal, the biggest business in town would pay the most toward low-cost housing funds, a company executive told the Memphis City Council last night. Frank Koch, vice-president of The Ace Company, protested the penalty housing fee suggested to the council by the city staff.

Do you think these 2 sentences are easier to read than the original 2 lead? Does the new paragraph explain more? It takes 5 lines rather than 4 in the original, but it meets the requirements of 6 lines maximum for a lead.

Notice the difference in sentence length. Count the words in the first sentence in lead 2. There are 35, not bad as long leads go. But tests have shown that understanding falls off after 20 words. Today, many editors prefer lead sentences containing no more than 30 words. The new version just meets that requirement: It has 28.

Notice how the shorter first sentence is achieved. In the third lead, neither the company name nor the vice-president's name or title are given. But the reader is given essential information: An executive of the biggest company in town tells the city council that his firm will pay the most money to low-cost housing funds if the council enacts a new proposal.

The second sentence names the names: person, company, penalty housing fee, and adds who made the proposal. Considerable information for a total of 46 words.

Practice writing some leads. Rewrite the following example, using the five Ws and one H as instructed.

Reporter Bill Jones, while waiting to cash his paycheck at the downtown branch of the National Bank in San Jose at 8:30 A.M., watched a man jump over the counter carrying a small brown bag. The man, who was wearing black gloves, shoved Jones aside and ran out the glass entrance doors. He leaped into a waiting car and sped off through the parking lot. When the bank manager ran up shouting that he had just been robbed of $100,000 after opening the bank safe, reporter Jones was unable to give him a description of the man or car.

Start with *who* (Unless you are instructed otherwise, give yourself 5 minutes for each lead.)

Perhaps you wrote: "Reporter Bill Jones watched a bank robber escape with $100,000...." The lead would begin with the name, in this case intriguing because the person was a reporter and should have been better prepared to supply details. However, often the name can be left until later unless the person is well known or is the important element of the action.

Now try *what*.

Perhaps you wrote: "A bank robber escaped with $100,000 from the National Bank...." There you have the essence of the action. That would be a strong, simple, hard news lead.

Try *why*.

Maybe you came up with: "After the National Bank manager opened the bank safe for the morning...."

Why can make an interesting lead, but in this case it is weak.

Now try *when*.

Did you write: "At 8:30 this morning, a man robbed the National Bank ..."? *When* is seldom the most important point leading off a story, but occasionally it may be the key element. For example, in this instance, perhaps the story might have been:

"In the first few moments of its opening day, the National Bank. . . ."

Now try *where*.

Likely you wrote: "The downtown branch of the National Bank of San Jose was robbed. . . ." In this story, *where* does not work well, primarily because it forces you to write in passive voice ("was robbed"). It is always better to choose active voice ("man robbed the bank") rather than passive. But as you can see, the *where* can be the important element to readers who keep their savings at this particular bank. Proximity counts.

Let us finish by trying *how*.

It is possible you had something like: A man who had just grabbed $100,000 after a National Bank manager opened his safe this morning jumped over the counter, shoved aside reporter Bill Jones, ran out the glass doors, leaped into his car, and sped away through the parking lot.

How often works well if the event is dramatic and can be told quickly and simply. Here the angle gets lengthy in the telling, though the lead certainly gives all the information.

Types of Leads

As you look at these different leads, what elements come through as important?

Drama?

Proximity?

Familiarity?

Unexpectedness?

Human interest?

Effects on reader?

Drama, unexpectedness, and human interest appear most important. Unless you know the bank manager, or Bill Jones, there is little familiarity. Proximity would affect you only if you lived or worked near the bank. And, since you probably assume the bank is insured for losses of $100,000, you are unlikely to feel affected by the robbery. But, if the bank had been robbed of $10 million, that might be another story!

Analyze your stories. Deciding what angle to use in the lead will determine whether you write a catchy, feature-type lead or a straight, factual, hard news lead. Though thinking about the five Ws is an easy way to break your lead ideas into various components, do not look upon the system as a formula. Newspapers today try many different approaches. Newspaper stories are competing with television and magazines, so arresting leads have become more important to some editors than simple summary leads.

Here are a few samples of different types of leads:

SAN FRANCISCO—If her name were Patricia Jones, said F. Lee Bailey, it all would have turned out differently. But with a name like Patricia Hearst, she didn't stand a chance, the flamboyant Boston lawyer said.

BELFAST, Northern Ireland—Mairead Corrigan puts her faith in God, and Betty Williams trusts in the common sense of ordinary people. Working together, they have achieved temporary peace in this strife-torn nation.

LOS ANGELES—The Duke is dead. John Wayne, who so embodied the national hero in a half-century of movies that he became a symbol of the strong, patriotic American, died of cancer last night at the age of 72.

Straight news leads should provide concrete detail to help the reader get into the story fast. Only the John Wayne obit lead above, does. Nonetheless, the other two delayed-feature leads work well. They have punch. The Belfast lead provided a refreshing angle to war news from Northern Ireland. The Patty Hearst lead provided unexpected name juxtaposition.

Avoid what are known as *label* leads—leads merely telling the reader that an event has taken place, such as "a meeting was held," or "Joe Blow made a speech." Highlight specific actions taken at the meeting, or main points made during the speech.

Below are two stories that ran in neighboring newspapers on the same meeting:

STORY 1

PALO ALTO—More than 200 concerned Palo Altans showed up Monday night for a special public meeting on the fate of their library system.

Library Director June Fleming two weeks ago had announced cost cutting proposals that could help the Proposition 13-plagued system save $225,000 a year.

The proposals, which if adopted would be implemented in fiscal year 1979–80, included:

• Closing the Children's Library at 1276 Harriet St., and consolidat-

STORY 2

Nearly 300 Palo Alto residents showed up Monday night at a "save our libraries" meeting, and promptly agreed to launch a petition drive to help do that.

Some residents suggested instituting a library use fee of about $15 a year for each family, while others just protested the "library reorganization" plan proposed by Head Librarian June Fleming.

"We don't want changes like this," Joseph Hirsch, 4149 Georgia Ave., declared. "Don't cut the libraries. We told them we didn't

ing that library's services into the central library's system.

• Closing the little-used College Terrace Library.

• Implementing a $3.50 registration fee for library users.

• Cutting library staff by nearly a third, from 35 to 24.

• Reducing service hours to accommodate available staffing and the needs of community members.

• Recruiting volunteers to carry out such services as extending the hours of local branches.

• Opening small minibranches in local supermarkets and shopping centers.

• De-emphasizing some of the seldom-used basic material at satellite libraries in favor of expanding those services at the central library.

"Proposition 13," said Mrs. Fleming, "has given us an opportunity to do things in a new and challenging way, but without any reductions in quality."

But many residents were skeptical that her changes could be made without downgrading the system.

Most were concerned about the closing of the children's library. Many thought that closure signaled a move away from the needs of children, and suggested that costs be cut elsewhere. Mrs. Fleming responded that the changes would improve the service to children by opening their library on Sundays and by allowing the children to use adult materials when they find it necessary.

"We are not trying to integrate the children's library into the main library reading room," she empha-

want Proposition 13. This plan is not acceptable."

The meeting, at the Lucie Stern Community Center, was coordinated by Gloria Horne, a children's shoestore manager, who is a founder of a new group, Concerned Citizens for Palo Alto Libraries (CCPAL).

The meeting began with Mrs. Fleming outlining the reorganization plan, which includes moving the Children's Library into the Main Library, closing the College Terrace Library and cutting back services at the Downtown and Mitchell Park branches, among other things.

Then Mrs. Horne began reading written questions for Mrs. Fleming to answer.

But one resident, Bernard Young, 966 Amarillo Ave., protested that procedure, saying that it was taking up time that residents wanted for making statements about the plan.

"What is the order of priority? I don't accept it," he said. He said the assignment to slash more than a quarter million dollars from the library budget—cutting it by 28%—was unfair to Mrs. Fleming.

The $15 a year family fee was proposed by Stuart Hansen, 184 Walter Hays Drive. "What better investment can be made for a penny and a half a day?" he asked.

But Enid Davis, a Los Altos librarian who lives at 1050 Newell Road, Palo Alto, objected that setting fees would change libraries into "elite private organizations" and would upset the American tradition of free public libraries.

Robert Debs, a former council

sized. "The two facilities would remain separate."

Other attendees said they were concerned that closing the College Terrace library would make use of the library system by many local residents difficult, especially senior citizens.

Mrs. Fleming responded that "consistently, over the years, College Terrace has declined greatly in usage. It seems to me that the obvious place to make reductions is where facilities are under-utilized and that means College Terrace." (*Source: San Jose Mercury News,* June 1979)

member, urged everyone to bring "all possible pressure" on City Council members, and posted a list of members' names and telephone numbers. Mrs. Horne said that letters might have more impact than phone calls, however. (*Source: Palo Alto Times,* June 1979)

Notice that Story 1 uses a label lead. It tells you only that Palo Alto citizens showed up for a meeting on the fate of their library system. The lead in Story 2, on the other hand, immediately tells you what actions those citizens are planning as a result of their gathering for the meeting.

Which lead gives you the essence of the meeting fastest?

Notice something else. Story 2 uses some partial quotations in the first sentence. You don't "hear" anybody speaking in Story 1 until almost halfway into the article. Quotations add color and interest to news stories, when 1) they are concise and to the point; 2) they summarize a view succinctly; and 3) are clear in meaning.

Be careful not to use long quotations. Sometimes you should paraphrase for brevity. If you do paraphrase, make sure that you attribute the idea to the speaker. Otherwise, the reader may think you are expressing your own opinion.

The following is a paraphrased lead quotation from a survivor of the People's Temple mass suicide in Jonestown, Guyana, a few years ago:

GEORGETOWN, Guyana—A man who witnessed the biggest mass suicide in recent history said yesterday that there was some hysteria and confusion as parents saw their children writhe in the throes of death from poisoning at the Jonestown settlement.

But Odell Rhodes of Detroit said most people quietly waited their turn to die. He said he saw perhaps 200 of the nearly 800 who died, drink cyanide or have it administered forcibly.

Perhaps the lead might have started with a quotation, had Rhodes made his point in a succinctly worded sentence. However, he probably spoke for several minutes before the reporter could grasp the essence of his remarks. So, it is would be wiser to paraphrase in the lead, saving some briefer, descriptive quotations for later—as indeed the reporter did.

Here is another paraphrase:

> WASHINGTON, D.C.—General Services Administration employees, not satisfied with normal kickbacks, created their own company so they could rake off more from government construction work, a federal prosecutor said yesterday.

You can see in the preceding example why an accusatory statement needs to be attributed promptly. However, whatever the nature of the lead quotation or paraphrase, always identify the speaker immediately for the reader.

Here are some samples of leads that start out with short quotations. The first is from the *New York Times* and the second, datelined Reno, Nevada, is from the *Peninsula Times-Tribune*.

> NEW YORK—"All good things must come to an end," the head of the Securities and Exchange Commission said yesterday, referring to the sudden halt to the rise in stock market prices.

> RENO—"I wasn't lost," Art Risser of Reno said today of his four-day ordeal in the Sierra snow.
> "I just couldn't find my way back."

These quotations are short and pithy enough to warrant lead position.

Order of Leads

Now, let us examine our two versions of the Palo Alto Library meetings from another vantage point.

Right after the lead in Story 1, the reporter launches into a summary of actions taken two weeks ago. You are far into the story before learning what actually took place at the meeting.

Always present the newest information first. Even when it is necessary to fill in background for the reader, save that information until later.

Notice how Story 2 handles the library closing proposals made by the librarian. The main points, published previously, were summarized quickly throughout the body of the story.

Common Errors

Be wary of numbers

Numbers stop readers. Analyze what the numbers signify, state that in your lead, and use the numbers later in the story to back up your lead idea. For example, the following information formed the basis of a five-paragraph story in a San Mateo, California newspaper:

A report from the California Department of Motor Vehicles stated that California had 17.9 million motor vehicles and 14.8 million drivers in 1978. The report predicted that there would be 29.16 motor vehicles and 22.6 million drivers in the state by the year 2005.

Private vehicles registered in San Mateo County numbered 380,007 in 1978. That figure was expected to jump to 607,110 in the year 2005.

The average driver age, throughout the state, was 39.5 years in 1978. In that same year, there were a million more male drivers than female drivers.

The reporter analyzed the information given in the report and then wrote a lead playing up the statewide trend. The second paragraph focused on the San Mateo figures to localize the story. Here are the two lead paragraphs, which took six lines:

California may need more motor vehicles like Georgia needs alligators, but they're coming anyway—another 11.26 million by the year 2005, according to a Department of Motor Vehicles (DMV) study.

Private vehicles registered in San Mateo County currently number 380,007, and that figure is expected to jump to 607,110 by the year 2005, the DMV predicted. (*Source: Redwood City Tribune,* July 1979)

The balance of the story went on to quote the head of the Highway Patrol Department on the predicted future car crush, and to present other figures from the DMV report.

Assumptions

Do not assume too much. Do not take for granted, for example, that a person speaks officially for an organization just because that person is affiliated with it.

You are affiliated with a particular college or university, but do you speak officially for that institution? Probably not.

Always identify speakers precisely. Make sure individuals cited are official spokespersons before stating that they are, and if they are not, state what they are.

Here, for example, is what might happen if Mary Smith, Joe Jones, and Betty Grey call a press conference at Podunk State College this morning to complain about the food served on campus. They state that they attend PSC and, on behalf of all 8000 registered students, want to complain about the low-quality food served in the student cafeteria.

They say the food is tasteless, nonnutritious, and overpriced. "It's revolting, in fact," says Mary Smith. "I wouldn't feed any of it to my pet rabbit."

The lead might read:

62 NEWSPAPER LEADS

> PODUNK—Cafeteria food at Podunk State College is tasteless, nonnutritious and overpriced, three students charged at a press conference this morning.
>
> "It's revolting, in fact," said one student, Mary Smith. "I wouldn't feed any of it to my pet rabbit."

Nothing said in the lead indicates that the students officially represent the 8000 students of PSC. This possibility would need checking.

Chapter 4 Exercises

Remember:

1. Analyze. Highlight the most interesting or most important details. Analyze the significance of numbers before using them. Don't use label leads.

2. Use strong, active verbs. Seek drama. (See Chapter 2.)

3. Write concisely. (See Chapter 2.)

4. Make sure the reader always knows who is talking and where the action took place. However, do not highlight these points unless they are the most important elements.

5. Do not assume too much.

6. Present newest information first; localize if necessary.

7. Use AP/UPI Stylebook form for datelines. (See Appendix A.)

Exercise 4.1

Write leads for the following stories. Try the leads two ways: First write one sentence only, no more than 40 words, or 4 typewritten lines (60 spaces). Then write the lead in more than 1 sentence, but no more than 6 typewritten lines total. You may need two paragraphs for the second lead. Rewrite for clarity as necessary. Use AP/UPI style.

Unless instructed otherwise, give yourself no more than 10 minutes for writing each lead.

1. John Mills, a professor of education at Ohio State University, gave a lecture before the Columbus, Ohio, Parents and Teachers Association yesterday. He said public school costs will skyrocket during the next few years. He suggested that parents and teachers should band together to see that money is spent wisely, preferably on teachers' salaries, rather than on such "frills as trips to museums." He said: "Parents can take their children to visit

museums; let salaries get high enough to attract strong teachers into public school systems."

2. Lawyers for the Plainfield, N. J., Board of Education sought court sanctions yesterday against leaders of the teachers' union for defying a back-to-work order issued last Wednesday. Meanwhile, this morning, teachers in this Union County community voted overwhelmingly to continue their walkout. The teachers' union, the Plainfield Education Association, urged their negotiators this morning to continue the fight for increased wages, medical fringe-benefits, and for an extra two hours a week class preparation time. The walkout started four days ago.

3. The Milwaukee City Council meets every Thursday night. At last night's regular Thursday meeting the City Council discussed plans to build a new City Hall. A staff report said the new building would cost $10 million. Several council members said they thought that was too much money to spend on a new City Hall. They said the building currently in use, which was built in 1925, could be refurbished for much less money. However, other council members protested that the old building no longer is safe and that it is too small for current needs. The City Council members voted 8 to 3 to hold a special public meeting on the subject next Wednesday night.

4. A lobbying organization said campaign reports submitted to the Federal Election Commission show that the bigger spender won 28 of the 33 contested races. Mark Green, director of Congress Watch, the name of the consumer lobbying organization which headquarters in Washington, D. C., said: "We expected a significant correlation between lavish spending and success but we were still somewhat surprised that it was as high as 85 percent."

5. Eddie Byers, 45, a cab driver in New York City, received a $25 parking ticket last June. On June 23, at 3 P.M., he went to the Parking Violations Bureau office to argue about the ticket. The next day he was arrested on charges of having robbed a home at 3 P.M. on June 23. Yesterday the robbery charges were dropped when his Legal Aid attorneys were finally able to prove that he had been in the Parking Violations Office arguing about the ticket at the time the robbery had occurred. Byers has spent all these months protesting his innocence. Had he been convicted, he might have spent 15 years in jail.

6. A check of the four major domestic auto companies in Detroit shows that domestic car sales had dipped 5.5 percent by the 10th of the month, compared to auto sales for the same period a year ago. Low stocks of some 1983 models contributed to the drop. In the first ten days of this month, Americans bought 238,373 new domestic cars from the four major U.S. automakers. A year ago, the tally for the same period was 252,148 cars. Through last month, auto sales had been up 1.9 percent from last year's figures.

7. The Federal Trade Commission is investigating children's commer-

cials. The FTC is considering the possibility of banning all television advertising aimed at children under eight. It also envisions putting restrictions on commercials which promote food that could cause dental cavities. The FTC will hold its first hearings on the subject next month in San Francisco. Two San Francisco women, who are members of the public interest group, Ban TV Ads, held a press conference yesterday. They said they will attend the FTC hearings and show the commissioners a study published by Ban TV Ads which shows that children under eight watch 20,000 commercials per year, most of them on Saturday morning children's shows. "On any given Saturday morning a child is exposed to four to seven advertisements every half hour for sugared cereals alone," one of the women said.

8. Today is Friday. Tuesday a woman jogger was murdered near the Lafayette reservoir in Salt Lake City. Her name was Mrs. Mary White, 40. The prime suspect is a middle-aged man with a "scruffy beard and long hair," the police announced this morning. Two neighbors and jogging companions told police yesterday that they had seen such a man rush off when they arrived to join Mrs. White for a jog last Tuesday. Not seeing her, they assumed she had left. They jogged without her and returned home. Yesterday morning they realized they should report this information to the police.

9. The Finnish Travel Agents Association, in Helsinki, Finland, has sent a formal letter of complaint to the New York Convention and Visitors Bureau. The agents complain in their letter that they have been unable to book hotel reservations for traveling Finns. New York City hotels are overcrowded and do not have rooms available unless the rooms are booked five months in advance, the letter states. The travel agents asked the Visitors Bureau to look into the matter.

10. John Gardner, founder of Common Cause, the public-affairs lobby, speaking in Washington, D.C., said he has surveyed political leaders, scholars and public interest groups across the country. They agree that the United States is getting more difficult to govern because of a piecemeal, inefficient system of authority for which the Presidency and Congress are partly to blame, he said. He also said that the nation is being whipsawed by special interest groups, resulting in a "paralysis in national policymaking."

11. John Peterson is a student at University of Minnesota. He is researching Japanese bombs which landed in South Dakota during World War II. He is headquartering in Madison, S.D. while doing his research. The bombs fell in South Dakota during May 1945. The Japanese had launched balloons with firebombs attached, hoping air currents would bring them over U.S. airspace and they would explode in western forests. The plan was partially successful. Several hundred bombs landed in and around Madison, Peterson has reported. He is looking for people who remember seeing the bombs explode. He said no one was killed by any of the bombs which landed in South Dakota.

12. The Agriculture Department put out its annual prediction on future

inflation trends. Department economists are predicting a sizable rise, 16 percent or more, in price of beef early next summer. Beef has risen 22 percent this year. That will translate into a rise in overall food prices next year of 7.5 percent, the economists said. Beef prices are not the only potential problem on next year's grocery list. Department analysts say sugar prices almost certainly will rise sharply as will dairy supplies also. According to their forecasts, the price crunch should come about mid-June next year.

13. Last month, Japan became the site for the opening of the world's 5000th McDonald's store. It was the 147th in Japan. McDonald's Co. of Japan was founded by Den Fujita, ten years ago. He is still president of McDonald's Co. of Japan, which headquarters in Tokyo. Den Fujita does not care much for hamburgers himself, but his family prefers them. He grew up eating a traditional Japanese diet of rice, fish, bean curd, fermented soybean soup and fresh pickled vegetables. He is 52 and still prefers that diet. However, on weekends, he says that when he asks his wife to make a Japanese meal for the family, she often refuses. Instead, she tells him he can cook for himself if he wishes, but she and the children are going to McDonald's.

14. Neil Armstrong was the first man to walk on the moon. Yesterday he left a hospital in Louisville, Ky. after having had his left ring finger reimplanted on his left hand. He was not wearing his wedding ring on his ring finger, however. Last Friday, Armstrong jumped from a truck at his home in Cincinnati and the wedding ring caught on a door. Part of the finger was pulled off. The finger was reimplanted by new microsurgery techniques. His surgeon said the surgery appeared to be a success, but it would take eight months before it's known whether Armstrong will regain complete sensation.

Chapter 5 Continuing the News Story

News Story Structure

The lead is the key to continuing the newspaper story. It determines the arrangement of the remaining information in the body of your story.

Often, different reporters analyze the same story differently. Each highlights a different element in the lead, causing the information flow in the body to differ also.

Suppose, for example, that you had three elements, A, B, and C, to cover. You could write a summary lead, mentioning all three. Then you would write more detail on each element, in descending order of importance.

On the other hand, if you decided B was the most important point and belonged in the lead, you would have to make a subsequent decision: Either finish explaining B before moving on to A and C or follow lead B with a brief mention of A and C. You could then return to B for a fuller explanation, followed by additional details about A and C.

The second alternative creates a choppier presentation than the first. However, sometimes the news content demands that approach. A few years ago, for instance, 4 planes crashed within 24 hours in different places in the United States. One was a military plane; another a private plane; the remaining two, commercial planes. A roundup story by the Associated Press led off with two elements: 4 planes had crashed in 24 hours; rescue operations were underway.

The second graf (paragraph) described the size and type of each plane and where each had crashed. Succeeding grafs told more details about each crash, starting with the military plane because it had carried the most passengers. The story finished with a roundup of rescue operations.

The following two versions of the same event illustrate how the lead influences information flow.

The event was a graduation ceremony at Stanford University (we will label graduation ceremony references as Element A). Then U.S. Ambassador to the United Nations Daniel P. Moynihan was the graduation day speaker. He asserted that the world faces nuclear weapons poisoning from growing stockpiles of plutonium (we will label his speech Element B). Moments after he began talking, 140 members of the graduating class walked out to protest views about blacks Moynihan had expressed several years earlier (we will label protest references Element C).

Here are two versions of the graduation event:

STORY 1

1. STANFORD—About 140 students, most of them black, walked out on United Nations Ambassador Daniel Patrick Moynihan as he rose to deliver the commencement address at Stanford University Sunday.

2. The protestors were joined by a handful of professors and spectators in sun-drenched Frost Amphitheater in a dramatic gesture of objection to selection of Moynihan as graduation speaker.

3. Black graduates said they consider Moynihan a "subtle racist."

4. But the colorful exercises went on without further interruption Sunday morning as 2,000 of Stanford's 4,000 degree recipients participated in the ceremony.

5. Moynihan, who was confirmed for the post just last week, delivered a gloomy assessment of the future of the world in this Nuclear Age.

6. A more upbeat message was presented by Stanford President Richard W. Lyman, who urged the

STORY 2

1. Daniel P. Moynihan, the new U.S. Ambassador to the United Nations, warned Stanford University's graduating class yesterday that the world faces "nuclear poisoning" from growing stockpiles of plutonium.

2. As Moynihan addressed Stanford's 84th annual commencement exercises, 140 members of the graduating class silently walked out in protest of his past, hotly controversial writings on black Americans.

3. Moynihan noted the "politeness" of the restrained demonstration, then went on with his first major address since the Senate confirmed his appointment to the United Nations last week.

4. "The prospect of nuclear disaster increasingly derives not from the preparations for war, but rather from the quest for peace," Moynihan said.

5. Nations seeking peaceful economic development are building

graduates to preserve their individuality despite the "excitement of shared goals" that marked student activism of four or five years ago.

7. Two professors, an administrator and two seniors were honored with Lloyd W. Dinkelspiel Awards for service to undergraduate education and three others won Walter J. Gores Awards for teaching excellence.

8. The Moynihan protest was spurred by past remarks by Moynihan about racial problems, the black graduates said in a leaflet distributed before the ceremony.

9. Moynihan advocated "benign neglect" of race problems as an adviser to former President Richard Nixon and, as a Labor Department official, wrote a report blaming most racial troubles on the disintegration of the Negro family.

10. "Daniel F. Moynihan has risen to the point where he has become extremely influential," the leaflet said.

11. "To those of us who are can look beyond the veil of eloquence and recognize the threat of 'benign neglect,' he is a symbol that must be spoken out against."

12. The diplomat's address was a somber note in the otherwise happy event marking the conclusion of the undergraduate careers of thousands who came to Stanford just as the campus tumult of the late 1960's was ending.

13. "What disheartens me," Moynihan said, "is the probability that the spread of plutonium around the world will lead to the gradual or precipitous—but in any event prox- nuclear power plants that turn out plutonium "as a by-product of the demand for energy," Moynihan said.

6. But, he warned, nations could fashion plutonium into nuclear weapons "within weeks, or at most months, should they desire them."

7. The developed nations cannot keep a "monopoly of nuclear energy," Moynihan said, and the United Nations is the only international forum that could find a way to separate "the production of energy from the proliferation of weapons."

8. If purely competitive, commercial sales of nuclear power plants continues, Moynihan asked, "Will human greed ever have written a more squalid history?"

9. Moynihan, a domestic advisor to presidents since John F. Kennedy, entered foreign affairs with his recent stint as ambassador to India.

10. But the students who walked out of commencement yesterday, many of them black, were protesting Moynihan's disputed theory that black families are too dominated by mothers and his famed memorandum recommending that President Richard Nixon follow a policy of "benign neglect" toward blacks.

11. (After a private communication on "benign neglect" became public in 1970, Moynihan was widely denounced by black leaders. But he replied that he was only suggesting there should be fewer "hysterics" over race issues.)

12. The protesting students, who left but returned after Moynihan's 15-minute speech, were among

imate—nuclear poisoning of the earth through the explosion of weapons fashioned from other plutonium."

14. "The prospect of nuclear disaster increasingly derives not from preparations for war, but rather from the quest for peace," he said.

15. "There is no reversing this spread of nuclear energy plants unless we decide to put an end here and now to economic growth in the world."

16. The only way out, he stressed, is through the United Nations.

17. He said a proposal made 29 years ago for an international authority to control all nuclear installations in the world ought now to be put into effect.

18. "There is no solution to the question which is not an international one," Moynihan said, "and no international setting save the United Nations in which such a solution . . . can ultimately be implemented."

19. Lyman, harkening back to the riotous days of 1968–71 during which he became president, advised the students:

20. "If hope and the excitement of shared goals were exhilarating, the weakening of individual responsibility and the glorification of anonymous solidarity were ominous.

21. "Self-righteousness, never an attractive human quality, is even more repellent—and more dangerous—when it is cloaked in anonymity."

22. After the group commencement involving about half of the 2,000 seniors and graduate students who went to sun-baked Frost Ampitheater to receive degrees. Half of those who received degrees skipped the formalities.

13. About 10,000 parents and friends watched the ceremony, many holding up commencement programs as sun-shades during the late-morning exercise.

14. Most of those graduating wore the somber black caps and gowns of tradition, but a few added sportier flourishes.

15. A law student wore a grand top hat. Several undergraduates displayed red banners of the United Farm Workers union. A student in cut-off jeans sipped beer during the speeches, and another wore a straw hat and a big rubber nose from a disguise kit.

16. The university's annual Lloyd P. Dinkelspiel Awards for service to undergraduates were presented to English professor Lawrence V. Ryan, history professor Gordon Wright, assistant dean of student affairs Alan B. Strain and seniors James M. Montoya of San Jose and Lise A. Pfeiffer of Los Angeles. (*Source: San Francisco Chronicle*, June 1975.)

4,000 qualified to receive degrees, diplomas were presented in individual ceremonies at the university's various schools. (*Source: San Jose Mercury,* June 1975)

Story 2 places the greatest emphasis on the contents of Moynihan's speech (B), with the protest a strong secondary lead (C). Relegated to the end position are descriptions of the commencement exercises (A).

Story 1 interprets the events somewhat differently. The protest receives key attention (C), followed by commencement exercises (A). Moynihan's remarks bring up the rear (B).

Before analyzing the 2 stories in more detail, we should note that Story 1 is about 15 lines longer than Story 2. Sometimes knowing that you have more space to tell your story affects how you tell it.

Story 2 moves along smoothly, with a minimum of switching back and forth. Diagramming the story, we would show B in the lead, immediately followed by C; a transition graf (3) acts as a bridge, followed by the 4 remaining grafs concerning Element A.

Story 1 begins with C for 3 grafs; uses a transition phrase to begin graf 4 on A; moves to Element B for 1 graf; uses another transition phrase at 6 to introduce 3 grafs on Element A; then spends 4 grafs on C; moves to 7 grafs on B; returns to spend the last 4 grafs on A.

Story 1 is unnecessarily choppy. It could have begun with C, moved to B, returned to finish details on C, then ended with as many grafs as necessary to provide information on A.

Just as there is no standard formula today for writing leads, neither is there a formula for organizing and writing the body of a newspaper story. Much will depend on the content of story, the editor's preference, space, and time pressure.

Transitions

Many papers around the country are moving toward feature-style writing, even for hard news events. Feature style often develops a story more slowly, in narrative or chronological order, with considerable color and background information supplied as the story moves along.

Whatever the style, however—whether feature style or inverted pyramid hard news style—a reporter must move from element to element, weaving all together as smoothly as possible. This integrating requires careful use of transitions.

The two graduation ceremony stories demonstrate different techniques for moving from one element to another. Story 2 uses transition paragraphs: Information from the preceding topic is combined with new information introducing the succeeding topic.

Note how the reporter uses Moynihan's comments in graf 3 on the demonstration (C) as a transition back to the ambassador's speech (B) after having

71 NEWS STORY STRUCTURE

described the protest (C) in the second graf. Much farther into the story, in graf 9, the reporter briefly describes Moynihan's background as a transition from his speech (B) to the protest (C).

That transition graf begins: "Moynihan, a domestic advisor to presidents since. . . ."

Several grafs later, in graf 12, another transition graf moves the story from the protest (C) to commencement events (A): "The protesting students, who left but returned after Moynihan's 15-minute speech were among 2000 seniors and graduate students who went to sun-baked. . . ."

Story 1 handles transitions in graf 6 with a few key words: "A more upbeat message was presented by . . ." moves the reader from Moynihan's speech (B) to the university president's remarks (A). Later, again, a few words reintroduce Moynihan's speech topic (B) in graf 12: "The diplomat's address was a somber note in the otherwise happy event. . . ."

Sometimes, especially in hard news stories, the reporter must move quickly from topic to topic without time to craft smooth transitions. Then the reporter must resort to mechanical linkages with such key words as: *however, in other action, elsewhere, meanwhile, for the most part,* and *following.*

Documenting the Story

The body of a newspaper story must provide answers to all questions raised in the reader's mind. This technique is called *documenting* your story. If, for example, you are writing about a fire, the body of the story must contain information on the cause of the fire, if known, or an explanation of why this detail is unavailable; the names, ages, and occupations of any persons hurt; an estimate of damage and the location of the fire, if that information is not used in the lead; how long it took to put out the fire; the owner of the property; and whether insurance will cover the damage.

Sometimes the questions raised in a reader's mind by a feature-type story are more subtle and must be anticipated by the reporter. A recent story from Southern California, for instance, described a man with a rare disease caused by fungus growing in his intestine that converted carbohydrates to alcohol. Shortly after eating starchy foods, he was apt to become drunk. An amusing article was written after he was convicted of driving while intoxicated by a Los Angeles jury that did not believe his defense. Nowhere in the story of his trial were readers told the circumstance of his arrest, which might have explained why the jurors chose to ignore medical testimony supporting his claim. This nagging puzzle left readers dissatisfied with an otherwise well-written human interest piece.

Chapter 5 Exercises

Remember:

1. Organize the information so one topic idea leads to another in smooth transition.

72 CONTINUING THE NEWS STORY

2. Use other transition techniques if you are unable to organize the story for obvious flow. These include mechanical linking phrases, or repetition of words and ideas expressed in the preceding graf.

3. Decide which of two possibilities suits each story: The most important information first, followed in descending order by subsequent information; or, the most intriguing information first, followed by an enticing presentation that includes all necessary information.

4. Answer all questions that might exist in the reader's mind.

Exercise 5.1

Diagram the following news stories, labeling each element with a letter of the alphabet (that is, A, B, C, D, and so on). Decide which element or elements you would place in the lead and which in descending paragraphs. Then write the story. (You may use any wording you consider appropriate.)

SALEM, Oregon—Police Chief Thomas Smith, 42, indicted yesterday on charges involving the falsifying of records, refused comment and Jordan Valley Mayor Ed Krupp said, "I'd rather have no comment. He has done a pretty good job."

The police chief of Jordan Valley, Oregon, population 210, apparently grossed a personal income of $102,117 last year, according to traffic-fine documents filed with the Oregon Department of Revenue.

In July 1978, the City Council awarded Smith, who spent 7 years as an Oregon state policeman, a 10-year contract to provide police services. He purchased a radar set, a Dodge, and hired an assistant for $800 a month, the documents said. Under the contract all fines are paid to Smith.

Smith, who has been accused of running a speed trap in the tiny town on the main highway between Boise, Idaho, and Reno, Nevada, was arraigned yesterday on charges of tampering with public records and making false statements on official documents.

Three counts accuse the chief of making false entries in expense account records and a fourth count accuses Smith of making false written statements when applying for certification as a police officer before the Oregon Board on Police Standards and Training.

Exercise 5.2

In January 1979, Richard Stand, 6, was asleep in his bed when the water heater leaked natural gas, starting a fire that spread quickly through the apartment.

The boy's grandmother, aunt, and two younger sisters escaped, but were unable to rescue Richard. The boy was saved by firefighters, but suffered third degree burns over 75 percent of his body. He was scarred and suffered respiratory damage in the blaze.

A Minneapolis jury yesterday gave him a $2.5 million settlement from the Minneapolis Housing Authority.

Richard's sister, Shellie Grim, 7, will receive $7,500 for the trauma she suffered in the fire.

Minneapolis Superior Court Judge Jay Stern approved the settlement yesterday.

Richard will receive $75,000 within a month, plus monthly payments of $1,000 for the rest of his life, with a built-in 3 percent annual cost-of-living increase.

The Stand children were represented by attorneys Marvin Black and Charles Allan, who claimed successfully that housing authority employees were negligent in repairing the water heater.

Richard will also be paid $25,000 on his eighteenth and twenty-first birthdays, $50,000 at age 26, $30,000 at age 32 and $30,000 when he reaches 36.

Richard's mother, Marilyn Stand, said she hopes the judge allows her to use some of the money to purchase a home for her family. They still live in a housing authority apartment.

Exercise 5.3

TALLAHASSEE, Florida—Before John Spenkelink was executed May 25, Florida's electric chair—called Old Sparky by inmates—had been idle since May 1964.

Governor Bob Graham signed death warrants for 2 of Florida's 133 death row inmates Tuesday, less than a month after John Spenkelink was executed in the electric chair.

Warden David Brierton scheduled the executions of convicted murderers Charles William Proffitt, 33, and Robert Sullivan, 31, for June 27.

Graham suggested clemency for two other death row inmates, Larry Leo Alford and Clifford Hallman, recommending their sentences be commuted to life in prison.

Attorneys for Sullivan and Proffitt said they were confident they can block the executions.

Reactions came quickly.

"I don't think two a month is too many," said state Representative David Lehman, a Democrat. "I think two a week would be better."

Proffitt was convicted in March 1976 by a jury which recommended death for the murder of a high school wrestling coach, stabbed March 13, 1974, while he slept beside his wife.

Scharlette Holdman, director of Florida Citizens Against the Death Penalty, said Graham was signing warrants for persons who have not exhausted legal remedies.

"He's trying to fulfill a commitment to make state murder routine," Ms. Holdman said.

Sullivan was sentenced to die for the April 9, 1973, killing of a restaurant manager. He was convicted and sentenced to death in November 1973.

The clemency recommendation for Alford and Hallman will be considered June 26 by the Florida cabinet. Three cabinet members must support Graham's recommendation before the sentences can be commuted.

Exercise 5.4

COLUMBIA, Missouri—The Columbia School Board met last night and concentrated on planning to cope with reduced income next year.

Trustees authorized SRI International to continue efforts to sell or lease a 59-acre, vacant school site in the Riverside area and the unused Terman School site downtown, along with several other empty sites.

The trustees voted 5–0 to appoint David Schwartz as the student representative to the board. Schwartz, 17, is a senior at Gavin High School. He replaces Kent Walker, student representative for the past 2 years, who will be attending Harvard University this fall.

James Vas Dias of the SRI staff said SRI still had to clear up a number of details before coming back to the school board with definite proposals for the unused school properties.

The discussion of the school sites revealed that talks between the school district and the city of Columbia on Tuesday included an offer by city officials to trade floor space in City Hall for the school district offices on a 3-acre site at 25 Churchill Avenue. The city is also having budget problems.

During a break in the meeting last night, Superintendent of Schools John Appelby confirmed that the offer had been made, but said no details were discussed. The offer was not accepted by school officials, he added.

Trustee Anne Martin said she didn't believe it would be to the district's advantage to move into city hall, where city officials have found they have too much space for city operations.

"We would need to know a great deal more," about the offer, trustee Donald Roper said.

A $34.8 million tentative budget, about $1 million less than the budget for the current fiscal year, was passed last night for the next fiscal year beginning in July.

Exercise 5.5

Skylab, a 6-year-old space station, has stopped functioning, left its original orbit circling Venus, and is now falling back to earth. National Aeronautics and Space Administration (NASA) engineers at the Houston manned space center are in charge of maneuvering Skylab safely back into earth's atmosphere, where most of it is expected to burn up. Some pieces, however, are expected to withstand atmospheric friction and land on earth.

Earlier today the Skylab space station was turned around in orbit in a key maneuver aimed at opening the way for an unprecedented attempt to keep it from falling over populous Europe and Asia next month.

The new orientation in orbit was designed to increase Skylab's resistance to the thin upper fringes of earth's atmosphere as the lab orbits the globe at about 17,000 miles per hour.

If it appears Skylab will begin its final descent during orbits that take it over densely populated regions of Europe and Asia, NASA will try to turn Skylab into a more streamlined position to decrease drag and thus extend its stay in space a few hours. This would change its reentry orbits to less populated areas.

Acting on instructions radioed up from earth during the night, the 78.5-ton orbiting laboratory changed into a position intended to balance the increasing forces of gravity and atmospheric drag, and to keep it from tumbling out of control.

The maneuver started at 8:50 A.M. Eastern Daylight Time (EDT), while the abandoned spacecraft was about 165 miles over the south

Pacific Ocean. Thirty minutes later, as Skylab passed over the Ascension Island tracking station in the south Atlantic, engineers confirmed that Skylab maneuvered as planned.

"Everything looks pretty good," reported control center spokesperson Robert Gordon in Houston. "All systems aboard Skylab look good."

He said it would take several hours of tracking to confirm that the 118-foot assembly remained in its new orbital orientation.

If successful, the maneuver was expected to keep the space station stable until the final hours before it reenters the atmosphere, now expected sometime between July 7 and July 25.

Such stability is required if engineers are to have a chance to keep Skylab from descending over heavily populated areas.

On the average, NASA estimates there is 1 chance in 252 that a piece of debris from Skylab would hit 1 person somewhere.

Exercise 5.6

OKLAHOMA CITY—An unidentified armed robbery suspect died early Wednesday after Oklahoma City police shot him in a gun battle at the end of a high-speed chase across the northern section of the city.

In a separate incident, Oklahoma City officers shot and critically wounded an auto theft suspect in a dawn shootout in adjacent Terra Heights.

Lieutenant Charles Higby of the department's robbery-homicide division said the dead man, whom he would not identify, had attempted to run over two officers who approached him as he sat in his car on Main Street.

In the second shooting, two officers said they chased a pair of suspected auto thieves to a house at 4201 Laurel Boulevard in Terra Heights and exchanged shots with one of the suspects. A police spokesperson said the unidentified suspect was wounded in the hand and stomach and was reported in critical condition after surgery in the jail ward at the County-Oklahoma City Medical Center.

The man shot and killed after the high-speed chase in the northern part of town was described as being in his 30s. He was said to have fled north from Main Street in his orange Ford Mustang, with police in pursuit at speeds up to 90 MPH. until he hit two cars, jumped a curb and halted at Victory Boulevard and Friar Street, according to investigators.

Higby said the suspect fired a single shot from a handgun at officers Thomas Ingledew and Frank de Cesare but missed. They fired three shots back, hitting the man at least once in the head, Higby said.

In the Terra Heights incident, both the wounded man and his companion were booked on suspicion of assault with a deadly weapon on a police officer, Higby said.

Police Department spokesperson, Commander William Booth, said both shooting incidents are under investigation, as is normal procedure after shootings in which officers are involved.

Exercise 5.7

NEW YORK—"I have hung up my gloves. It's time to get out," drawled Muhammed Ali, insisting his announced retirement is no farce this time, after at least a couple false alarms.

With his children laughing and playing behind him, Ali recited what he says he has contributed to boxing since first winning the title as Cassius Clay on February 25, 1964, when he stopped Sonny Liston in the seventh round.

"I brought a whole world into boxing which had never followed it, including the communist world and black Africa. I am the first man to predict the exact round in which his opponent will fall."

"I'm in a position that I can go no further in boxing," the 37-year-old Ali told a news conference.

"It's something I got to do," Ali said. "When I was 26-years-old I could chew up and spit out guys like Larry Holmes, Earnie Shavers, Gerrie Coetzee. But now I'm 37 and if I trained for a few weeks I could still whip them. But I don't want to kill myself training for 15 rounds. . . ."

"I have other battles to fight. I'm going to Russia in two weeks. I am going to talk with President Carter. There are more pleasing things to do than beat up people."

Ali noted he currently weighs 234 pounds.

In 1967, Ali refused induction into the U.S. Army at Houston on religious grounds and was convicted of draft evasion. He was fined $10,000 and sentenced to 5 years in prison. But he was never jailed because of an appeal and the U.S. Supreme Court eventually overturned his conviction.

"I would do the same today," he said of the moral stand for which he was stripped of his title in 1968.

Exercise 5.8

PALO ALTO, California—"If you can't ride a bike, then you can't do this," Chris declares.

The scene is a small parking lot in Palo Alto at the southwest corner of Ramona Street and Channing Avenue. The clown-like truck was a gift from a woman who won it in a drawing about a month ago.

Jimmy became an overnight celebrity in the neighborhood and occasionally lets his muppet friends streak around in circles "for 3 or 4 minutes" at a time.

Saturday afternoon Jimmy and his tight circle of racing-car disciples were tooting around in the parking lot while Jimmy's father, Jim Suetos, fixed big cars a few blocks away at his job with Paddleford Oldsmobile.

Jimmy, with his baseball cap turned backward, mulled over Jason's request, ruled the kid "is too small; maybe next year," and then changed his mind. Jason was ecstatic.

The truck, which tops out at 15 miles per hour, whirled around in an erratic circle—nearly striking a couple of the kids as they shouted out last minute directions on how to apply the brakes.

"If he doesn't know how to use the brakes, get out of his way!" shouted Jimmy's father as he approached the scene. Jason finally figured out how to stop the diminutive contraption, and the others took their turns entering the cockpit and the thrilling world of race car driving.

"It's completely safe," Suetos said. "You really can't tip it over or anything . . . it's not meant to drive in the streets."

It's designed for people the size of Munchkins in *The Wizard of Oz*, but it makes them feel like big shots in the real world of grown-ups.

Pint-sized Jimmy Suetos, 11, chewed the life out of his bubble gum as 4 buddies tried to weasle a ride in his new 3-horsepower, 1-quart gas tank, 76-inch long, fiberglass truck.

"I want to drive it, Jimmy," begged Jason Brown, 6, of San Jose.

"Eh," teased Jimmy, "I might let Paul drive it." Paul, aged 7, is Jason's big brother.

"He can't even ride a bicycle," snaps Chris Walter, 10, also of San Jose. Chris has driven the truck "lots of times," and "it's scary for some but not for me."

"So what if I can't ride a bike," Jason sniffed.

The vehicle was purchased by Mike Delaney, owner of Motor Car Supply Company of Palo Alto, for $500 as a promotional gimmick to attract customers to his grand opening last January.

The truck, which weighs a mere 150 pounds, was manufactured by F. W. and Associates, Inc., of Tempe, Arizona. It is really a go-cart encased in the fiberglass body of a truck.

Chapter 6 # Interviewing and Observing

Speaking to a university audience about the news media, a speaker made harsh comments about the number of reporters who go on assignments knowing little about the subjects they are to cover. A young reporter for a radio station said to him after the speech: "Look, I agree with what you said. But consider my problems. I got here late for your speech because I had to tape an interview downtown an hour ago. Now I'm supposed to ask you a question or two for the afternoon news show. Forty-five minutes from now I'm due at the Sheraton for another interview. I don't have time to get ready for half the things I cover."

This story reflects a basic problem, especially in radio and television, which usually try to cover too many events too fast with too few reporters. Newspaper reporters usually operate on less pressured schedules and aim at more complete reports, but they are sometimes as ill-prepared as the radio reporter, and often for intertwined reasons. Radio and television are much faster reporting news than the newspapers. Thus, the newspaper must give a feature slant to many stories to compete, rather than using the stark news story.

To make certain that you can become a good feature writer and magazine writer, use the following guidelines.

Interviewing

You must gather at least three times as much information as you can use. Writers who have collected more information than they need are free of the need to use everything they have. They can *select,* and selection is the key to all successful writing. Instead of relating a tasteless anecdote and one that actually reveals character, the writer must be able to choose 5 revealing anecdotes from a stock of 12.

If you are writing an important, long profile of a person, do not be content to ask him questions and record what he says. Interview your subject more than once, especially when you can see the person at work or at play. Then you can *observe* the subject. Again, when you are writing a profile, never be content to talk only to the interviewee. Interview two or three people who know the subject. The more information you collect, the better your story will be.

How to Interview

An easygoing, conversational technique is valuable. Interviewees usually are so disarmed by the conversational approach that they talk more freely than they might have done had the interviewer been either more formal or more aggressive.

An entirely different interview atmosphere is created by the tough, aggressive interviewer who bores in with rifle-shot questions, hoping to upset the interviewee to the point that he defensively says much more than he had intended to say. This approach, however, often results in the interviewee's putting up his guard and revealing as little as possible—even about matters that he would not have minded discussing under more relaxed circumstances. In any event, a young reporter seldom is successful in this more aggressive mode. Remember this: If you must ask tough questions, ask them near the end of the interview.

Prepare for the Interview

Always learn as much as possible about your subject before the appointment. Those who are not actually incensed by an interviewer's ignorance will almost surely be uncomfortable with one who demonstrates a lack of homework. Doing the homework—learning at least the basic facts about an interviewee—is a compliment to the subject and will encourage response. Author John Gunther has warned: "One thing is never, never, never to ask a man about his own first name, job, or title. These the interviewer should know beforehand." (*Source:* John Gunther, "An Exercise in Self-Education," *Harper's,* April 1961, p. 41.) And, of course, much more.

In preparing questions, however, remember that an interview is a human, not a bookkeeping, situation. Most professional interviewers have a few questions ready, in mind or jotted in a notebook, but not many of them prepare a long list of questions. Growth and continuity in an interview stem from conversation. Transitions should be natural. Questions should grow logically from the discussion, one answer suggesting another question. The interviewer who knows, 1-2-3-4, what to ask may miss the opportunity to pose a good question arising during the course of the interview.

Take Notes

Professional interviewers disagree on when and how to take notes. Interviewees may become self-conscious when they see their words being written. Some freeze. These are cogent arguments against tape-recording interviews,* but many writers are turning to the recorders. Other interviewees are uneasy when notes are *not* taken, fearing that the interviewer (especially an obvious beginner) will later try, ineptly, to remember what was said. At least a few interviewers follow this rule: Take notes freely—or use a recorder—in talking with those who are accustomed to speaking: teachers, politicians, civic leaders, entertainers, and the like. Be wary with those who are not in public life, for few can avoid tightening up in the presence of a notebook or tape recorder, thus preventing the natural flavor the interviewer wants. One writer says: "Flipping out the notebook the minute you flush the quarry has never worked too well for me. It scares some subjects. The best excuse I find for breaking out the pad is a bit of blue-eyed admiration for some happy observation they've just made. I may try, 'Say, that's good. I want to be sure I get that down just right.' And write. The notebook now spells reassurance."

Encourage a Response

The ideal interview will find a halfway point between monologue and dialogue. If the interviewee talks in an endless monologue, leading points may be missed. Most interviewees must be steered. But if the interview is a real dialogue, you are doing half the talking and, as a result, showing off and probably irritating your subject. This is the most delicate point in interviewing—the balance between commenting appropriately on an answer in developing the next question, and yet not seeming to dominate the interview. A comment is effective in connection with at least a few questions, for you are never more likely to draw a full response than when you make it clear, modestly, that you are knowledgeable. The interviewee develops confidence that his responses will be reported in a meaningful context and thus speaks more freely. It is a cardinal error, however, for you to fail to ask questions because you fear exposing your ignorance of particular points. If you knew *everything,* there would be no reason for an interview.

It usually pays to wind up an interview with a comment like, "My hindsight is better than my foresight. When I check over my notes, I'll undoubtedly find that there are questions I'll wish I had asked. May I come back with another question or two?" This keeps the door open and suggests to the inter-

---

*If you want to use a tape recorder, remember this: Many beginning reporters use the recorder for a time, then give up. It takes much more time to translate what was said from the recorder than from taking notes. Also, your recorder may fail at the wrong time. Some professional reporters will take notes while recording the speakers—and seldom listen to their recorders. They use their recorders as backups, especially when the speakers question the way the reporters have written their stories.

viewee that he is dealing with a careful writer. One writer has observed: "I make it a habit to ask the source a broad leading question toward the end of the interview—something like, 'Is there anything I haven't asked you that you think I ought to ask or that you are anxious to answer?' It sometimes opens up whole new fields of exploration that I didn't even know existed."

Respect Confidences

Finally, it is important to remember that those who conduct interviews will probably be asked to keep some information confidential. This request occurs when subjects suddenly decide they have been indiscreet or have been so lured by the interviewer that more has been revealed than should have been. The interviewer and interviewee should determine at the beginning what kind of and how much information will be disclosed.

If you have never conducted a formal interview and know little about conventional techniques, you may be a better interviewer than one who has conducted many interviews and has carefully studied the insights and experiences of professional interviewers. Interviewing has a highly personal character, and curiosity, intelligence, and warmth are all valuable assets. Studying interviewing techniques, however, can certainly help improve your interviewing style.

Observing

Observation is vital. Like interviewing, direct observation yields liveliness—paragraphs that have a lift and freshness. Early in his career, Bruce Bliven had the good fortune to work under Fremont Older, a demanding San Francisco editor with "a personality so vigorous that you could feel his presence through a brick wall." Deciding that one dull reporter could write compellingly only by immersing himself in his subject, Older assigned him to write about the Salvation Army and gave him all the time he needed to research and write captivatingly. But after three weeks with the Army, the reporter turned in his usual flavorless stuff. "Didn't you *observe* anything?" Older bellowed. "At night, for instance, *where did they hang the bass drum?*" The reporter did not know. He was fired.

This kind of concentration is essential to good writing largely because we become too accustomed to our environment. Familiarity breeds indifference. This was demonstrated strikingly in a series of studies: Students proved themselves incapable of describing the entrance hall of their university. They had seen the entrance countless times, but it had never registered clearly in their minds.

How can you train yourself to see sharply? First, you must recognize the common pitfalls of observation:

1. *The process of distortion.* In attempting to be a good observer, you should remind yourself that human perception is not

infallible, and that deeply embedded habits, interests, and sentiments are likely to affect the way you absorb new information. Thus, you are forced to simplify and select—or distort—what you observe. Remembering this tendency toward distortion should cause you to go slowly.

2. *Emotional states.* Most of us have learned to discount some of our unfounded impressions. We dismiss them with "Well, I guess I was pretty emotional then." The most accurate observations normally are those recalled immediately after an event. But if the event has placed emotional stress on the observer, he may be more subject to the distortion caused by emotion. This problem can often be resolved by recording impressions of an event immediately after it occurs, thus capturing details that might be forgotten. Later, at a more tranquil time, you can assess your first account and evaluate any possible distortion arising from your emotional state at the time of the event.

3. *Significant details.* As mentioned before, to concentrate on the important visual details is a difficult job. You, as an observer, must decide beforehand which forms, events, or details are worth your attention. Your task as an observer would be hopeless if you did not have in mind, or even on paper, your intended focus. Train yourself to concentrate on what is significant for your purpose. The ability, or the will, to concentrate varies. This is why some football coaches are better than others at scouting upcoming opponents and at picking out small, but crucial, details of interior line play—while nearly everyone else in the stadium is watching the ball. But anyone with vision can learn to focus it.

4. *Distortions of perspective.* The most obvious method of avoiding distortion is to recognize that any single perspective is necessarily limited and must be supplemented with others. Careful researchers are usually quick to recognize that they must consider other perspectives when they are weighing another observer's report, but they may not be so quick to supplement their own observations. Nearly all observers are too ready to trust the evidence they have seen. Wilbur Schramm, a thorough investigator, says that whenever possible he arranges to have another researcher accompany him for observing and interviewing. He has learned that checking one impression against another often yields surprising and useful results.

It is easier to identify these enemies of valid observation than it is to conquer them. But isolating them and recognizing their power is your first step in countering their effects. Observers who know they are subject to vagueness of vision, or to overly strong personal perspective and attitudes, are at least on guard against the most obvious distortions.

Chapter 6 Exercises

Remember:

When doing the following exercises, keep in mind:

1. You must prepare for the interview.
2. Conversational techniques usually work best.
3. Observe details you may wish to use when writing your article.

Exercise 6.1

Below is a summary of Katharine Graham's career. After reading it list 20 questions that you, as a feature writer or a magazine writer, would ask her in order to write a 1000-word profile.

Katharine Graham (1917–   ) is the chair of the board of the *Washington Post*. Born the daughter of the late Eugene Meyer and Agnes Meyer, she first attended Vassar. She transferred to the University of Chicago and was graduated in 1938.

Mrs. Graham first worked as a reporter for the *San Francisco News,* then joined the editorial staff of the *Washington Post* in 1939. She continued working in the Sunday, circulation, and editorial departments until 1945. She was married to Philip L. Graham in 1940, and they had four children: Elizabeth Morris (Mrs. Elizabeth Weymouth), Donald Edward, William Welch, and Stephen Meyer. Mr. Graham died in 1963.

Mrs. Graham became widely known after taking over as publisher of the *Post* in 1968. Her company owns two other newspapers in Trenton, New Jersey, *Newsweek* magazine, and four television and radio stations. The *Post* has become widely known for its adversary relationship with government officials, especially in the Watergate controversy that brought President Richard M. Nixon to resign. The power of the *Washington Post* has been increased substantially with the agreement that brings it together with the *Los Angeles Times* in the Los Angeles Times-Washington Post News Service, used by more than 300 newspapers.

Exercise 6.2

Below is information about and an interview with a popular university professor. Pose yourself as a student asking the questions in the interview. Write a feature story of about 700 words, based primarily on the interview.

Professor Gene Beach, a professor of economics at your university, is over 60. He is 6 feet tall, weighs 180 pounds, has blue eyes, and his hair, which was once brown, is almost white. He is handsome. Even when he is teaching large classes—more than 300 students—he treats the class as a seminar. When Beach walks into a 340-seat auditorium at 9 A.M., he sits down at a table edge. Instead of launching into a lecture, he invites questions on any economic issue the students choose: from the textbook, television, or newspaper. For the first 15 minutes, any such question is fair game. "Inviting questions at the beginning of a class loosens things up a bit, and keeps the course in touch with the real world," Beach said. In interviewing him (you are the student interviewer, below), you think this way: "He's amiable and enthusiastic and is able to answer any question I can ask." As the interview continues, it seems to you that he is serious, but relaxed.

Student: Are there any rules that you observe as a teacher?
Beach: There are three basic rules a good classroom teacher should follow:

First, teach students to think through problems for themselves. Never give pat answers, teach concepts and how to use them. This frequently frustrates students, who want pat answers. But the important thing is to make them think for themselves.

Second, know precisely what you want the student to learn, and focus the teaching on those essential concepts or ways of solving problems. If a teacher doesn't know clearly what he wants the student to learn, it's unlikely the student will learn it. A related rule is, don't try to teach too much. Trying to cram a lot in usually results in less learning, not more.

Third, motivation is important. When bright students are motivated to learn, they do. Without real motivation to learn, few students can achieve much.

Student: Some of the people taking your courses are scared of you. Do you know that you frighten some people?
Beach: (His stern face breaks into a remarkably warm smile, and his chuckle is rich.) I used to scare them, but I'm getting softer in my old age.

Student: Do you consider yourself a tough teacher?
Beach: I used to be tough; I used to drive them all the time into thinking for themselves "Why?" "Why?" "Why?"

I feel students ought to work hard. This may be the most important time of their lives. I keep at them to think clearly. But they learn pretty quickly that the stern look is just a facade.

They know I've been around a lot of years, and served as economic consultant to the Federal Reserve Board, the Treasury, and businesses, and I suppose that may influence their attitude to me.

Student: If you are not so tough now, are you getting just as good results out of the students?

Beach: That depends on the particular student. A first-rate student ought to be led to work hard or be driven hard. Some of the students clam up if you push them to justify their reasoning or their positions. They grow scared and tense.

Student: How do you cope with the problem of keeping the right balance in teaching between the brighter students and the laggards?

Beach: It's a question of interest and motivation, not ability, especially with the graduate students. Every student can do the work.

Student: Do you feel on edge before a lecture?

Beach: Sure. Every good teacher has to self-hype a bit, especially for big classes. We all want to do a good job. I believe in careful preparation. After all these years I cannot teach a class without preparing. I generally put in two or three hours before going into the classroom.

Student: Are your courses the same every year?

Beach: Oh no. The basic analytical economics changes some each year. The applications and examples change a lot.

Student: Do you use notes?

Beach: Some. A well-prepared teacher ought to have the plans for the class pretty well laid out in his head.

Student: What is the biggest mistake a teacher can make?

Beach: Trying to cram the heads of students with masses of technical detail and facts. The important thing is to teach concepts and principles, and how to apply them to differing situations, especially to what I call complex, ill-structured problems.

Economics is hard to teach because students come looking for answers. The worst thing is to give a pat answer, for the student will memorize the answer and then later slap it onto another problem which is different. Tomorrow will have new problems which need new answers.

Students get very frustrated about this sometimes. Some say I am not being helpful. Thinking for oneself is a painful process to learn, but it pays off.

Student: Is there any crucial period in a course?

Beach: Yes, the first few days. You should avoid jumping on any of the students during that period. That makes them nervous, and they will stay silent the whole course.
Student: In a class of 340 people it must be impossible to get to know many of them.
Beach: By the end of the big elementary course I may know 20 or so students tolerably well. The lack of personal contact is the worst thing about teaching large classes.

With the smaller graduate classes of 66 each in the Business School I generally get to know maybe half of them fairly well. But those classes are still too big. A small seminar of first-class students is a real joy.
Student: Are the best students those who are most vocal and visible?
Beach: Sometimes. Sometimes not. Some of the best students sit quietly without participating, and then turn in a paper that is superior to all the others. The student who is falling behind is just as likely to say nothing.
Student: Do you make yourself freely available after class?
Beach: I try not to turn students away. I try to be here for students on Wednesdays, and to schedule appointments for other days.
Student: If learning to think for oneself is the most important thing for a student to learn, what is the most important rule for a teacher?
Beach: To work out exactly what ideas he wants to put across. The worst thing he can do is to pump a lot of only vaguely relevant and organized facts into students' heads.
Student: So the key for both teachers and students is to learn how to reason?
Beach: (Forty years of experience light up his smile.) You've reasoned it out.

Exercise 6.3

Anticipating the things that will demand your observation can make you a better reporter. Consider each of the following situations and decide what details you would look for in each. List at least five areas of observation for each situation.

1. You are interviewing the head of your campus computer center in her office. Your story concerns the varied uses various academic departments have for the computer. What will you look for in the way of detail to flesh out your piece?

2. You are interviewing the head of a national teachers' union, who has recently proposed that all public school teachers be given the right to strike. You meet him at the airport, where he

has a one-hour layover. What kind of detail can you gather in a situation like this one?

3. You are spending a day on the road with Orville Drall, a politician running for congress. His administrative assistant is along to drive the two of you through the district. You stop at court houses, post offices, drug stores, and other local businesses and gathering places. What details will you gather on a road trip like this?

Exercise 6.4

In this exercise you assume the role of a reporter for a San Francisco daily newspaper. Your city editor hands you two news releases. "Check all this out," he tells you. "Do some digging and broaden the scope of the story some." Read the two releases below. Next, list additional sources you will contact before you write the story. Naturally you will want to contact Oceanic Gas and Electric Company and the environmental coalition for further information, but you will also want to contact other officials and affected people. List at least five more sources you will try. Finally, write a lead paragraph based only on the information in the news releases, and then speculate what information from each source might prompt you to change the lead.

```
Oceanic Gas and Electric Company
Corporate Headquarters
San Francisco, California


For Further Information: Rag Muffin
415-111-1111, ext. 1111


              Press Release
   OG&E Plans New Plant, New Jobs Expected

   Oceanic Gas and Electric Company today an-
nounced plans for a new coal-fired electricity
generating station to be built near Eureka.
   The plant, which will cost nearly $1 bil-
lion, is scheduled to go into operation in
1985.
   The decision to build a coal-burning fa-
cility was reached after evaluating other op-
tions such as natural gas, nuclear and hydro-
electric.
```

Construction will begin as soon as the necessary permits are received from appropriate federal, state, and local government bodies. It is estimated that the construction project will provide nearly 2500 jobs. The permanent work force at the plant will be approximately 500 employees.

Northern California Environmental Coalition
2229 Redwood Bluff Road
San Francisco
415-999-9919

For Immediate Release

    The Northern California Environmental Coalition said today it will move to block Oceanic Gas and Electric Company's plan to build a coal-powered generating plant near Eureka.
    Henry Black, spokesperson for the group, said the decision was made during a conference call among the coalition's board of directors.
    "The board was unanimous in its opposition pending further study," Black said. "It is not clear yet what action we will take, but court proceedings are a definite possibility if the plant is not relocated to a less environmentally fragile area."
    Black said the board of directors was skeptical about the power company's claim that the generating plant would create additional jobs for the Eureka area.
    "Every time one of these corporate giants wants another expensive boondoggle, it claims the project will bring new jobs," Black said. "In fact, the jobs will last only during construction and will not help stabilize the area economy over the long run."
    The coalition is composed of environmental and conservation organizations, including the Sierra Club, the Izaak Walton League and the Wilderness Society.

Chapter 7 **Creating Color in News Stories**

Good news writers concern themselves almost as much with colorful presentation as they do with thoroughness and accuracy. The serious news article is worthless without the second two attributes, but it may go unread without the first.

In the late 1800s, news stories were sometimes fattened with detail and fanciful language. Gradually this gave way to lean stories, quickly told, with a minimum of extra information. This trend, in turn, has reversed itself again in recent years.

Readers weaned on television and picture magazines demand more visual imagery in hard news as well as features. Quick, revealing minutiae, which add flavor and texture to a scene, have crept back into stories. However, unlike earlier times, calorie-rich descriptions are ladled up with restraint.

An account in 1870 of the murder of a San Francisco lawyer who, while embracing his wife after returning from Europe was shot from behind, opened this way:

> The old adage, "Hell hath no fury like a woman scorned," was amply exemplified yesterday on the Oakland ferry when an attorney type of profession sworn to support the Commonwealth. . . . (*Source:* Will Irwin, "The American Newspaper," *Collier's,* February 1911)

The reader had to read one-half the column before discovering someone had been murdered, three-quarters of the column before learning who

95 CREATING COLOR IN NEWS STORIES

had been murdered, and into the next column before reading who had committed the murder.

In much more recent times, the murder of a son by his father made the front page of the *Washington Post*. This story, too, possessed considerable drama and was filled with human interest. Here are the opening grafs: (the names are changed.)

> The police emergency line rang at 5:50 Saturday afternoon and a man identified himself to the operator as [John Mark Saunders] and said he had just shot his son.
> Gaithersburg ambulance attendants found 26-year-old [John Cole Saunders] lying on a blood-drenched kitchen floor, but neighbors, told of the slaying, said their sympathies were with the father. "It's a miracle," one of them remarked, "that it had not happened sooner."

Within another three paragraphs readers were told of the son's drug addiction, his constant demand for money from his parents, and more about neighbors' reactions. By the sixth graf, the reader learned the father had been charged with murder, and released on a $25,000 personal bond. Like the 1800s story, this murder was told with emphasis on gore and tension, but unlike the earlier story, you learned the key facts fast.

The *Washington Post* story started with a common device for adding color to a news or feature story: the scene-setting anecdote ("The police emergency line rang at 5:50. . . ."). Here is another example from a *Christian Science Monitor* story titled "U.S.S.R. Packages Politics Best."

> When the Soviet housewife goes shopping, she carries a traditional net bag. She calls it an "avoska"—a "maybe-bag," from the word "avos," "perhaps."
> Last winter and this spring, when the drought caused potato shortages and warnings against waste of bread, the name 'maybe-bag' might have had some significance. But heavy purchases of American grain averted serious shortages, and now, with a record crop in the bins, Soviet citizens are eating pretty well. The net bag is full.

This story, without becoming overblown, establishes a visual scene on which the reporter can paint political details that stand out for the reader.

The *Wall Street Journal* has elevated the anecdote to an art form that has been much copied. Here are a few *WSJ* examples of short vignettes, or scenes, which highlight the news angle:

> Dr. Felix Salerno doesn't usually take a break in his 8 A.M. to 8 P.M. working day at the Hunterdon Medical Center in Flemington, N.J. But yesterday he did—to look for gasoline so he could get home last night.
> In Norwalk, Ohio, Pat and Joe Makowski are busily revising their earlier

plans to drive to Cape Cod, Mass., for vacation. For fear of difficulty in finding gasoline along the way, they will make only a shorter trip. "It's a real letdown, but it'll be a nice, little, short trip," Mrs. Makowski says.

Such disruptions in the lives of Americans have become widespread as the gasoline shortages that hit California in April have spread to the East Coast and through Americans' consciousness.

On a warm Sunday afternoon earlier this month, several hundred diners sat in a Winnetka, Ill., restaurant mopping their brows and desperately waving for a waitress's attention.

Harry Klingeman, owner of the Indian Trail restaurant, had raised the thermostat to 80 degrees Fahrenheit as a test. He wanted to find out how his customers will react if President Carter sticks to his pledge to require temperatures of no lower than 80 in most public buildings this summer.

"My customers won't buy it," Mr. Klingeman says. "They're coming to the restaurant to get out of the hot kitchen. Customers are purchasing comfort" as well as food when they go out.

Mr. Klingeman is one of the many people doing a slow boil as the government moves to put limits on how cool they can be this summer and how warm next winter. Under standby authority approved by Congress in May, the President can restrict thermostats to 80 for cooling and 65 for heating in all commercial, industrial and nonresidential public buildings. (*Source: Wall Street Journal,* July 1979)

Examples, sometimes closely related to anecdotes, also add color and pertinency to stories. Here are two, the first from the *Wall Street Journal* and the second from *Newsday*:

In selling his five-bedroom home near San Diego last month for $114,950, engineer Robert Lewis figures his real-estate agent saved him about $6,000.

In recent weeks, a seven-piece band known as "Jim Chapin and the Jazz Tree" has performed in elementary schools in Valley Stream and East Williston. The band runs through a 45-minute medley of tunes, demonstrating the development of American jazz, and pupils are encouraged to participate at appropriate moments with shouts of "boo-wah" and "ba-ba-ba-doo."

Historical allusions, as well as metaphors and similes, are other typical methods of adding color. A *San Jose Mercury* article on the findings of a Voyager space shot used these entertaining references:

To the ancient Greeks, Io was a beautiful maiden loved by Zeus and turned by a jealous Hera into a heifer guarded by the 100-eyed Argus.

To scientists gathered at NASA's jet propulsion laboratory, the name Io represents one of the strangest and most fascinating bodies in the solar system.

The innermost of the large satellites of Jupiter, Io has been described as looking like a corroded ballbearing or a bright orange pizza.

"Future history" enlivened a political account in *Newsday* of the visit of Pope John Paul II to Poland, his homeland:

But John Paul's pilgrimage—the first visit by a reigning Pope to a Communist country—was marked by open challenge to official atheism. That, and the enormous popular response he drew, make it unlikely authorities would ever permit a return trip. Even in death he will not come back. A space is reserved for his name on the tombstone marking his parents' grave in Krakow, but the church of Rome buries its Pontiffs beneath St. Peter's Basilica in the Vatican.

Not all stories, however, devote several grafs to colorful anecdotes, examples, or historical allusions. When the story must move faster, a few turns of phrase or brief observations heighten drama or personalize the story. Following are examples:

From a story on returning evacuees after the Three Mile Island Nucleur Power accident in Pennsylvania a few years ago: "As she straightened the hood on her son's parka, she said, 'I don't think these children should be back yet.'"

From a story on Alfred Kahn, head of the Civil Aeronautics Board: "He shredded red tape into confetti."

From a story on presidential press conference: "Standing relaxed in the sunbright Rose Garden, the breeze riffling his hair, he parried. . . ."

From a story on the late Egyptian President Anwar Sadat's visit to the United States: "Sadat ducked into a helicopter for the hop to the South Lawn."

From a story on Defense Secretary Harold Brown's selling of the Salt II treaty to senators: "Brown appeared with Secretary of State Cyrus Vance before a standing room only crowd in the marble-columned Caucus Room of the Russell Senate Office Building, scene of the Watergate hearings and many other historic confrontations."

98 CREATING COLOR IN NEWS STORIES

From a story on a major air crash in San Diego: "Smoke rose quickly into San Diego's sunny but smoggy skies."

From a story on the administrative habits of the new Pope: ". . . pallium of office draped around his shoulders . . . he ruffled the Vatican's starchy bureaucracy."

From a story on supermarket chains: ". . . the not-so-great Atlantic and Pacific Tea Company."

From a story on federal spending and inflation: ". . . beating the bloat out of the federal budget."

From a story on a press conference during the Three Mile Island nuclear power accident: "Denton (a Nuclear Regulatory Commission official) was wearing his long days on his face. There was a shadow of beard, a sleepy look. Long sideburns and the receding hairline highlighted the white gauntness. He tensed a bit."

From a story on stripper Tempest Storm: "The small dressing room contained a tired wood dresser and single-sized brass bed. The bedsheet had a streak of orange lipstick, left from the previous user of the room."

As the preceding examples show, revealing detail adds spice to otherwise straightforward stories. Showing rather than telling creates imagery that captures your attention. The few words depicting the Rose Garden or the Senate Caucus room for example, provide immediacy. So does the streak of orange lipstick on Tempest Storm's bedsheet and the shadow of beard on Denton's face.

Having Sadat "duck" into the helicopter implies his physical vigor without specifically describing that personal attribute. The mother straightening her son's parka shows her nervousness more sharply than writing that she was nervous.

Similarly, a turn of phrase, such as Kahn's shredding "red tape into confetti" or playing upon the Pope's pallium as a substitute for "mantle of office," effectively conjures visual pictures. The words "beating the bloat . . . ," which also gain rhythm from alliteration, work visually, too.

Colorful writing demands that reporters absorb details that can be interspersed in stories at appropriate moments. When writing, you may restrict observed details to only a word or phrase, or enlarge them to complete paragraph-long anecdotes. Either way, pertinent observations enhance news and feature stories by providing material a reader can relate to personally.

When you are gathering information, pay attention to people's clothes, facial expressions, body and speech mannerisms; to background scenery; to props such as furniture, cars, office books, pictures on the wall; to sounds and smells; even to tactile impressions such as smooth or rough textures, hot or cold surfaces.

In attempting to write imaginatively you should carefully avoid repeating clichés unless you are able to put an unexpected twist on them. Here's one example, from *Time:* "As statues go, Lusaka's bronze monument to Empire Builder Cecil Rhodes is pretty run-of-the-horse. . . ."

Newsweek took another approach in poking fun at tired phrases. In a story quoting Tony Dorsett, Dallas Cowboy football star, the writer quoted Dorsett: " 'I knew there was no tomorrow. This was for all the marbles. But I can't cry over spilled milk,' he said, shattering the record for consecutive cliches."

Quotations also enliven stories. Quotations add piquancy, or personalize the news. The following few quotations, for example, are guaranteed to pique reader interest:

"Now when I bore people at a party they think it's their fault." (Henry Kissinger)

"Being in politics is like being a football coach. You have to be smart enough to understand the game and dumb enough to think it's important." (Eugene McCarthy)

"Roast beef medium is not only a food. It's a philosophy." (Edna Ferber)

"Once you've seen one redwood tree, you've seen them all." (Ronald Reagan)

"Amateurs hope. Professionals work." (Garson Kanin)

"I would rather score a touchdown than make love to the prettiest girl in the world." (Paul Hornung)

These quotations provide a sense of the speaker that would otherwise take a writer several paragraphs to match. Similarly, quotations taken from people at the scene of a disaster or during the heat of a debate provide an immediacy not easily imparted in longer descriptive phrases. You have read exclamations of horror from people who have observed air crashs or car wrecks. They usually read like this:

"All of a sudden I heard this loud boom, then there were bodies all over the place."

"I was driving along the freeway and suddenly I saw the plane begin to nosedive. I thought it was going to hit the car. The next moment there was a flash of fire, like an atomic bomb, as the plane hit the ground."

"It was terrible, people were crying and moaning. I rushed over and started pulling people from the car."

When the space satellite Skylab fell from the sky in July 1979, it excited descriptions such as the following:

> "A train on fire with bits of fire burning all the way down the carriages, that's what it was like," Smith said. "There were golds, yellow, reds—we were damn lucky to see it." (*Source:* New York Times News Service, July 1979)

And another:

> "It was an incredible sight," said John Seller, a rancher in Australia's vast outback. "Hundreds of shining lights dropping all around the homestead . . . we could hear the noise of wind in the air as bigger pieces passed over us. Just after the last pieces dropped out of sight, the whole house shook three times. . . ." (*Source:* New York Times News Service, July 1979)

Even in less dramatic circumstances, the personal comment brings you into the story. Here are some examples:

"I am outraged by this politically motivated grand jury inquisition," Kopp said. "Joe Freitas is just trying to grab a cheap headline and salvage his own sinking political career at my expense." (*Source: San Francisco Chronicle*, June 1979.) Obviously, this is from an account of a grand jury probe of a politician.

"He just went right down the line for the railroad," lamented PUC attorney Vincent Mackenzie of the decision by Judge Robert Wallace. This is from a story on the decision of a Washington, D. C., administrative law judge to dispense with a train commuter service.

"She hasn't changed that much—still the cheapest, most gratifying and fun-filled of all bigtime sports entertainment," the president of the Chicago White Sox said. At age 65, Bill Veeck's life is still dominated by baseball, according to an interview he gave in Sarasota, Florida.

"The way I see it," said a bartender in Goldsboro, looking out his door at the cooling towers a mile and half away, "the damn thing worked. They had a problem, and they took care of it. Who got hurt?" This is from a story describing local attitudes to nuclear power after the Three Mile Island event in Pennsylvania.

"And so, before I leave you, I wish to give one more look at Krakow, this Krakow in which every stone and every brick is dear to me," he said, his voice hoarse and tired after nine days of public preaching, singing, bantering. Pope John Paul II was quoted in his last speech before leaving his homeland, Poland, after an historic visit.

Note that in both the Pope quotation and the one from the bartender at Three Mile Island, additional color is provided by describing the Pope's voice and the bartender's view from his door. Substituting the "said" with descriptive words such as lamented, decried, sobbed, muttered, shouted, or whispered also creates stronger imagery, but such words must be used judiciously and with precision.

One other caution when quoting: Keep the quotation short. If the speaker rambles, lift out only the "sexy" portion that makes a point, heightens drama, or entertains.

Chapter 7 Exercises

Remember:

1. Show, do not tell.
2. Use examples and anecdotes.
3. Reach for visual words and turns of phrase.
4. Employ metaphors and similes.
5. Record revealing details that recall for the reader sight, sound, smell, and touch.
6. Personalize experiences by using appropriate quotations.
7. Heighten drama through judicious quotations.

Exercise 7.1

Search through copies of Newsweek, Time, People, *the* New Yorker, Christian Science Monitor, Wall Street Journal, Los Angeles Times, New York Times, *and the* Washington Post *to find and list 10 examples of each of the following:*

1. Visual words
2. Turns of phrase; twists on clichés
3. Revealing detail
4. Anecdotes and examples
5. Historical allusions

6. Spicy quotations
7. Quotations that personalize an experience

Exercise 7.2 *Select an issue of* Time *or* Newsweek. *Then go to the library or otherwise acquire access to a good daily newspaper. Find at least five stories that were covered both in the newsmagazine and in the newspaper. Then select at least five elements of color from each newsmagazine story. Check these elements against the newspaper stories. Prepare a short memorandum summarizing the differences in approach taken by the newspaper and the newsmagazine on each story.*

Exercise 7.3 *This is a timed exercise. Here is a list of 30 words. They are divided into 15 obvious pairs. In 10 minutes, see how many synonyms you can think of for each word. You will find that colorful writing is varied writing. You should strive for unstrained variation.*

big

little

tall

short

bright

dull

famous

unknown

fast

slow

rough

smooth

find

lose

come

go

rise

sink

smart

dumb

shout

whisper

good

bad

grow

shrink

help

hurt

funny

sad

Exercise 7.4 *Colorful writing is sensual writing. Not necessarily sexy, but sensual in the broad sense: When readers read your work they should imagine they are hearing, tasting, feeling, seeing, or smelling whatever you are writing about. Once I had a dacquiri that felt like a centipede tap-dancing across my tongue. Here is your assignment: Take no more than 15 minutes and collect 2 bright sensual examples for each of your 5 senses. Then sit down at your typewriter and make your observations come to life on paper. Your campus should be ideal for this endeavor. Smell, for instance, can be found in the student dining facility. If that is not enough for you, try the locker room at the gymnasium.*

Exercise 7.5 *Here is the first part of a story on a teacher's strike in Oakland. Rewrite it, improving the "show" and tightening the copy.*

A LAZY SCHOOL DAY IN OAKLAND

The bap-bap-bap-thud of a volleyball being dribbled and then thrown against a wall echoed yesterday from the third floor of an Oakland high school that was severely depleted of classroom activity.

A tremendously large female student was wielding the ball with no one available—or willing—to interrupt.

One middle-aged substitute teacher who was making $100 for this first day of the Oakland teachers strike did risk a fairly long look her way—mostly in admiration for the way the volleyball seemed reduced to the dimensions of a softball in her hands.

But when she glared back with a "you wanta make something of it look," he shrugged and double-stepped down the stairs.

That sort of related attitude toward the educational process prevailed at most secondary schools across the town—though there were exceptions, particularly in a high-achieving hill school or two.

The disorganization—striking teachers called it chaos—was generally attributed to the fact that the district simply could not get anywhere near enough substitutes to the schools.

Exercise 7.6

Here are two feature stories dealing with the same subject—a two-headed goat. Both are fair pieces of journalism, but neither is a perfect example of "show, do not tell." Carefully go through each. Select the color elements (including quotations) you consider most appropriate for the story. Then rewrite the story in 400 words or less. Remember: Being colorful is desirable, but take care not to be offensively cute.

Patricia Costa, a Santa Rosa animal breeder, had her hands and her bathtub full yesterday—with a two-headed baby goat named Hedy Lamarr.

"Hedy is so top-heavy she can't stand up," said Costa, who has a three-bedroom ranch house and a farm where she keeps 35 normal goats, 14 pigs and—at last count—100 rabbits.

"The bathtub in the house seems to be the safest place where she can just lay around . . . Fortunately, we have a separate shower for the rest of the family."

Already attracting interest from university researchers, the bizarre she-goat is the daughter of a nanny known as Goaty-Goat. A perfectly healthy twin brother also was born Wednesday evening, on a farm near Novato. Hedy was sent to Costa, an expert in the care of goats.

Before any doubting experts could say "Bah," the two-headed rarity was authenticated by agricultural researchers from the University of California at Davis.

Dr. Ed Price, a UC geneticist who specializes in goats, said the phenomenon occasionally occurs in births among farm animals. Almost invariably, however, the two-headed creatures die within minutes of birth.

"She's still very much alive and kicking 24 hours later," said an exhausted Costa as she watched Hedy flailing away in the bathtub.

Her husband, Bob, a Pacific Gas and Electric Co. worker, took the day off so he could help her turn Hedy over in the bathtub crib "every hour on the hour."

"The poor thing can't roll over herself and we're afraid she might get bedsores or bathsores," the goat breeder said.

"One problem is that she seems to have two brains as well as two heads, and that can be confusing," she added.

For one thing, she noted, one of Hedy's brains "appears to be more dominant than the other, so every time she lies down the strong mind takes charge and tries to flip her over."

Costa said she has been feeding Hedy from a bottle with milk from Goaty-Goat. Mama goat, it turned out, wouldn't have a thing to do with the two-headed infant. (*Source: Peninsula Times Tribune* (Palo Alto), January 26, 1979. Reprinted by permission)

Goaty-Goat and her offspring have starred in a doubleheader that has attracted the attention of farmers all around Novato and of veterinary science experts all the way from Davis to San Luis Obispo.

Goaty-Goat is one of four nannies on a small farm east of Novato run by Bert Balladine and his cousin, Glenn Schneider, a secretary for the state Supreme Court.

In addition to the four nannies, there are some horses, cows and sheep on the place.

Until yesterday morning, the place was a model of bucolic calm.

Then Goaty-Goat delivered.

Twins.

Not all that common, for a nanny to have twins, but not all that rare either.

The first born, Balladine said, was a fine, healthy male, arriving about 8 A.M.

About an hour later Goaty-Goat delivered the punch line: a two-headed female.

Oh, you poor kid!

Goaty-Goat rejected her little two-headed offspring and refused to nurse it.

"I wanted to destroy it," Balladine said. "It wasn't a pretty thing to see. Normally, a kid can stand up just a little while after birth. But this thing's head was so heavy it was out of balance.

"I didn't think she would last very long. But then I thought she might be of some value to science, so I got in touch with Pat Costa right away."

Costa, widely known Santa Rosa goat breeder and member of a breeders' association, got right down to the Novato farm.

Goaty-Goat's two-headed daughter was, in Balladine's words, "healthy, kicking and both heads were crying for something to eat."

Balladine and Costa got some milk from the mother and other goats and fed the two-headed kid from a bottle.

One mouth at a time.

Then they arranged to take the two-headed kid to the West Side Veterinary Clinic in Santa Rosa, where it was checked out by Dr. Robert Fielder.

"She's really doing well," Costa said. "She's nice and big and strong and has a good appetite and should survive."

The kid was named Hedy Lamarr. Costa said Hedy supposedly means two heads in German.

Goaty-Goaty-Goaty-Goaty Goat had been suggested. But whether she will live long enough for a christening is a question.

As Balladine pointed out, "It's very unusual in a case like this for an animal to live more than 48 hours."

He added: "If she survives I'd like to put her in the hands of some scientists and see what we can learn."

Dr. Ed Price, a University of California at Davis geneticist who specializes in goats, said the kid was a rarity and that he was amazed she had survived so long.

Births of two-headed creatures occur occasionally among farm animals, he said, but in most cases they die within minutes.

He once observed a two-headed calf, he said, and has seen a two-headed caribou fetus preserved in a University of Alaska museum.

Dr. Lyle McNeal, of California Polytechnic University, San Luis Obispo agreed such a birth among goats or sheep is quite rare.

It could be due to a genetic aberration, he said, or to some nutritional problem that developed while the fetus was growing within its mother.

Balladine, meanwhile, said ruefully: "I wish it had never happened to me. All the farmers around here say they never heard of anything like it. There's been people coming around here all day."

And what about the father?

The old buck is on loan to a neighboring farm, Balladine said.

Not even a "baa" for his two-headed daughter. (*Source: San Francisco Examiner,* January 1979. Reprinted by permission)

Exercise 7.7

Almost every college campus has a computer center. And almost every computer center is a pretty interesting place. Often you will find some interesting people there, too. Go to your local computer center. Put yourself in one location, a good one that lets you see what is going on. Before you leave, take at least 50 separate notes on what you see, hear, feel, smell, and so forth. Then go to your typewriter and prepare a 500-word piece on the computer center. Be sure to unify your piece with

107   EXERCISE 7.7

some angle or theme. And here is the real twist: Try to write your story without using adverbs or adjectives. *Give yourself 100 points, and subtract 5 for each adverb or adjective you must use. Articles—a, and, the, and so on—do not count. Anything more than 75 points is an admirable score.*

Chapter 8 **Feature Stories**

To make certain you understand features, let us review briefly the various types of news writing, then feature stories.

The most common type of news story is the *straight* or *hard news* report—also known as the *objective report*—which is a timely account of an event. A newspaper report of a speech is usually straight news. Because it covers only what happened during a brief period, straight news provides a valuable focus. It is valuable also because it makes such limited demands on reporters that they can come close to presenting an objective report of verifiable fact.

The *depth report* is a step beyond straight news. Instead of merely trying to mirror the highlights of an event, the reporter gathers additional information that is independent of the event but related to it. A reporter who covers a speech on medical practices in China may consult experts and reference sources, then present the speaker's words in a larger framework. In some cases, additional information is placed in the report on the speech; in others, it is reported separately. In either case, depth reporting calls for transmitting information, not the reporter's opinion. Verifiable fact is as pivotal in depth reporting as it is in straight news reporting.

Interpretive reports—also known as *news analyses*—are another step beyond straight news. These usually focus on an issue, problem, or controversy. Here, too, the substance is verifiable fact, not opinion. But instead of presenting facts as straight news or a depth report and hoping the facts speak for themselves, the interpretive reporter clarifies, explains, analyzes. The interpretive report usually focuses on why: Why did the president take that trip, appoint that man, make that statement? What is the real meaning of the event?

Investigative reporting, sometimes called *muckraking,* is the practice of opening closed doors and closed mouths. As in interpretive reporting, the focus is on problems, issues, and controversies. In fact, interpretive and investigative reports are the same in cases where the reporter must unearth hidden information in order to clarify, explain, and analyze. Normally, though, interpretive reporters have relatively little trouble finding facts because they are endeavoring to explain public events, and they can usually find many sources who are happy to help them. (In fact, the danger in all reporting is that a source may want to provide information serving its own private interests.) In contrast, the investigative reporter must try to discover facts that have been hidden for a purpose—often an illegal or unethical purpose.

Features differ from the news reports itemized above primarily in their intent. A news report ordinarily presents information that is likely to concern readers, but a feature is usually designed to capture their interest. The feature reporter casts a wide net in search for facts, sometimes pulling in and using things a news reporter would consider frivolous. The feature writer's report provides a reading experience that depends more on style, grace, and humor than on the importance of the information.

Like all other writing, journalistic forms overlap, especially in metropolitan newspapers. Traces of depth or investigative reporting may appear in a feature, sometimes quite strongly. An interpretive report may have both feature and investigative elements. Often, a feature may seem to be weighted as heavily with matters of concern as with matters of light interest.

Imagine that university administrators, discovering that too little dormitory space is available for all the students who want to live on the campus, have leased 100 trailer homes and have parked them on the edge of the dormitory area to house 400 students.

Assigned to write a feature, you look for the color and flavor of trailer life. Do trailer residents live differently from other students? How? Have they painted their homes in wild colors? Are they planting gardens? Who does the cooking—and with what results?

Are those enough possibilities? On many newspapers, from the campus daily to the metropolitan paper, those are sufficient, provided you bring color to the story and are a close observer. However, there is much more to writing features. A reader says: "Entertain me while you educate me. Make me laugh. Make me cry. I want to escape from the narrow confines of my life, while deriving moral satisfaction from the hope that I am learning at the same time."

The Feature Slant

There is one rule for all features: The story must be endlessly interesting. The feature is as important in the middle as it was at the beginning, as important at the end as it was in the middle and at the beginning. You must tell your story clearly and simply. It must be readable. The following guidelines should help with the central problem—making your writing clear and readable.

Sentence Structure This is the basis of readability in nearly all sentences. Usually, sentences should be constructed like this: subject, verb, object. That may sound simple, but many sentences begin with clauses or adjectives. Beginning writers often like to twist their sentences for effect. They should do this rarely. The overarching rule is that nearly all sentences should be as simple and direct as possible.

Sentence Length Generally, the shorter, the more readable the sentences will be. It is true, of course, that if you write for *Harper's* magazine, for example, you can write in a more complicated form—as long as you can control it. But if you write for newspapers or for widely circulated magazines, as a rule you must keep your sentences short.

Concreteness Wherever possible, you should use concrete words instead of abstract words. The following excerpt of the abstractions of James M. Landis, who was an assistant to President Franklin Roosevelt, and the revision made by the president is a good illustration. Landis wrote:

> Such preparations shall be made as will completely obscure all Federal buildings and non-Federal buildings occupied by the Federal Government during an air raid for any period of time from visibility by reason of internal or external illumination. Such obscuration may be obtained either by blackout construction or by termination of the illumination. This will, of course, require that in building areas in which production must continue during the blackout, construction must be provided that internal illumination may continue.

President Roosevelt said to rewrite it this way:

> Tell them that in buildings where they have to keep the work going to put something across the window. In buildings where they can afford to let the work stop for a while, turn out the lights.

Verbs Making the verb do the work of adjectives is always preferable. The verb expresses action, and if it is carefully chosen, it can even describe personality. For example, "The four men were on hand in the office." All the reader learns from this is the number and location of the men. But if you say, "The four men sprawled in the office," you have conveyed more about the personalities of these men.

Adjectives The fewer adjectives a writer uses, the more readable the style. For example, "The sharp-eyed, gray-haired general's sharp eyes flashed as he got up and shook his head," could be better put this way: "The general's sharp eyes flashed as he rose and shook his gray head."

Story Structure

All beginning writers are told that a lead must catch and hold their readers. If possible, a feature lead should be a startling, witty, or pithy statement. It is usually a mistake to devote the beginning to summing up a story, as a straight news story often does. That is the death of the feature.

Transitions

Learning to link the paragraphs in a way that pulls the reader on is a skill that distinguishes the professional from the amateur. After the first paragraph, what comes next? A beginning writer can learn much by studying *Time* and *Newsweek*. Both magazines stress the importance of transitions.

How can you use those tips about feature writing? In the following section, you'll find the most commonly used types of feature stories.

Types of Feature Stories

News Features

More and more often, the newspapers are recognizing that feature stories are part of their news mission, not entertainment. Thus, the editors have their reporters become part-time feature writers by converting a news event into a feature. The following paragraph begins the way a news feature might read:

> In oil-rich Saudi Arabia, an absolute monarchy where royalty payments are more than a figure of speech, the king has argued for years that his nation should own part of the production facilities and operations of the Western-owned oil company that has a concession in his realm. Last week, Saudi Arabia agreed to pay an amount estimated to top $500 million for a one-fourth interest in the oil and gas producing operations of American-Arabian Oil Company in Saudi Arabia. . . .

Color Stories

The color feature plays up the descriptive elements of a news event. The feature writer is assigned to cover the color, flavor, and excitement of large crowds—instead of focusing his or her attention on the players. The spectators, the cheering sections, the yell leaders, the half-time performance, and the mascots are likely to be the focal elements of a sports color story, instead of the players. The feature writer covers the election sidebar in much the same way. While the election reporter is concentrating on results, the feature story writer describes the manner and mood of the voters as they enter the election booths. He or she looks for quotable signs that herald the voters, listens to the sound trucks making last-minute appeals, and records the candidates' reactions on the last day.

Personality Sketches or Profiles

People are interested in people. That is why newspapers ask for long stories; because the editors realize that the writer must spell out the significance of the subject. Here are the essentials:

1. *What the subject says.* You should use quotations and paraphrase.

2. *What the subject does.* The subject's actions, including anecdotes that illuminate him or her, are necessary.

3. *Description of the subject.* Include not only such routine facts as height, weight, and color of eyes and hair, but also write about how the subject walks, talks, gestures, and makes small movements.

4. *History of the subject.* Although what the subject is like *now* is the most important aspect, failing to color in his or her background may suggest that the subject was always this way—that the subject was never in the process of *becoming.* Ideally, historical tracing helps to show how the subject became what he or she is.

5. *What others*—friends and detractors—*think and say about the subject.*

Human Interest

Although the human interest story was once described as a "sob story," that is no longer applicable. Human interest features are those that involve the readers emotionally: stimulating or depressing them, angering or amusing them, awakening sympathy or distaste. In order to avoid writing a sob story, you must write with restraint, describing exactly what the subject does. For example:

> Guadalupe Morones bent his head low over the blunt pencil which moved with so little skill across the rough notebook paper. He let his breath out hard—so hard you knew he'd been holding it the way a diver holds onto air the second before it's time to cut the water. Guadalupe's hands, gnarled with work and years until they took on the look of two dark knots in an oak tree, stopped.
> "I can't go on," Guadalupe said in the tongue of his birth. "I must stop and see if the hand will let me write."
> Now, each Thursday morning Guadalupe drives into town with his son, Jesus, and learns about things like the year the *Mayflower* crossed the Atlantic and how Thomas Jefferson stayed up late nights helping to put words into the American Revolution.
> Guadalupe is working hard to be an American. . . .
> (*Source:* Marj Wightmen, *Austin American-Statesman,* February 26, 1961. Reprinted by permission)

Seasonal Stories

In most newspaper offices, there is always a need for someone who can fashion features out of seasons and holidays. We have the four seasons—autumn, winter, spring, and summer—and also such holidays as Christmas, New

Year's Day, St. Patrick's Day, St. Valentine's Day, and so on. Learning to master the kind of style required by this assignment depends on the controlled imagination of the writer. For example, read the following story about St. Valentine's Day, which was written by a writer who decided to take a fresh look at what has happened to this observance.

> Your hubby eats at work all year,
> So he ain't too bad-lookin',
> But you look like a nightmare, dear.
> 'Cause you eat your own cookin'.

These sentimental lines commemorate a Christian martyr named St. Valentine who lived during the third century.

This isn't the only bit of doggerel that has bounced through the mails carrying an unusual note of love and cheer for St. Valentine's Day.

There are, of course, the traditional couplets, most of them in keeping with the original spirit of St. Valentine's Day:

> The string of hearts above
> Tells you of my love.

But these garden-variety sentiments have been yielding a bigger and bigger place on the stationery counters to insulting missives, which come replete with matching illustrations.

A scattergun survey of local card-selling establishments failed to turn up any reason for the appearance of the supposedly humorous valentines. Perhaps the joke-cards came into being because verse-writers ran out of ways to say "I love you" in rhyme.

Or perhaps "Valentine Insult Cards" began because of general confusion about the origin of the day itself. Even Webster's Dictionary is bewildered:

> It was a very old notion that on this day birds began to mate. The custom of sending love tokens at this time has no actual connection with the saint, whose name was probably introduced through some mistake.

Obviously, the way to determine whether it was a mistake to make February 14 St. Valentine's Day, and to proclaim it a day for love, is to go to the tomb where his remains are buried and shout these lines from a Valentine joke card:

> I love your chin, your lantern jaw,
> My valentine, my mother-in-law.

If St. Valentine turns over in his grave, it was not a mistake.

How-To-Do-Its   One of the most durable forms, the how-to-do-it, is flourishing today, perhaps because of inflation. The possibilities are endless: They range from how to stop smoking to how to build a better garage—and that represents only a small fraction! Although you as a writer may begin with an inventive lead, you must curb your imagination, because nearly all of the how-to-do-it story must be painfully attuned to teaching the readers how they must perform. For example, note the way the writer begins to describe how to find gold:

> Gold mining can be hard, back-breaking work that requires long hours of concentrated effort, cold wet feet, and a lot of luck. Or it can be a marvelous way to spend a spring afternoon by the side of a streambed, soaking in the sun and the wildflowers in bloom. The difference is how hard you want to work for your find. The choice is yours.

After finishing writing this lead, the writer lists the utensils needed, then begins to describe painstakingly exactly how the readers must work: "Submerge the pan in the riverbed by keeping the rim level with top of the water, being careful not to lose any of the contents. . . ."

Descriptives

You must take the readers somewhere, in effect, and build a mental picture of a scene that they might never be able to visit in their lifetimes. Or it could be that you can describe a place so attractively that many of the readers will want to go there. Also, on occasion, you can be writing a descriptive as an effective way of exposing a wrong by presenting a seamy picture, such as a slum dwelling or the threatened destruction of a wilderness. Here are the essentials:

1. Focus on distinctive characteristics. By carefully selecting the features to describe, you can sketch a picture that sets forth the unique quality of a place.

2. Phrase carefully. Descriptions depend largely on the way words are put together to achieve their effect. Read carefully again the section of this chapter on visual writing.

3. Make the story a reading and viewing experience. The success of a description is not determined by whether the readers *learn,* in the sense that they learn facts or ideas from other kinds of stories. Success pivots almost entirely on whether readers finish reading a description with the feeling that they have been through a satisfying experience. The most evocative descriptions—those fashioned by writers who have developed and refined a talent for using visual words—are also a viewing experience.

Informatives

Although nearly all stories are informative, those that have this name ordinarily take the readers behind the scenes of an unusual technological process or public service. For example, an informative might describe how the university keeps tabs on everyone's grades through their college years. Or it could be that an informative will describe how a railroad keeps track of its wandering freight cars. Here are the essentials:

1. Unearthing facts. Most informatives cover subjects that could be explored by anyone. Few are so high-toned that only the specialist can investigate and understand. The writer of an informative customarily unearths the facts beneath ordinary phenomena.

2. Dressing up the facts. The facts must be interesting; the writer must select them carefully and present them pleasingly. This is true of all writing, of course, but it is especially important in writing an informative because the unadorned presentation of facts about everyday institutions is likely to bore readers. One way to dress them up is to be aware that readers are usually more interested in people than in things. When facts about things can be presented in relation to people—the people who use the things, the people who produce them, and so on—interest heightens.

3. Dissection. One of the purposes of an informative is to examine. Writing an informative calls for writing that shines a bright light on the central matter and dissects it with words.

4. Clarity and unity foremost. As the writer of an informative, you must work for extreme clarity. Sentences must march along decisively, major point following major point in a way that seems inevitable.

These are the essential stylistic qualities; you must leaven your work with devices that lend color and flavor.

Chapter 8 Exercises

Remember:

1. The feature story must be endlessly interesting; the middle and the end must be as interesting as the beginning.

2. Most features must stress the descriptive elements, especially the color story.

3. Clarity and unity are foremost. Check carefully the transitions from sentence to sentence and paragraph to paragraph.

116 FEATURE STORIES

Exercise 8.1   *Four sets of visual words appear in the following paragraph, which is taken from "Shooting an Elephant" by George Orwell. Orwell used the middle word in each set. Write a short paragraph describing the different pictures drawn by each word in each set.*

>He looked suddenly [shattered—stricken—smashed], [smaller—shrunken—lessened], immensely old, as though the frightful impact of the bullet had paralyzed him without knocking him down. At last, after what seemed a long time—it might have been five seconds—he [sank—sagged—drooped] flabbily to his knees. His mouth [drooled—slobbered—gushed]. An enormous senility seemed to have settled on him.

Exercise 8.2   A class of journalism students was given an assignment to create *new* clichés by completing the following:

1. as comfortable as . . .
2. as jumpy as . . .
3. as wild as . . .
4. as smooth as . . .
5. as exciting as . . .

The students created new clichés by writing these:

as comfortable as a bachelor changing a diaper.

as comfortable as King Kong with rabies.

as jumpy as a pregnant nun.

as wild as a cat caught in a garbage disposal unit.

as wild as a dope addict writing poetry.

as smooth as a farm-to-market road in Tibet.

as smooth as riding a three-legged horse through a rock quarry.

as exciting as a wet noodle.

as exciting as the society page in *Pravda*.

117 EXERCISE 8.3

Your assignment is to create new clichés for these:

1. as fast as . . .
2. as colorful as . . .
3. as relaxing as . . .
4. as difficult as . . .
5. as rugged as . . .
6. as heavy as . . .
7. as light as . . .
8. as graceful as . . .

Exercise 8.3 *Write two leads for each of the following sets of information. Make the first lead hard news. Make the second a feature lead.*

1. You are working the rewrite desk. Several wire reports arrive detailing a rocket crash in the West. Your editor throws them at you. Thinking you will impress him, you write a hard news lead and a feature, too. Here is the information.

Last night (Wednesday) people in Washington, Idaho, and Montana reported seeing a bright object flash across the sky. Thursday morning Reginald Balk, a spokesperson for the Pentagon in Washington, D.C., said the flash was not a comet but was part of a Soviet rocket launched yesterday. The Pentagon official said the rocket had been tracked by military radar as it descended. The rocket was part of the launch assembly for Cosmos 854. The rocket, which fell in Montana, has not been recovered, Balk said.

2. It is Wednesday evening. You are in the *St. Louis Babbler* city room. Things are quiet. You are reading Dashiell Hammett, thinking wryly that he might make you a better investigative reporter. The city editor calls and says one of the city supervisors—Dan Kopp—has been hit in the face with a pie. You promptly get Kopp on the telephone at home, where he has just arrived. He offers this.

"I had just arrived at 2501 Bryant. It was about 8 P.M. We were having a Mission Planning Commission meeting. This guy in a battered fedora suddenly ran up to me on the street and smashed a pie into me. It bounced off my right shoulder. The organizers of the meeting were horrified, but I just

118   FEATURE STORIES

took off my coat and we went ahead with the meeting. I didn't call the police. It didn't seem like I was in any real danger."

Just as you hang up, the city editor puts you onto another line, where someone is asking for the reporter doing the pie story. The man identifies himself as Aaron Kay and says: "It was me that got Kopp with the pie. I wanted to protest his asshole attitude about the International Hotel. This time it was banana cream."

You ask him whether you have heard his name somewhere before.

"Probably," he says. "I've hit Moynihan and a bunch of others. I'm an officer in the Yippies, you know."

3. You are in Albany writing for the *New York Babbler.* It is Tuesday, and you are preparing this story for Wednesday morning's editions. Your first piece of information is the following written statement, issued Monday by the New York Department of Alcoholic Beverage Control (ABC).

"Officials of the Department of Alcoholic Beverage Control announced Monday that proposed rules against the sale of spirits at sports facilities, with the exception of stationary refreshment stands, will not be adopted.

"The department decision came after public hearings on the proposal. The department will continue to monitor the situation to determine if further hearings are warranted."

You consult the files of the *Babbler* and learn that the ABC had wanted to stop grandstand vendors from selling beer at baseball games. ABC feared the salespeople were letting underaged youth pour down the suds. One hearing was held in April on the proposed rules change. Another was held in June. Both were at the Capitol in Albany. At both the *Babbler* reported "vehement protests" against the change. One beer vendor at the June hearing said:

"The suggestion that we are selling beer to children is ridiculous. We police ourselves. We have in the past, and we will continue to do so."

You call the ABC and talk to Hobart Dryman, an assistant public information officer. He says only: "The department wants to let the statement speak for itself. We really don't think there is anything else to be said right now."

Exercise 8.4

The University of Missouri has just awarded you the highest graduate fellowship in journalism. Because the award came to $3000, and was based on general intelligence and on writing ability, you had strong competition. More than 100 other students from around the country applied.

Write a third-person factual feature story on yourself in at least 600 words.

List five people you would have interviewed if you had not been the person yourself. (Incidentally, if you had not been the person and had interviewed some of the people, you might have been shocked by their answers.)

Exercise 8.5

As a feature writer, you must go to one of these campus buildings: (1) the most beautiful; (2) the most ramshackle; or (3) the busiest. Take notes on the building. Go there at the time when the students are going from class to class. Take notes on how some of them hurry, some are lethargic, and so on. Then, when the next class starts, go into the largest classroom and take notes on how the teacher performs, and how the students perform (or do not perform).

After taking these notes, type a feature story of at least 500 words in which you focus on visual writing. Decide whether you will focus on the building, the students going from class to class, the classroom, or how the teacher and the students perform.

Exercise 8.6

As a feature writer, you are sitting quietly in the newsroom of the *Oakland Tribune* (California), minding your own business, drinking coffee, working the crossword puzzle, using the Wide Area Telephone Service (WATS) line to check up on some old school friends.

Suddenly, the city editor looms large over your desk. It seems that in his opinion the students up the road in Berkeley are at it again. This time they want to make people pay to use the streets that were paved with public funds. He wants you to do a 500-word feature story on the proposal for tomorrow's paper.

Write the story using the information below. Tell in the story what the actions would mean, both in terms of changed life-styles and in any possible resulting conflict.

The first thing you do is to go to the *Tribune*'s library: There you found stories about Singapore's traffic control plan. Singapore is the only city in the world that now charges motorists for the privilege of driving on city streets.

You then do some checking and find that the Berkeley City Council is now studying a proposal to implement the daily fee for drivers using city streets. The scheme was put forth by the U. S. Urban Mass Transportation Administration (UMTA). The UMTA suggested several possible ways of going about it: Charging a daily fee of $1 to $2 for driving on city streets; charging a similar fee for driving on Tunnel Road, which is the main traffic artery linking Berkeley with communities to the south; or charging a similar fee for driving on streets where traffic is heavy.

You called the UMTA in Washington, D. C. An agency spokesperson said that the agency had presented the idea to several other cities, including San Francisco, but none was receptive. The agency turned to Berkeley, he said, because of the city's history of innovative approaches to traffic control.

The money generated by the pay-as-you-drive plan would be used to buy buses and build parking lots on the outskirts of the city. People could then use the buses to get downtown and around the city, thus avoiding the street use fee. The aim of the plan would be to further reduce traffic in the city.

Berkeley has already set up a controversial program barricading some streets to keep traffic out of parts of the city.

The City Council is expected to decide within six months whether to go ahead with the program.

You call John Durham, an outspoken critic of traffic control plans in Berkeley. He says, "They'll never implement it. The community would rise up in arms and throw out the government completely."

You call Mark Stephens, a spokesperson for the Associated Students of the University of California at Berkeley. He says that the plan amounts to a "thinly disguised regressive tax."

You call the mayor of Berkeley, Warren Widener. He agrees that the plan would be regressive, but hopes any plan adopted would be flexible enough to soften the financial blow. He also states that he likes the plan. "We have to do something to keep our city from strangling in traffic," he commented. He said the plan could succeed because "Berkeley is special."

Finally, you call Tom Davis of the California Department of Transportation to see what the state has to say about it. He says the state law would have to be changed to allow Berkeley to assess a use fee for driving on its streets.

Chapter 9 # Completing the News

Seldom is the news complete with the first version of the facts you gather. Late-breaking facts or additional information putting a local angle on a story require the updating and altering of leads. In addition, editors often instruct reporters to write sidebar stories after the main story has been written. Sidebars highlight special angles minimized or omitted from the story.

Updating

Newspaper copy, especially that on the front page, will be updated for each edition. This requires three or four versions of the same story. Wire copy may have dozens of versions, because stories get updated minute by minute if necessary.

When the Skylab space station was scheduled to fall from the skies in the summer of 1979, for example, NASA officials changed their predictions almost hourly about when the satellite was scheduled to crash to earth. Dutifully, throughout the day for many days, news stories reflected each updated prediction.

When Skylab finally fell on July 11, 1979, wire services issued minute by minute updates on the details as they became known. Here are three new leads on New York Times News Service stories that moved minutes apart: (Time given in 2400)

    7/11/79 19:31:   The Skylab space station, at 77 tons the largest object ever orbited, flashed through the atmosphere and

122 COMPLETING THE NEWS

                        disintegrated in a blaze of fireworks over the Indian Ocean Wednesday, showering tons of debris across the Great Australian Desert, one of the world's most remote places.

7/11/79 19.35:   Although the bulk of Skylab crashed into the Indian Ocean miles off the southwestern tip of Western Australia, some large pieces hurtled on over the port of Esperance and the gold-mining town of Kalgoolie.

7/11/79 19.36:   The Skylab space station, at 77 tons the largest object ever orbited, flashed over the Indian Ocean Wednesday, showering tons of debris across the Great Australian Desert—one of the world's most remote places. Space agency officials Wednesday placed the point of impact above the gold mining town of Kalgoolie, about 400 miles inland from the Indian Ocean. (*Source:* New York Times News Service, July 11, 1979)

Stories such as disasters, labor negotiations, kidnapings, key political events, and significant public occurrences are reported on a continuing updated basis for days at a time. (Or even years; John F. Kennedy's assassination was still being probed in government and the news media 11 years after the event.) Second-day stories, the label given to continuing stories, often contain few new facts. But reporters must strive to present scraps of fresh information in lead grafs to entice readers into the story yet again.

Localizing

Because newspapers want to attract local readers, every effort is made to give local significance to national and statewide news. Many times the local angle is developed as an addition to the main story. In this case, the local information is placed high in the story, perhaps in the lead or second graf. For example, during spring 1979 an oil crisis hit the United States. Many news stories across the nation incorporated local reactions with descriptions of the national scene. Leads such as: "Here as elsewhere around the nation, gas lines began forming at 5 A.M. . . ." were common.

Another common way to handle localizing is through sidebar stories. A second story, often run prominently in a box, describes local reaction. When the president ordered thermostats lowered to 78 degrees during summer to conserve the energy used in air conditioning, separate stories ran in many papers outlining local attitudes.

Sidebars

Sidebar stories complete the news for readers by providing extra information. They usually have a special angle, such as the local reactions mentioned earlier, or background information on people or places. Sidebar stories on Australian geography, for example, were run alongside stories on Skylab's descent, once NASA predicted the space station might hit Australia. Sometimes sidebar stories are created from titillating bits you have gathered but cannot fit easily into the main story.

Many sidebars are short color stories, providing mood and atmosphere for the longer, main story. Sidebar stories typically run near the main story, are boxed, or have tags or tielines (brief inserts) that advise readers "related to story on page...." or "see other stories...." Though sidebars are generally 500 words or less, they include sufficient key details to make them complete stories in themselves.

Chapter 9 Exercises

The following exercises will give you experience in common newspaper devices for rounding out, or completing, news stories by adding updated information, localized information, or sidebar stories.

Remember:

1. Updated stories must contain the newest information in the lead, even if the balance of the story is virtually the same as that which appeared in an earlier version.

2. Many state and national stories can be made more interesting to local readers by reporting local reactions. This information should be placed high in the story.

3. Sidebar stories should be complete in themselves, even though they may be placed close to the main story. Frequently, sidebar stories are more lighthearted than the main story.

Exercise 9.1

Here is the information for a series of second day stories—in this case extending over 10 days. Write a new lead, no more than 3 or 4 sentences maximum, for each date listed below. You are writing for a morning paper, so you are always reporting on the previous day's activities.

Amid gas lines, looming fuel shortages, soaring prices, and prediction of recession in late spring and early summer 1982, the U.S. president's popularity with the American public had plunged to a Gallup poll rating of 23 percent, lower than any president's to that time.

In late June, with the Organization of Petroleum Exporting Countries (OPEC) boosting the price of oil 50 percent, the president canceled vacation plans and returned from an economic summit with Western leaders in Japan to make some visible efforts to deal with the energy situation.

Telling his aides he wanted a "bold and forceful" energy program that would be quickly approved by Congress, the president announced plans to broadcast a speech July 5.

On July 3 he left Washington with his wife for Camp David to work on the speech. But after getting a draft on July 4, he ordered press secretary Jerry Powell to notify reporters that the talk would be canceled. The reason, Powell reported, was that the president did not believe the country or Congress would react favorably to yet another energy speech.

Thereafter, for 11 days he remained at Camp David, meeting with a variety of official and unofficial persons. Until the last day, the media were kept at "the bottom of the mountain" to watch the president's secretive activities "on the mountaintop." Reporters questioned everyone who came down the mountain to learn what they could of the "domestic summit" as the informal meetings were dubbed.

Following is a synopsis of what reporters learned on key days.

Thursday, July 5: The president canceled a weekend trip to Louisville, Kentucky, where he had planned to address a gathering of governors. Instead, he went fishing and Powell announced plans for the "summit." Governors express disappointment.

Friday, July 6: The president met with the first group, his inner circle of advisers, followed later in the day by the first of the outsiders, a group of governors led by Julian Carroll of Kentucky. "He's listening," Carroll reported.

Saturday, July 7: The president held several more meetings. One, which went past midnight, included Washington lawyer and former adviser to earlier presidents Clark Clifford, and black leader Jesse Jackson. Both spoke later of a "civilizational crisis" and predicted major changes in congressional action and the president's key advisers.

Sunday, July 8: The president met with oil industry figures and others, including the president of the Massachusetts Institute of Technology. The vice-president, who had seen the president early in the day, spoke in Washington of a massive program to produce synthetic fuel.

Monday, July 9: The president told a group of Senate and House members that Saudi Arabia had agreed to increase oil production temporarily, and publicly thanked the Arab nation. The president met late into the night with key congressional Democrats. They indicated the president intended to address the nation soon on more than just energy problems.

Tuesday, July 10: The president met with economic advisers from past administrations, union chiefs, and business executives. Powell announced that the president would not lift retail price controls on gasoline, and would set a new speech date shortly.

Wednesday, July 11: More economic meetings with industry people from all fields were held. An unofficial count by news people indicated the president had met with more than 130 persons by this time. Powell announced that the president would address the nation over TV on Sunday, July 15, at 10 P.M. EDT.

Thursday, July 12: The president made a surprise evening visit to seek the advice of five blue-collar families in Carnegie, Pennsylvania. They told him the country is in a state of decline, and that people are hungry for leadership. "We gave it to him straight," the host, William Fisher, told reporters who learned of the visit after the president returned to Camp David.

Friday, July 13: Another unannounced trip, this one to meet retired and professional couples in Martinsburg, West Virginia. Among those visited: Marvin and Virginia Porterfield. Then back at Camp David the president held a luncheon with more than a dozen journalists who described him as deeply troubled by the nation's lack of faith in his leadership, but determined to make major changes and turn things around for himself and the country. The president said he realized his abrupt cancellation of his July 5 speech added to the doubts about his leadership. The reporters found him looking fit.

Saturday, July 14: The president flew back to the White House in the evening. Powell said the chief executive spent most of the day at Camp David working on his Sunday evening address. There are still no firm hints on what he will say, but opinion appears to be on the side of "nothing too startling." The president is said to realize his protracted meetings have probably created exaggerated expectations.

Exercise 9.2

A tornado hit Cheyenne, Wyoming at 3:40 P.M. on a Monday. The following story, filed late Monday night, ran in the Tuesday morning papers. New information on the wires by mid-morning Tuesday was added for the Tuesday afternoon editions. Update the morning story, using important new facts and dropping unnecessary information. Keep the updated story to 500 words.

CHEYENNE, Wyoming (AP)—A slow-moving tornado rolled through two subdivisions and a trailer park in northern Cheyenne Monday, destroying hundreds of dwellings and causing what a sheriff's dispatcher called "substantial" injuries. The National Weather Service said at least one person was killed.

Expensive brick homes were flattened in the Buffalo Ridge area, with only fireplaces and chimneys left standing. At the Cheyenne Trailer Court, only debris could be seen.

Hundreds of houses had windows blown out and roofs knocked off. Heavy debris was scattered all over the north side of the city.

There were unconfirmed reports that some persons were still trapped in their wrecked homes hours after the tornado struck.

Laramie County Memorial Hospital—one of three hospitals in this state capital of 60,000 persons—reported receiving "several severe injury" cases.

Joe Pettigo, a spokesman for the National Weather Service, said the 50-yard-wide tornado came in from the west at 3:40 P.M. MDT and carved a swath about four miles long through the city before moving off to the southeast toward Colorado.

He called it "a very significant tornado" and said it caused "several million dollars damage."

The weather service said in a storm report that one fatality had been confirmed, but it gave no details.

The tornado also rolled through the National Guard Armory at the northern end of the municipal airport and narrowly missed the governor's mansion.

Willis Larson, a spokesman for the Wyoming Disaster and Civil Defense agency, said "we just don't know anything yet. It's just a total chaotic mess."

Police, firemen and National Guardsmen all were asked to report for duty.

Three hours after the storm passed through the city, traffic was backed up, power lines were down, and communications were partially disrupted. Mountain Bell said its circuits into Cheyenne were overloaded and asked people to hold telephone calls to emergencies.

Missy Dehner, a Wyoming Highway Patrol employee, said she watched the tornado from the department building and saw it knock a semitrailer truck off Interstate 25.

"It got real dark and there was a big huge grayish cloud swirling around way up over by the highway department," she said. "There was a whirlpool of dirt . . . when it started to come down, I went downstairs into the basement. It moved east and went across . . . threw a couple dumpsters, hit some power lines and knocked the power out."

Willis said two C-130 cargo planes on the ground at the Cheyenne Municipal Airport were destroyed.

He said at least one light plane on the ground at the airport was blown away. "It got sucked into the funnel and people saw it coming out of the clouds," he said. (*Source:* Associated Press, July 1979)

New information for the afternoon papers:

National Weather Service spokespeople confirmed that this was the first tornado in Cheyenne's history. Residents resumed sifting through rubble of more than 200 homes early this morning (Tuesday). They were being allowed back into the northern residential areas ravaged by the Monday twister. They looked for belongings and began the sad task of cleaning up. Nearly 40 persons were injured, and 7 remained hospitalized today. A 14-month-old boy, David McKinnon, died instantly of head injuries when his family's mobile home northeast of Cheyenne was demolished, officials said. The boy's mother, Linda McKinnon, and a brother, Mat, were reported in serious condition at Laramie County Memorial Hospital this morning. Two other unidentified victims were listed as stable at Memorial Hospital, and three patients at DePaul Hospital were reported in satisfactory condition today.

"No one ever thought we would ever have a tornado in Cheyenne, Wyoming," Mayor Don Erickson said, "but we had one." The mayor said the tornado's funnel cut across a 2-block wide area for 4 to 5 miles within the city limits.

As the twister came towards Cheyenne, Norma McClellan urged her two teen-age children to get in the car and outrun it, but her son disagreed. The family took shelter in its basement, and when the sound ended, came upstairs to find the home destroyed. Nearby, three children alone in their home took the same action. "The Lord was good to us," said their mother, Diana Coles. About a mile east of the McClellan and Coles homes, Joe Griego was searching through the rubble of his home. His wife was crawling across the rubble. "I've got to go get my diamond earnings," she said. "They're the only thing I have left."

Governor Ed Herschler asked the president to declare the 200 ravaged blocks disaster areas, qualifying residents for emergency federal relief, Erickson said.

Exercise 9.3

For the next two items, write a lead localizing a national story. Keep in mind that you have to present a sense of the national story as well as the local angle. Decide whether to combine the two elements, or to put one first, followed by the other.

1. A strike by the American Airline Employees Union hit Allright Airlines at noon today. Throughout the country, Allright employs 70,000 people in 25 different cities. A spokesman for AAEU in New York says the strike may be a long one because Allright is refusing to negotiate. The wire story from New York gives details of union demands, disrupted air schedules, and the fact that Allright carries 100,000 passengers a day on its flights.

To localize this national story you gather the following facts: 14,000 passengers a day leave your local airport on Allright Airlines. Of Allright's total employees, 7,000 work at your local airport. Merchants estimate that Allright employees account for 20 percent of their daily business. All local AAEU members have already walked off their jobs. There are large crowds of airline passengers stranded at the airport who had been scheduled out on two Allright flights after the strike started; 12 more flights are scheduled for the rest of the day.

2. The ABC Brands Company has recalled all of its Brand X canned string beans because botulism has been discovered in its Series E batch, sent to retailers three months ago. The wire story from Kansas City, headquarters of ABC Brands, says a company spokesperson said that its canned goods

are first distributed to regional warehouses, then reshipped from there. Retailers may have received the canned goods within the last two months, or may not have received the Series E shipment yet. Normally, retail stocks turn over about every two months on string beans. The company advises consumers to check their Brand X cans of string beans, looking for the Series E mark just to the right and bottom of the company logo. If they find they have Series E, they should either throw the cans away or return them to supermarket retailers who will refund their money. Supermarkets and other grocery retailers are being notified by telegram to remove Series E Brand X string beans from their shelves.

You check the regional distributor nearest your community and learn that 20,000 cases of Series E were received 2.5 months ago. About 7,000 cases are still left, which means that the others are in local stores or in consumers' homes. You check Lucy's, the largest supermarket chain in your area. A spokesperson says they have not yet had a chance to determine how much of the company's Series E has been sold.

Exercise 9.4

Music conductor Arthur Hampton, of Atlanta's Second Symphony orchestra, was for 50 years considered king of symphony pops concerts all over the world. He has just died, at age 90, in Atlanta. Long obituaries and features will run. You have been asked to write a local sidebar for your community paper. Use whatever city name is appropriate. Here are the local facts.

Arthur Hampton had a second home for 2 decades with your city's symphony orchestra. Local music critics frequently hailed him as "champion of classical music for people who hate classical music." Hampton, who had cut 35 best-selling records over his 50 years as conductor, used the local symphony for 5 of those records. One is titled "These Are the Sounds."

For 17 years, from 1960 through 1977, Hampton directed benefit concerts for the Children's Health Council here, which raised about $100,000 per concert. Since Hampton's retirement in 1979, local efforts to hold Pops concerts to raise money for CHC have brought poor results.

Hampton's fame and magnetic personality filled the local Civic Amphitheatre with overflowing crowds for about 9 concerts every year during his season here. The outdoor Amphitheatre holds 12,000 who would lounge on the grass in late afternoon sunlight to munch fried chicken, sip wine, and soak up the varied fare of light classics and orchestrated pops. The typical Hampton audience would whistle and sing along after the maestro and orchestra had left the stage.

Early in 1979, Hampton's doctor finally ordered him to slow down, and he reluctantly canceled his local Pops season. He returned to this community only once again, as a visitor to his good friend, violinist George Lenzwig, in the summer of 1979. "I'm back, aren't I," he told reporters then. "I'm always coming back." But he did not make it back.

Many people noted changes in his programming through the years. Local critics decried his move from overtures, tone poems and light classical works to arrangements of movie scores and Broadway shows. But local audiences never deserted him; his popularity kept growing through the years.

Exercise 9.5

You have just written a story on a research report that states that two teachers sharing a single job can bring important benefits to students, parents, schools, as well as the teachers themselves. The research study covered 9 school districts surrounding your community, where 44 teachers are sharing 22 jobs. The study showed that school superintendents said job sharing brought "greater enthusiasm and excitement" to teaching, and that students benefited from having more than one expert in a classroom. The study also indicated that those who share jobs produce more satisfactory results than individuals who simply work part-time alone, returning home after a specified number of hours.

Your editor tells you to phone someone who is job sharing to write a short sidebar. You do so and gather the following information. Use it to write the sidebar.

Blanche Gifford has worked in the Whisman District elementary schools for seven years. She had worked for five years full-time. Then she had her first child two years ago. She could not decide whether to quit or keep working. She did not want to turn her child over to a babysitter every day, but she liked her job and was afraid she would get bored at home. She discussed her problem with her school principal, Ed Sherman. He told her another teacher in the district was facing the same problem. He suggested she talk with the other teacher, Pat David. Maybe the two of them could work something out. He would be content if they wanted to share a class, he said. Pat and Blanche decided sharing a teaching load would be an ideal solution to their problem of motherhood and career. They agreed to work half days. One would teach the morning sessions; the other the afternoon. This way, each would be away from home only three hours a day. They have been extremely happy with the arrangement. "I work hard my three hours," Blanche says. "I really work a little extra at home, too, preparing for classes. But I'm at home, so I don't mind."

Pat David echoes these sentiments. "It's been marvelous. I can have my career and my time with my child. Job sharing has been a perfect solution for me."

Exercise 9.6   *Your college football team has just won its first bid to play in the Orange Bowl. You are the sports contributor to the local paper. The editor asks you to write a sidebar on the head coach, Jack Nelson, to run alongside a history of the team's wins and losses this season. Use the facts below.*

Head coach Jack Nelson was born in Cleveland, Ohio, 48 years ago. He was an All-Ohio player while attending John Hay High School, then went on to play seven years for Paul Brown's Cleveland Browns. He entered coaching as an assistant in 1963 for Sid Gillman's Los Angeles Chargers in the then new American Football League.

Nelson grew up playing backlot baseball every spare moment. Everyone who knew him was surprised when he went out for football after entering high school. He has never given up his interest in baseball, and still spends hours coaching his two sons, aged 14 and 16, on the fine points of throwing a fastball. "Baseball is fun, but it is not a serious game like football," he has been quoted as saying.

He is extremely serious about football. In fact, despite his devotion to his players and the good rapport he establishes with them, he is noted for his lack of humor. He has a reputation for being respected, if not well liked, by his players. But none of them criticize him. "There's no point joking with him," halfback Ricky Jones has said. "All he wants to talk about is how to improve your game. But his suggestions are always helpful and he never says anything mean."

Nelson joined college football teams 10 years ago, when he became associate coach at Willamette College. He helped its team rack up three season wins in the Midwestern Association between 1975 and 1979. After joining your college for the 1980 season, he led your team to a 1–11 loss record in his first year as a head coach. There was some talk among alumni supporters that he should be fired, but this was squelched as the team's record improved in subsequent seasons. With the bid to the Orange Bowl, his players appear willing to forgive him his dour remarks at the end of each game, win or lose.

Chapter 10 # Speeches, Meetings, and News Conferences

Advance Stories

The advance story is the easiest possible news story to write. In the case of a speaker, you can write this:

> Marcella Ying, a long-time resident of the People's Republic of China, will speak Thursday on "Teaching English in China."
> The speech will be made at 4:15 P.M. in the Polich Room, Lou Cubberly Building.

If the speaker is important, such as a U. S. senator, you can add many paragraphs. In any case, this structure of who, what, where, and when can be used again and again.

In writing an advance story on a meeting or a news conference, you can use the above story as a model, substituting the name of the group that is to meet or the speaker at a news conference. If a meeting is important, you should add whether the public is admitted. In a few cases, you should also add whether there will be an admission charge.

News Stories

When you are writing a story about a speech, a meeting, or a press conference, use this question as a guide: What is the most important and interesting thing said?

You can abandon that question in very few cases. It could be that the speaker or speakers do not say anything much. You should then decide not to write the story, or switch to a feature lead. For example, one imaginative student who covered a speech by Dr. Louis Baer decided that a feature lead would attract readers. He wrote:

> Take two aspirin tablets, rest in bed, and read the Book of Job.
> An unlikely prescription? Not if you're a patient of Dr. Louis Baer.

The reporter then went on to describe how Dr. Baer, a professor of clinical medicine, prescribed Descartes and the Book of Job as well as penicillin to his patients.

In most cases, however, you should ask yourself: What is the most important and interesting fact? To test what you have already learned, in the following columns you will find a published newspaper story and an effort by a beginning student to write the same story. After reading the two columns—no further—try to determine which is published and which is amateur.

Clara Luck, who has gone the full political circle from Franklin Roosevelt to Ronald Reagan, painted a melancholy picture of Democratic Party prospects in a local address Tuesday.	Yesterday Clara Luck—author, skindiver, and former congresswoman—spoke to a full house in Stephens Auditorium. Her topic was "The Future of the Two-Party System."
The Democrats aren't moribund yet, but barring a major disaster such as war or depression it will be at least 20 years before it will recover again, Mrs. Luck predicted.	Mrs. Luck began by saying that the two-party system started when the issue of states' rights collided with the stronger executive power. She brought out that this is important because "Any party is deeply involved with its past."
The Republicans will remain in power as long as they maintain peace, she declared, and while she sees the vague outlines of war in the future, the chances of economic calamity seem to be growing.	Mrs. Luck, a staunch Republican, admitted that "There is a whale of a lot more Democrats than Republicans," and that "The recipe for disaster of a political party is a split." She went on to say, "If the conservative wing of the party will not accept liberal leadership, and the liberal wing of the party will not accept conservative leadership, the only alternative is to return to a 'Me-too' position."
Mrs. Luck, former Republican congresswoman from Connecticut, analyzed "The Future of the Two-Party System" in an hour-long speech to nearly 500 in Stephens Auditorium.	
"The future of the Democratic Party is not very bright," she emphatically stated. "A charismatic leader—such as General Eisenhower—may save it, but the trouble is	She mentioned that since there are 6 or 7 Democrats in every 10 registered voters, that the only hope

you usually have to have a world war to produce one."

Mrs. Luck asserted the Democrats would probably have survived the Korean War and remained in power except for the charismatic figure of Eisenhower.

"The only hope for the Democratic Party as matters stand," she continued, "is the failure of the Republican Party . . . something that none of us patriots wants to see."

If a depression or "a long and wounding war" were to occur, "the Democrats will bounce back," she said.

"If peace and prosperity are developed by the Republicans, they will remain in power for 20 years, or as long as they maintain them," Mrs. Luck said.

She pointed out. . . .

for the Democratic Party as it stands today would be a failure of the Republican Party. By "failure" she said she meant, "Another depression or a long and wounding war."

"Crises offer both danger and opportunity," she said. It was the men in history who excelled in a crisis that we remember today as outstanding presidents. Mrs. Luck did not feel that the two-party system was on its way out, but that the Republicans, as near as she could see, might very well be in power for the next 20 years.

In a humorous vein, Mrs. Luck mentioned Alma Maters of presidents. Harvard has had six men in the White House; Princeton, one. . . .

Which one was published? If you voted for the story in the right column, pay careful attention to the next few paragraphs: You were wrong. Even though the story in the left column was published, it has no special flair; it is routine. Nonetheless, you should have voted for the story in the left column for these reasons:

Paragraphing. Even without reading anything—as though you looked at the page from a distance—you should have noticed that the story in the left column was paragraphed in a way that you should already know: short paragraphs for a news story.

Leads. The lead in the right column reported the correct item to begin an advance story—the topic of her speech. The lead at the left sums up what Mrs. Luck said.

Order. As you should judge from reading the story at the right, the second paragraph starts with the speaker's beginnings ("Mrs. Luck began by saying . . ."). Never let the speaker dictate in what order you should write the story. If the most important fact is stated in the middle of the speech, or at the end—or even in response to a question after the speech—begin with that.

Quotations. Note that the story at the left first quotes Mrs. Luck directly with, "The future of the Democratic Party is not very bright." Then note that the story at the right first quotes her directly with, "Any party is deeply involved with its past." Because Mrs. Luck is an important politician, her prediction (left column) is important. The reporter of the story in the left column is first interested in what she said about a timely event, the prospects of the party.

Error. The reporter in the right column errs by ending the fourth paragraph with a closed quotation. That is an error because the reporter begins the next paragraph with a quotation. As a reader, you should have thought: "The reporter is introducing a different speaker." Because the reporter did not actually introduce another speaker, he should have deleted the quotation marks at the end of the fourth paragraph. That indicates that Mrs. Luck is still speaking when the next paragraph begins with a quotation mark.

Although the stories already quoted report only on a speech story, you should remember the form and the comments. They tell you, generally, how you should report a meeting or a news conference. Even though many people may speak at a single meeting, and even though at large news conferences many reporters may ask many questions that the speaker answers, you should think of this above all: What was said that is important? If you are not able to decide which is the most important, thinking that three different speakers at a meeting said something vital, you should arrange your story this way:

In a meeting of the City Council last night, three strong opponents of the new ordinance said:

1. What seems to be the most important item, stated in a sentence or two.
2. What also seems to be the most important item, stated in a sentence or two.
3. What also seems to be the most important in a sentence or two. Then, double back by writing details of the first. Then details of the second, then details of the third. Then finish your story with anything else that seems appropriate.

The most important factor in writing speech stories, meeting stories, or news conferences, is quoting—and quoting accurately. If you write a story and do not use direct quotations—or even if you use only a few words of quotations—most readers will doubt your story. "Is that what the speaker said?" they will ask, shaking their heads.

Because you are a student, you have probably taken many notes during lectures from your teachers. Even though you may take general notes, not quoting the teachers directly, it will be fairly easy for you to note the important things a speaker has said. As for the mechanics of note taking, most reporters devise their own shorthand: *imp.* for *important,* *w* for *with,* *w/o* for *without,* and so on. Practice taking quotations directly. When you become accustomed to taking direct quotations, after listening to two or three speeches you will probably be able to single out the most important things the speaker emphasizes.

The importance of learning to take quotations must be emphasized. Keep in mind:

1. Few readers trust stories that are all (or mostly) paraphrased.
2. Quotations help recreate an event.
3. Quotations help present the flavor of an event.
4. If the speaker's words are worth remembering, you can write a story worth remembering.

Gathering Information

Gathering information for advance stories, speeches, and meetings is often more routine than other forms of newspaper reporting.

Information for advance stories frequently comes from press releases announcing the upcoming meeting, speech, or news conference. The press release may be complete, or may require that you phone one or two people for additional information. Usually the name and phone numbers of the people who can supply more information will be listed on the press release. If not, the correct organization or person to phone is usually obvious from the release itself.

If you need to gather background information on a speaker, your newspaper's morgue may provide sufficient data. If the speaker is famous, the newspaper library or a public library will usually have biographical data in one of many *Who's Who* reference books. (*Who's Who in American Scientists* and *Who's Who in American Women* are but two examples.) Libraries, especially those associated with colleges or universities, may have copies of articles or books that the speaker has written. If you have the time, it is useful to skim this material, as well as news reports of any previous speeches the speaker delivered. Many modern newspapers have extended information services available through computer networks. These provide previous speech stories on some speakers, if your own newspaper's morgue does not have such clippings.

If you have any doubts about what a speaker said, always try to catch him or her immediately afterwards, asking for a clarification. Most speakers are happy to oblige; they want their words reported accurately.

Gathering information before a meeting may be a bit more complex. You may need to contact at least two persons, if not more, to adequately prepare yourself. The person in charge of the meeting—a mayor, for a city council meeting, for example; or the chair of a professional meeting such as the American Bar Association, will usually prove helpful in advising you what key subjects are likely to interest your readership. Executive secretaries of associations, or city managers—in other words, staff people for the group holding the meeting—are also excellent sources.

These same people will prove useful during and after a meeting, if you need help in deciding what important action took place. Sometimes inexperienced reporters are unfamiliar with the history of an ongoing group, such as the Board of Education; they will write better stories if they understand whether a topic hotly debated has been around a long while or is new, or whether some seemingly subtle discussion really has more significance than initially appears.

However, the reporter must always be alert to particular biases the person providing background information may have. That is the reason for seeking more than one opinion.

Your newspaper's morgue should also be a good source for learning the background of any ongoing local meetings. So will the minutes of those meetings, often available at local libraries as well as at the group's headquarters.

Many public and private groups, associations, and professional bodies have press information officers who can be helpful to both inexperienced and experienced reporters.

News conferences are almost always organized by specialized press information persons. They will usually be the best and fastest source for learning the details of upcoming conferences, or supplying extra information during and after a conference.

Chapter 10 Exercises

Before performing the following exercises, check yourself on these highlights.

Remember:

1. To grasp the complexities of this chapter, begin with the simplest part: advance stories.

2. In writing news stories about speeches that do not seem important, consider using a feature lead.

3. Study carefully the two stories about Clara Luck's speech. You can determine what to avoid by reading the analysis.

4. Quotations are often the center of these kinds of stories. Study the four points made about quoting speakers.

5. You can grasp the overall essence of gathering information by studying the end of this chapter.

Exercise 10.1   *Write short advance stories based on the following information.*

1. John Todd will speak today. He is a mayor of a city, Redwood Lanes, Washington, and will speak before the local Optimist Club at 7 P.M. in Driscoll Hotel. He will talk about "The Ever-Crowded City." He has been the mayor for eight years, having been reelected to the post three times. He is married and has three sons and one daughter. Although he is a member of the Rotary Club, he consented to speak to the Optimist Club during his visit here.

2. The state Orange Growers Association will hold its biennial convention beginning next week. The convention will be held for three days, Monday through Wednesday. A vice-president, local resident Bill McNeese, said that the meeting will be larger than ever. He estimates that more than 500 orange growers will convene. The meeting will be held locally, in the Smith Hotel. McNeese said that the crowd will be large because they will be protesting the restrictions on the orange growers brought by the governor.

3. Governor Jerry Maisel has decided to stage his first news conference in three months. It will be held in the Executive Office Building, Room 302. The conference will begin at 10 A.M. tomorrow. He will begin with a major announcement, protesting the way the president of the United States is hampering the state by giving too much attention to the Department of Defense. After his announcement, he will be questioned by the reporters for the media.

Exercise 10.2   *In the left column below, write a criticism of the story published in the right column. Read again the stories published side by side earlier in this chapter, and the comments to determine what kind of criticism you should make. Add any criticism that you think is justifiable.*

(For example: This lead is not appropriate. Younger's injury is not serious. The writer should have begun with what Younger said and saved the injury until a later paragraph.)

Because he had injured his leg in getting out of a car before his speech, Bill Younger, a candidate for governor, almost hobbled. Then he made his campaign speech to a capacity crowd at the Commonwealth Club on 13 October 1978.

Younger began by outlining his campaign platform for governor by relating economic issues to the problems of the state surplus in tax dollars, the energy shortage, and the housing shortage. Younger proposed to "give them (the taxpayers) back their surplus. Give them back their money. It isn't the government's right to collect more money than it needs." Predicted to be "$10 billion" by the end of the year, Younger called the surplus "Obscene." He went on to say that the "most insidious thing about the surplus is that it enables the legislature to spend money anyway it wants" despite the taxpayer's wishes.

A strong proponent of Proposition 13 before its acceptance, Younger wants to refund extra tax dollars based upon an outside audit.

He also proposes to trim the government down, stating that "Where government action is necessary, expedite it; where it's not, eliminate it." First to be axed, if elected, would be the Energy Commission at a saving of $20 million dollars. Younger supports immediate development of nuclear power plants. He wants to "put Sun Desert back on track" along with the Diablo Valley project. Basing his responses upon the scientific support of Edwin Teller and other scientists, Younger reassured the audience that nuclear wastes can be safely disposed of in the desert. He suggests that more extensive exploration and drilling for off-shore gas is essential if we are to avoid increasing reliance upon foreign oil. "We don't want someone over there to turn the spigot off. That would be a great tragedy." Unless new sources of energy are cultivated now, Younger predicts that "We are going to have a significant power shortage in the mid-1980s."

Repeating his theme that government controls and expenditures should be limited, Younger proposed several reforms for the housing industry. He would fire Gene Quinn, provide a one-stop building permit, increase renters' allowance . . . He also says that he would tighten up the law so that municipalities cannot cheat Proposition 13's effects by increasing service fees.

His goal is to develop housing so that homes are no longer priced out of the typical homeowner's reach. For, in Younger's words, "Homes are the foundation upon which we build society."

When questioned about the quality of California prisons, Evelle Younger spoke in characteristically hard-line terms: "Prisons are not pleasant places . . . But given the character of the people in them, I believe that our correctional officers do the best job possible . . . If you're realistic, you know that prisons are not places to rehabilitate prisoners . . . The purpose of prisons is to protect the good guys from the bad, at least for a little time."

The most important thing he said, with which I can agree, was warning that "Americans are great problem solvers, but great procrastinators, too," Younger concluded his speech with the hope that the audience would "worry a little more about these problems than when you came in."

Exercise 10.3 *You were assigned to cover a speech today at noon. The speech is being given at the Royal Inn at the airport. The speaker is Richard F. Brown, publisher of the Austin, Texas,* American-Statesman, *who spoke to the annual convention of the Midwest Political Science Association. Write a story of 500 words for tomorrow morning's newspaper. The speech text is as follows:*

"The role, the function, of the press in our system of government is probably the least understood of all our democratic processes. Not only by the average citizen, but by many of the highest leaders in government and business. And this is true almost 200 years after the rights of free speech and free press were created by our Constitution.

"Basically, of course, we recognize that the newspaper today is—and always has been—very much like a messenger of the Roman era. When he brought bad news from the battlefield he was killed. None of us likes to hear bad news and we live in days when news of rampant crime, moral decay, drugs, dying cities, pollution, racial strife, and war is the ordinary and not the exception, as it was in earlier periods of our history.

"There are those—and I am sure there are some in this audience—who would argue that newspapers print too much of all this; that we seldom find the space to print the quote good news unquote. There is so much bad news, they say, that it almost overwhelms us.

"Well, let me give you the plain truth. The bad news would indeed overwhelm us if we weren't made aware of it by newspapers and the other media.

"The news media are often dismayed by the fact that the public and many leaders of government, though understanding that role, choose to ignore the constituted role of newspapers and the other media in our society.

"There seems to be prevalent in the country today an attitude that the news media should be partners of government on whatever level—local, state, or national—in achieving whatever goals or purposes those who govern choose to reach.

"To the contrary, the Constitution insured the freedom of press in America so that the human failing of those who govern would always have the press to fill the role of antagonist; to quiz, to challenge, to hold up for public view and discussion the errors and misdoings of elected officials.

"This is not to say that the news media should not or cannot support and help develop the forces of public opinion to help achieve those goals of government which are worthy. But in no sense is the press obligated to say what a government official—no matter how high his office—happens to think it should say.

"The growing threat to freedom of press and speech in the United States today is a danger that is difficult to define and explain to people outside our profession.

"But there exists in America today a cacophony—a chorus of harsh and irresponsible attacks—against newspapers and the news media that surpasses in intensity and severity anything we have experienced in our past.

"Part of this climate of unreasoning anger with the press, of course, is part of the pattern of the unreasoning temper of our times.

"First, the political atmosphere is charged with emotion as it has seldom been in America.

"Second, the average person—as part of his misconceptions about the role of the media—has developed a belief that those who publish newspapers or magazines or own radio or television stations are the franchise holders of freedom of speech and press.

"Too many people think that the full burden of defending and preserving those freedoms also belongs to publishers and broadcast station owners.

"The truth, of course, is that the rights of speech and press belong to every one of us and the news media are nothing more than the channels through which those rights are given expression. But the increasing erosion of the free flow of ideas and information and the critical role of the press in serving as a watchdog over government and authority is not restricted to the federal level.

"I would remind you of the fact that when the Bill of Rights was written by the same men who conceived our form of government and wrote our Constitution, those men insisted on the rights of free speech and free press because they did not trust their own power and authority.

"If for any reason you do not have confidence in the press of this country I suggest you think hard about whether you should trust those who stay close to and represent the public—the news media—or those few who represent government. And I would remind you that in our very recent past—as through the past 200 years—the vigilant force in our society has been the press, not those who govern."

Exercise 10.4

The following opinions on business regulation appeared originally in Saturday Review. *Assume for this exercise that each was expressed in a public forum on regulation. The forum was held on a Thursday in Cleveland. It was sponsored by the Public Debate Society, a local civic group. Read each opinion. Select material for a story. Write it, keeping it under 750 words.*

GARY HART
DEMOCRATIC SENATOR FROM COLORADO

The regulation of American business is becoming excessive. Many regulations are inefficient, costly to implement, and often stifle innovation.

The challenge is to maintain the benefits regulations were intended to achieve while cutting down on their cost.

One way to cut the cost of regulation is to simplify compliance. For example, a company in Colorado wishing to make synthetic oil from oil shale must first obtain 18 permits from the federal government and 20 from state and local agencies. In addition, the same company needs 27 more permits to begin a housing project adjacent to its mining operation. Surely the public could be served just as well, if not better, if some of these 65 requirements were combined.

Second, we need to revise the regulatory process itself. Regulations have been designed to induce actions which may not be profitable for individual firms but which are desirable from society's perspective. Environmental regulations are an example. Neither the cost of destroying the environment nor the profit from cleaning it up appear on the balance sheet of any corporation, so we have devised regulations to protect public health and safety.

We need to provide economic incentives for cleaning up the environment, and to replace the volume of regulations with a simpler pollution fee.

Under such a system, polluters would pay a fee for every unit of untreated pollution discharged into the environment. Regulators would no longer dictate to each firm how much pollution to abate or how to achieve the standard. Instead, fees would be set high enough to provide efficient economic incentives so that most firms would comply.

For genuine public health hazards, involving, for example, toxic chemicals and heavy metals, economic incentives are not the answer, outright prohibition still is. But a system of economic incentives and disincentives to combat pollution deserves to be tried as a serious alternative to the burden of regulation.

A. W. CLAUSEN
PRESIDENT, BANK OF AMERICA

It is safe to say that we are overregulated when we begin to suffer from the following paradox: Our economic and social regulation seriously impedes our economic and social progress. This paradox is at work now.

In fiscal year 1979, the federal government has budgeted $4.8 billion for 41 regulatory agencies. The overriding concern, however, is not that $4.8 billion but the cost to business of complying with these federal regulations. A study by Murray Weidenbaum, a former Undersecretary of the Treasury who now heads Washington University's Center for the Study of American Business, found that compliance costs are generally 20 times greater than the government's regulatory budget.

Clearly, the appropriate level of regulation for our society can best be determined through cooperative effort among government, business, and the public. To get that effort off to the right start, representatives of each sector must dispense with the traditional rhetoric that tends to polarize viewpoints on the issue, and proposed regulations and regulatory structures must begin with a "zero-base budget" approach.

RALPH NADER
CONSUMER ADVOCATE

Regulation does not present a threat to the American economy; not regulating does. Health and safety standards are the best economic investment that we can make in this country. Every life and every limb we save, every disease that we prevent, represents not only a human achievement but also a reduction in the gigantically inflationary cost of medical and hospital care. The cost of neglecting health and safety requirements can be calculated in loss of worker productivity, and in such insurance costs as workmen's compensation.

The claim that regulation is costing business upwards of $100 billion is sheer nonsense. Not only are the figures as phony as a three-dollar bill, but they include none of the returns, such as public-health benefits.

Businessmen also complain that regulation stifles innovation. The exact opposite is true. EPA and OSHA regulations have stimulated tremendous innovation in health and safety products. In the September 14, 1978, issue of the *Journal of Commerce,* Eugene Melnitchenko, a vice-president at US Trust, Inc. observed that OSHA regulations had served as a great boon to chemical specialty companies, who are thriving in the detoxification business.

In fact, regulation provides the largest source of new jobs in industry today. Regulation has created perhaps a million jobs, and eliminated no more than 15 to 20,000.

HERBERT SCHMERTZ
VICE-PRESIDENT, PUBLIC AFFAIRS
MOBIL OIL CORPORATION

As an energy company, Mobil has experienced the never-never land of Catch-22 created by excessive government regulation. Consider these examples:

In resolving electricity-generation needs, the nuclear option stands out as the best and most logical. Nuclear power is totally predictable; one can know exactly how much power will be available from a given facility at a given date. Its safety record is excellent, and there's little environmental disruption. But in spite of these virtues, conflicting and sometimes retroactive regulations have reduced orders for new installations from 44 in 1973 to only three in 1977. I know of none in 1978.

EPA and other government regulators are making it extremely difficult to construct a new refinery or even expand an existing one. The permit-gathering process can easily take between 18 and 36 months, involving federal, state, and local agencies.

How to untangle the morass? First, the president should appoint a commission of citizens from outside government to review all federal regulations five years old or older. Second, legislation should be enacted to schedule the demise of all regulations and regulatory agencies whose charters have not been periodically renewed by Congress.

LLOYD MCBRIDE
PRESIDENT, UNITED STEELWORKERS OF AMERICA

The steel industry estimates that it will have to spend over $4 billion between now and 1985 on pollution control. Yet that is roughly one-tenth of what the industry figures it must spend on plant modernization and capacity expansion during those same years to continue growing and remain profitable.

Moreover, we should not lose sight of the fact that we are facing a mammoth health, social, and economic problem. A recent government study connects as many as 20 percent of all cancer deaths to occupational exposures.

But we need not rely on such cost-benefit justifications for protecting workplace and public health. Congress has rightly established as public policy the need to work toward removal, or at least minimization, of these hazards wherever possible from the plant environment, the surrounding air, the waterways, and other media. Congress has not required that action await cost-benefit analyses. Such a computation would not only waste time and money, but would yield inconclusive figures.

All this is not to say that regulations should not be cost-effective and feasible. Having defined the safe health level related to a particular pollutant, we must then find the best means of attaining it. Despite popular misconceptions, OSHA's health standards do reflect these criteria. EPA is bending over backwards to tailor its enforcement strategies to individual industries.

JACK KEMP
REPUBLICAN CONGRESSMAN FROM NEW YORK

The reason we have so much regulation these days is that the whole national "economic pie" has been shrinking. When this happens the bigger guys try to protect their share of the pie by pushing regulations in the name of helping the little guys, knowing that regulations always have the effect of squeezing and ultimately eliminating the competition.

The big oil companies can afford to hire the lawyers and accountants necessary to deal with complex energy regulations. The big retail chains have to pay high wages and guarantee warranties, so it is not only no skin off their noses to support high minimum wages and stiff warranty legislation; and it also eliminates the small competitors.

My advocacy of federal tax rate reduction, less government regulation, and a monetary standard to help end inflation addresses these problems indirectly, which is the only way I think they can be addressed effectively.

Exercise 10.5

Use the following speech to write a story of about 300 words. The speaker is Katharine Graham, chair of the Washington Post. *The main thrust of her speech is the accountability of the press. Graham spoke before the faculty and students in Stephens Hall last night.*

"The news is an independent business. That fact flows from the First Amendment, from the conviction of the founding fathers that the agencies of news in a free society should not be in the hands of government nor subject to control by presidents or Congress. This meant that the great public responsibility of conveying information was entrusted to free, private individuals and the organizations they could establish and maintain in the competitive marketplace.

"The corollary is that the health of a news company as a business—as a private company—and the quality of its products—its ability to serve the public—are intertwined and interdependent.

"A newspaper has responsibilities to three masters: its owners and stockholders; the public; and a standard of journalism which is in some respects the most demanding taskmaster of them all. These responsibilities may sometimes seem to pull in opposite directions. But in the long run, I firmly believe that it all comes together; good journalism is good public service and good business. For all three really involve the same thing: to publish a newspaper which, day after day, is informative, interesting, and consistently accurate and fair.

"Fairness is a hard concept to define, especially because the term is often invoked when critics of the press really mean something else. Often when people complain that a story is unfair, or that a newspaper is biased or slanted, what they really mean is that it doesn't exactly reflect their own point of view or stick to the particular material they would like to see in print. In other words, readers can be very biased themselves, and very quick to equate their own preferences with the facts.

"Of course we never do a perfect job—and even if we did, one day, we'd have to start all over again the next morning. But I think it's the nature of the news business to be continually unfinished. After all, the First Amendment wasn't designed to make journalists rich and happy. It was intended to give the public the independent, vigorous, and controversial press which is indispensable in a free society. (Courtesy, Katharine Graham. Reprinted by permission)

Chapter 11

Stories from Announcements

Many years ago, you could be almost certain that your name would be printed in the local newspaper at three different times: your birth, your marriage, and your death. In a metropolitan city, of course, that would not be feasible because of all the residents. Nonetheless, in a small town, or even in a medium-sized city, you could be fairly certain that your name would appear at least those three times.

Newspapers have changed—and are still changing.

Births

Many of the small-town papers once published births this way:

> It's cigars for everybody in the office of John Clancy, popular insurance man. His wife, Mrs. Jane Clancy, has just given birth to their first bouncing baby at County Hospital.
> According to Clancy, the baby, Ann Marie, already has an Irish smile.

Perhaps parents, in no mood to analyze whether babies actually bounce, liked this style. Many editors now realize, however, that only the family, relatives, and close friends will share the spirit of such writing. Moreover, in straining to make every birth as blessed an event for readers as well as for parents, the reporters need time to compose the paragraphs. Now most editors decree that births will be announced this way, published under a standard heading:

NEW ARRIVALS:

DEAN, ABIGAIL ANN, a daughter for Mr. and Mrs. Robert Dean of 2178 East University Lane, arrived May 26.

In both small-town newspapers and metropolitan newspapers, only the births of the very prominent are saluted by anything more than such routine announcements.

Weddings

To the dismay of many brides, the wedding story that once bore a young couple into marriage on waves of frothy prose now has all the turbulence of a glass of water. Some brides wail that they plan to save their wedding stories all their lives—and why couldn't you at least write "pretty"? Most editors have decided that if every bride is described as "pretty," "beautiful," or "attractive," then the words are meaningless.

Most often wedding stories will be published from a wedding form (see the Exercises, p. 151). The stories are spare, simple—the kind that a police reporter would be able to write provided one could be persuaded to help.

In most newspapers, a wedding story like the following would be published:

> Catherine A. Sanger of Vian City and former Kansas City resident Steven Alexander of St. Louis exchanged vows December 16 at Red Bluff Presbyterian Church. The Rev. Dean Rowley officiated at the 2 P.M. ceremony.
>
> Jean Sanger of Vian City acted as her sister's maid of honor. Loretta Nelson of South Jacksonville also attended the bride.
>
> Stan Alexander of Salinas stood with his brother as best man. Ushers were the bride's brother, Philip Sanger, Richard Silva of Alachua, and the bridegroom's brother-in-law, Chuck Noroian of Alachua.
>
> A reception at Red Bluff Woman's Club was attended by 50 guests following the ceremony.
>
> The bride is the daughter of Mr. and Mrs. Val Sanger. She is a graduate of Vian City High School and Georgia State University, where she received a B.S. degree in agricultural education. Prior to her marriage, she was employed with the Flower Boutique in Red Bluff.
>
> Alexander is the son of Mr. and Mrs. Alvin Alexander of Salinas. He is a graduate of North Salinas High School and the University of Georgia, where he received a B.S. degree in agriculture. He is an agriculture instructor at Red Bluff High School.
>
> Following a honeymoon, the couple will live in Red Bluff.

Obituaries

Although the publication of stories on births and weddings has been simplified, the obituaries are published much as they have been for years. Only those who are prominent—a politician, a movie star, an athletic star, an executive of a corporation, and so on—will be given much space. Otherwise, the obituary will be published from a form furnished by a funeral home (see the Exercises, p. 152). A story like the following will be published:

> Russell E. Jones, retired operating engineer for the Kaiser Plant, died unexpectedly Wednesday morning at Kaiser Medical Center. He was 70 years old.
>
> A native of George, Iowa, he was a veteran of World War II. Jones was a Baton Rouge resident since 1944, and made his home at 514 Alvin Drive. He retired in 1973 as operating engineer for the Kaiser Plant and was a member of American Legion Post 31 and Operating Engineer Local 3.
>
> He is survived by his widow, Gertrude Jones of the family home; his mother Sophie Jones of Sioux Falls, South Dakota; a son, Rodger Jones of Sumter, South Carolina; a daughter, Mrs. Marilyn Janes of Aptos and a sister, Violet Jones of Sioux Falls, South Dakota.
>
> He was preceded in death by a son, Howard E. Jones, in 1976. Friends may call at the Laporte Funeral Home.
>
> Funeral services will be held at 2:30 P.M. Saturday in the Laporte Chapel. The Rev. Paul Danielson, pastor of the Corral de Tierra Church of the Good Shepherd, will officiate.
>
> Burial will be in the Queen of Heaven Memories cemetery.
>
> Memorials are preferred to a favorite charity.

Writing an obituary from a form takes little time—and little experience. You may be assigned to write obituaries on your first newspaper job. If your first obituary is not about a prominent person, think of the audience: primarily relatives and friends. When writing about the death of a man, his name, age, and usually the reason for his death should be featured in the lead. Next, sketch the history of the man in a sentence or two, then tell when and where he moved to the city. Also, write about his primary occupation and his primary memberships in social organizations. Then list his near relatives and their locations. Finally, finish the obituary by writing when and where he will be buried and who will officiate.

When the deceased has been important, the editor will take that story out of the regular column and have it printed as a separate story on the obituaries page or the front page. In such cases, even though you will be furnished with a form from the funeral home, check the morgue, looking for stories printed about the deceased. Then interview anyone who knew the deceased well.

When, in 1979, the *New York Times* published an obituary of Mary Campbell, an executive for the Condé Nast Publications, the reporter gathered information from the chair, S. I. Newhouse, and Alexander Liberman, creative director of the company. The reporter began by using the form, then added this:

"Mary Campbell has touched the life of nearly every fashion journalist in America today—profoundly, in many cases—with her uncanny feeling for the potential of people," S. I. Newhouse, chairman of the Condé Nast Publications, said yesterday. "She played a major role in shaping Condé Nast and, in consequence, the world of design and fashion."

Later in that story, the reporter quoted Liberman:

"She had an extraordinary sensitivity to creative people, and was the anchor for those who edit magazines," said Alexander Liberman, creative director of Condé Nast Publications. "She was the personal friend of all the people involved, who would go to her to pour out their problems and discuss with her what was on their minds." (Copyright 1979 by the New York Times Company. Reprinted by permission)

Award-Winners

Ordinarily, in writing stories about award-winners, you should write the news story routinely. For example:

John Hinds, 17, son of Shirley and Jack Hinds of Minneapolis, recently became Troop 31's twenty-fourth Eagle Scout during ceremonies at the Union Presbyterian Church.

John, a senior at Jackson High School, has participated in four 50-mile backpack trips with his troop, serving as Senior Patrol Leader on the most recent one. He is a member of the Order of the Arrow, and during his six years of active membership in Troop 31 he has served as a Patrol Leader, Quartermaster, Assistant Senior Patrol Leader, and Senior Patrol Leader.

For his Eagle project, John organized and carried out a blood drive for the American Red Cross at Lee Shopping Center. Of the 33 prospective donors who turned out, 24 were accepted and donated and of those, 16 were first-time donors.

Also, as you can judge, the following story is also routine:

The Smith Family Foundation has awarded a 3-year, $50,000 grant to the university to develop analytical tools to help solve complex medical problems.

Twenty-six medical, engineering, and business students will tackle complicated medical problems such as the importance of annual check-ups and other preventive measures, the use of expensive and risky diagnostic tests, and the preferred therapy for certain diseases.

They will focus both on solving real problems and on developing techniques that can be used to analyze other problems, according to Dr. David Johnson, associate professor in the schools of engineering and medicine, and program director for the project.

Their findings will be submitted to appropriate organizations, such as the State Department of Health, the Food and Drug Administration, or the American Hospital Association.

When you are writing a story of an important award, do not be satisfied with a routine story, one that you can type in 20 minutes. Look carefully into the information supplied to you, then interview someone who is in authority.

Chapter 11 Exercises

Remember:

1. Although announcements may seem routine work, be careful in spelling the names.

2. When you are writing announcements, make certain whether or not the subject or subjects are prominent.

3. Remember that writing announcement stories may be your first job on a newspaper. They may be your first test as a professional.

Exercise 11.1

Find each of the following using your local newspaper (or a newspaper from the nearest city):

1. *Birth announcements*
2. *Weddings*
3. *Obituaries*

Match the first birth announcement published in this chapter against those in the newspaper. Do the same with the weddings and the obituaries. Which is longer? Which is more likely to editorialize (as when John Clancy is called the "popular insurance man" in an example in this chapter)? Does your analysis of the newspaper tell you that it is going in the direction of the other contemporary newspapers: clipped, unemotional, no editorializing? Why or why not?

Exercise 11.2

Although most newspapers have their birth announcements in one clipped sentence, some papers continue to use the old-fashioned form. In some cases, you may be faced with this form. Write a news story from the following information. Remember, you can make a story out of this form by linking the information in sentences, cutting such facts as December 2, 1979, adding the correct day, and the like.

BIRTH ANNOUNCEMENT

Mr. and Mrs. **John Laidlaw** of **1046 Ross Street, Billings, Montana,** announce the birth of a son or daughter or twins **James John Laidlaw** on **December 2, 1979**. Mrs. **Laidlaw** is the former **Miss Jane Phillips**.

The baby **is the first child**.

The grandparents are **Mr. and Mrs. John Phillips of 943 Middlefield Road, Providence, Rhode Island; and Mr. and Mrs. William Laidlaw, 743 Ross Road, Billings, Montana.**

Because wedding stories are usually written from a form, they sometimes seem to have a paralyzing sameness. Read the wedding stories in your local newspaper (or one from the nearest city). Examine the leads of three wedding stories, then, using some additional information in the stories, rewrite the leads, favoring variation. You can avoid that by varying sentences and playing up different aspects. For example, these leads indicate avenues to variation:

The Rev. Manning Jinies, minister of the First Baptist Church, read the nuptial service at which his youngest daughter, Mary Jane, and William Johns were married Saturday.

Gold vases of white larkspur and Madonna lilies and palms decked the sanctuary of St. John the Baptist Catholic Church where Eileen Wilts and Robert McGary exchanged vows.

152 STORIES FROM ANNOUNCEMENTS

The ivory slipper satin wedding gown which was worn by the former Susan Bay to become Mrs. Norris Johnson was worn again by her sister, June Bay, for her marriage to Paul Weston yesterday.

Exercise 11.3 *Use the following information, provided by a funeral home, to write an obituary of the deceased.*

RIVERTON FUNERAL HOME
OBITUARY FORM

Name of Deceased **John Charles Flowers**

Address **8123 Lytton Place**

City and State **Savannah, Georgia**

Age **59**

Date and Time of Death **8:30 a.m. November 7, 1978**

Cause of Death **Cancer**

Time and Date of Funeral **3 p.m. Friday, November 10**

Place of Funeral **First Methodist Church**

Place of Burial **Alta Mesa Cemetery**

Officiating Clergyman **The Rev. Virgil Manning**

Place of Birth **Gainesville, Georgia**

Places and Lengths of Residences **He lived in Gainesville until he was 16, then moved to Savannah with his parents.**

Occupation **Manager of A.J. Cleaners**

Did Deceased Ever Hold Public Office (When and What Office)? **No.**

Name and Address of Surviving Wife (or Husband) **Wife, Iris**

Maiden Name (if Married Woman) _____

153   EXERCISE 11.4

> Marriage, When and to Whom <u>Married Iris Preston in Atlanta, Georgia, in 1951</u>
>
> Names, Addresses of Children <u>George, New York, N.Y.</u>
> <u>John, Jr., Newport Beach, California</u>
> <u>Margaret Harriet, at home</u>
>
> Names, Addresses of Surviving Brothers and Sisters <u>William, Bloomington, Minnesota</u>
>
> Number of Grandchildren (Great, etc.) <u>3</u>
> Names, Address of Parents (If Living) <u>Dead</u>
>
> Additional Information <u>He became active in scouting at the end of World War II. He served as an associate post adviser and scoutmaster and had been an assistant scoutmaster of Troop 14. In 1973 Mr. Flowers was presented the Silver Beaver, scouting's highest award, in recognition of devoted service to the Boy Scouts of America. Also, at the end of World War II, he began to work at A.J. Cleaners. He became manager of that business in the mid-1960s.</u>

Exercise 11.4   *Although Walter Lippmann died in 1974, you are to write an obituary as though it happened yesterday. Read the following information, then use any appropriate sources to extend that, including Lippmann's books cited in the last paragraph. Use quotations and descriptions. Write an obituary of at least 800 words.*

154 STORIES FROM ANNOUNCEMENTS

Walter Lippmann (1889–1974), an American writer and political philosopher, won worldwide fame. Born in New York City, the only child of a wealthy Jewish couple, he became a brilliant student quite early. At Harvard University, while still a student, he became well known to such noted philosophers as William James and George Santayana. He was graduated in 1910 after three years of study.

Lippmann's brief career as a socialist ended early when he served as an executive secretary to the Reverend George R. Lunn, the Socialist mayor of Schenectady, New York. He decided after working four months for Mayor Lunn that socialism was sterile. He worked for *Everybody's* magazine in 1911, then helped found the liberal *New Republic* in 1914. During World War I, he served in several government posts, and gave President Woodrow Wilson eight of the president's Fourteen Points.

In 1921, he began his long service to newspapers, joining the *New York World*. He became editor of the *World* in 1929. The *World* ceased publication in 1931. On September 8, 1931, he began to write his famous column, "Today and Tomorrow," which he continued writing until 1967. Syndicated in hundreds of newspapers, he became widely known for reasoned conservatism.

During the 36 years of writing his column, Lippmann became recognized as a conservative in the highest classical tradition. He was a strong advocate of the principle of a law higher than the will of a people, the law of reason, which is the same as the law of nature. He always favored statesmanship over politics. His prose was always written with sound elegance.

Using his column as the basis for his books, Lippmann published many widely noted books, among them *A Preface to Politics* (1913), *Drift and Mastery* (1914), *The Stakes of Diplomacy* (1915), *Public Opinion* (1922), *A Preface to Morals* (1929), *The New Imperative* (1935), and *The Public Philosophy* (1955).

Exercise 11.5   *Write your own obituary. Use only the facts except the reason for your death.*

Chapter 12 # Rewrites and Press Releases

Rewrites

Frequently, you will have to rewrite stories from wire copy, from earlier editions, from press releases, and from information phoned in by fellow reporters. Usually you will be under tight deadline pressure and will need to write fast.

Wire copy is rewritten for several reasons:

to combine stories

to add local information

to shorten

to highlight a different angle

Normally stories from earlier editions of the same paper will take only a new lead and a new *insert*. An insert is that portion of the story that adds new information but does not go in the lead. Often the new material is inserted between the lead and the old body (sometimes called *B-copy*), but may be inserted anywhere appropriate. However, sometimes the whole story will be rewritten to change emphasis or improve writing.

Newspapers that publish both a morning and afternoon paper often rewrite a morning story for the afternoon paper. Where possible, the afternoon paper will add new facts to the lead to make the story appear new. However, that is not always possible. Then the rewrite reporter must rearrange the story sufficiently to create a fresh impression on the reader who may have caught the story in the morning paper.

Briefs are a common form of rewrites on many papers. Papers frequently run columns labeled "Highlights of the News," "Roundup," "Digest," or "News in Brief" wherein stories from all over the world have been reduced to about 200 words each. These columns appear in all sections of papers and may be grouped by subject.

When rewriting for any reason, remember to write concisely and brightly. And highlight key facts, especially those that will interest local readers.

Press Releases

Press releases are the genesis of substantial portions of the news we encounter every day. These releases stem from environmental groups, politicians, governmental bodies, businesses, the Parent-Teacher Association, Boy Scouts, labor organizations, even individual citizens with an interesting issue. Sometimes the releases are nothing more than announcements of coming events or puffery on a group's activities. Other times they announce major new scientific breakthroughs or changes in government policy.

Releases come into newsrooms by the thousands. When they serve their purpose best, they stimulate story ideas which reporters follow up by checking a variety of sources. All too often, however, releases find their way into news accounts verbatim without even a single phone call having been made to probe for additional facts.

Press releases commonly gloss over facts that are the real news; they attempt to tout as news what is favorable to the organization or individual concerned. A financial release issued by the Boeing Company, Seattle, a few years ago highlighted the firms' increase in sales but buried the information that profits and incoming orders had declined and that the firm was planning layoffs in the months ahead. For Seattle citizens who are highly dependent on Boeing's well being (the company is the community's largest employer), the latter was important information that should have been checked more fully. But a local paper ran the release word for word.

Rewriting press releases is much the same as rewriting news stories that need condensing and additional information. Even when the release appears complete and well written—and many are—check for more facts, new facts, last-minute facts. At the very least, get a personalized quotation you can use to make your story different from your competition, which may run the story as is.

As in most rewriting and updating, the new information you gather should be placed high in the story.

Chapter 12 Exercises

Remember:

1. Write concisely. Condense information when necessary.
2. Add latest information high in the story.
3. Check to make sure a press release is not overlooking significant information that should be included in the story.

The following six exercises consist of several press releases plus additional information that you are to suppose you gathered after making a telephone call or two. Write stories incorporating the release and the new information. Write concisely, highlighting latest information and local information you garnered from your phone calls.

Exercise 12.1

You are writing for a Seattle newspaper. You phone Donald E. Prewett and ask what are some special interests of Washington electronics companies that the new WEMA council intends concentrating on in the immediate future. He replies:

"Well, first of all we need to attract more electronics companies to the area so we have a bigger employment pool in Washington. Electronics companies are clean operations which do not pollute the atmosphere, but at the same time they employ large numbers of people at all levels: college graduates and blue collar workers for the assembly lines. Washington needs more industry like that to keep our growing population employed. So what we'll do first, is to start a promotion campaign to sell the virtues of locating electronics businesses in Washington."

NEWS RELEASE

Contact: Licia Thomson
(415) 327-9300

FOR IMMEDIATE RELEASE

<u>DONALD PREWETT ELECTED</u>

<u>WEMA COUNCIL CHAIRMAN</u>

SEATTLE, WASHINGTON Donald E. Prewett, executive vice president of Phase Linear Corp., Lynnwood, has been elected chairman of the Washington Council of WEMA, the trade association representing nearly 900 electronics companies in 34 states.

Other new officers are Vice Chairman Harold H. Kawaguchi, senior vice president of Physio-Control Corp., Redmond, and Secretary-Treasurer John F. Bowker, president of Opcon, Inc., Everett.

During 1984, the three will coordinate council activities of special interest to Washington electronics company executives, including monthly dinner meetings and educational workshops.

Both Prewett and Kawaguchi have also been elected 1984 directors of WEMA, representing the Washington Council. As WEMA directors, they will participate in policy decisions governing the nation's largest electronics trade association. The new board meets for the first time November 22 in Scottsdale, Arizona.

Founded in 1943, WEMA provides electronics companies with a variety of advanced management education programs, industry statistical surveys and a united voice in legislative matters affecting the electronics industries.

> In addition to the Washington Council, WEMA has ten other councils located in: the Southwest, Arizona, Colorado, Oregon, New England and five in California.
>
> # # #
>
> 1600 EL CAMINO REAL • PALO ALTO, CALIFORNIA 94306 • TELEPHONE (415) 327-9300

Exercise 12.2

You phone the Watts Company utility in your city to get a local angle on the new fuel cell SRI is developing for the Department of Energy. You are writing the story for your local morning paper. You reach John Jones, vice-president of the Watts Company and ask him whether the utility is likely to be interested in the coal/air fuel cell, if it is developed further. His reply:

"Sure, we'd be interested if it is developed within the next 12 months. That's the problem. I doubt that the idea will become economically feasible within the near future and we're under the gun from DOE to stop using oil and switch to some other fuel, especially coal. So we're investigating ways of powering our plants to produce electricity for this community which won't cost an arm and a leg. Using coal as a fuel means you've got to spend lots of money preventing polluting gases from escaping into the atmosphere because environmental restrictions are so tight these days. People don't realize how expensive that is; how in the end they're going to pay for it. The coal/air battery sounds marvelous if what they claim for it is true. But I have my doubts it will be ready in time for us to incorporate in our rebuilt plants. We've got to start rebuilding within a year."

NEWS RELEASE

CONTACTS: Susan E. Atkins, Ext. 3754
Home: (415) 552-5571
John C. Miller, Ext. 3034
Home: (415) 948-0893

RELEASE DATE: April 16, 1979

Washington Contact:
Donna M. Swenson
(703) 524-2053
Home: (703) 569-0433

COAL/AIR FUEL CELL CALLED CLEANER, MORE EFFICIENT WAY TO RUN POWER PLANTS

Menlo Park, CA A power plant that burns coal but is flameless . . . that produces electricity more efficiently and at lower cost than steam turbine generators . . . that operates without polluting the atmosphere . . .

A prototype coal/air fuel cell for such a plant has been developed and tested successfully during the past two years at SRI International under sponsorship of the Department of Energy. Although the technology must undergo further research and development, the fuel cell, which is a replenishable battery for the generation of electricity, holds early promise as an alternative method for running the power plants of the future.

The fuel cell uses the same raw materials—coal and air—as the traditional coal-fired steam turbine generator but these materials react electrochemically, as in a battery, and produce nearly twice as much energy from the same amount of coal. While the steam turbine uses 30% of energy available in the coal, the fuel cell makes use of 55%, according to a recent SRI report prepared for DOE.

In a coal/air fuel cell, treated coal is surrounded by an electrolyte, a mixture of carbonate salts in a molten state at 700° C.

Carbon from the coal serves as an electrode to form carbon dioxide, and in the process creates electricity.

There are no stack gases, and therefore no fumes or particulates and no nitrogen oxides to generate smog. The sulphur released from the coal is trapped in the electrolyte and is ultimately recovered.

(Over)

SRI International

333 Ravenswood Ave. • Menlo Park, California 94025 • (415) 326-6200 • Cable: STANRES, Menlo Park • TWX: 910-373-1246

2/2/2

"Electrochemical burning of coal is clean and it is efficient—those are its two great assets," said Dr. Leonard Nanis, who heads the electrochemistry program at SRI's Materials Research Center and who pioneered the concept with Dr. Robert Weaver.

Another asset is that the coal/air fuel cell reduces dependency on petroleum (many power plants today are oil-fired), and relies instead on our abundance of coal.

A power plant based on the coal/air fuel cell would be less expensive than any other type of power plant, according to the report. A present-day steam plant of 500-megawatt size costs $1000 per kilowatt to construct including the cost of stack gas scrubbing to reduce pollution. A 500-megawatt electrochemical power plant would cost $758 per kilowatt.

> Future research will focus on building a
> coal/air fuel cell in a working model of an
> electrochemical power plant, Dr. Nanis said.
> SRI International, formerly Stanford
> Research Institute, is an independent
> nonprofit organization that performs contract
> research for clients in business and
> government worldwide.
>
> \#   \#   \#

Exercise 12.3   You are writing this story in June 1983 for your local paper. Your editor tells you to place a call to Washington, D. C., to see if the Electronic Industries Association (EIA) has estimates on whether electronic equipment exports in 1983 will show an increase in its trade surplus over the 1982 figures. You phone Kelly Mansfield. She says: "Sorry, we won't get those figures until about six months from now. It takes that long to compile them." Your editor then tells you to call the president of the ABC Electronics Company in New Jersey to see if he can come up with a guess. You phone David Apple, president of ABC, and he tells you: "There's no way of telling this early in the year. However, I know everybody's feeling pretty good about this year's exports so far." Your editor tells you to go ahead and write the story from the release, playing up the trade surplus angle.

NEWS RELEASE

electronic industries association

For Release
June 6, 1983

Contact: Kelly Mansfield
202/457-4980

SALES OF ELECTRONICS UP 15 PERCENT IN 1982

Washington, D.C. U.S. factory sales of electronic equipment, systems and components totalled $64.9 billion in 1982, representing an increase of nearly 15 percent over the previous year, according to the 1983 Electronic Market Data Book, just released by the Electronic Industries Association.

More than one-third of the sales were in the industrial electronic equipment category which grew by 18 percent over 1981. The other major electronic industries also showed healthy growth in 1982 with sales of consumer electronics increasing nearly 15 percent, electronic components 14 percent and communications equipment 12 percent.

Some $13.3 billion of electronic products, or about 20 percent of total sales, were exported in 1982. This gave the U.S. a trade surplus of $2.6 billion in electronic products while the nation experienced an overall trade deficit of $34 billion.

Canada was the largest customer for U.S. electronics in 1982. It imported $1.6 billion of electronic products followed by the United Kingdom and West Germany with about $1.2 billion each. These three countries accounted for more than 30 percent of U.S. electronic exports.

Japan was the largest exporter of electronics to the U.S. with products valued at more than $4.6 billion. This represents 44 percent of the total amount of electronic products brought into the U.S. Taiwan, with $1.1 billion, and Mexico, with almost $800 million, were the second and third largest exporters of electronics to the U.S. Together, the three nations accounted for more than 60 percent of the electronic products brought into the U.S.

(more)

2001 Eye Street N.W., Washington, D.C. 20006 (202) 457-4981

    Employment in the electronic industries grew by 9 percent in 1982, to more than 1.3 million workers. This growth rate was almost double the increase in overall U.S. employment.
    The Electronic Market Data Book is published annually by the Electronic Industries Association and contains detailed information on sales, foreign trade, research and development, employment and U.S. government markets. Covering the many diverse products of the electronic industries, the Electronic Market Data Book is based on company data provided to EIA, supplemented by selected government and private sources.
    The 130-page 1983 edition may be obtained from the EIA Marketing Services Department, 2001 Eye Street, NW, Washington, D.C. 20006. The single copy price is $25 for EIA members and $50 for non-members.

#   #   #

Exercise 12.4

You write for a Chicago weekly newspaper. The editor tells you to rewrite this release, emphasizing McIntyre's Chicago background. You check the Office of Management and Budget (OMB) information office and learn that McIntyre grew up at 50 South Dorchester in the Hyde Park section of the city and went to Hyde Park Elementary and Hyde Park High School.

EXECUTIVE OFFICE OF THE PRESIDENT

OFFICE OF MANAGEMENT AND BUDGET

WASHINGTON, D.C. 20503

```
FOR IMMEDIATE RELEASE      OMB-32
AUGUST 23, 1978            INFORMATION OFFICE
                           395-4747/4854
```

James T. McIntyre, Jr., Director of the Office of Management and Budget, today announced the appointment of Van Doorn Ooms to be Assistant Director for Economic Policy. Ooms has been chief economist for the Senate Budget Committee.

McIntyre said Ooms "brings to OMB a wealth of talent and experience that will be distinct assets in economic policy, economic forecasting and program analyses for budget issues. His work at OMB will augment studies done for the President's Economic Policy Group in the international as well as domestic area. Ooms will work closely with OMB's outstanding staff of economists and with me."

Ooms is expected to join OMB around October 1.

> Ooms was born in Chicago on October 29, 1934. He received his undergraduate degree from Amherst College in 1956, graduating summa cum laude. He attended Oxford University in England as a Rhodes Scholar from 1956-59 (where he received First Class Honours), received his master's degree from Yale University in 1960 and his doctorate from Yale in 1965.
>
> He taught economics at Yale University and for a year served as planning adviser of an economic planning unit for the Government of Malaysia. From 1968-76, Ooms was a professor of economics at Swarthmore College, Swarthmore, Pennsylvania.
>
> Ooms joined the Senate Budget Committee staff in 1976. He became the committee's chief economist a year later.
>
> He is the author of numerous publications, including "Models of Comparative Export Performance." He was coauthor of "The International Economy and the Federal Budget" and also coauthor of "The Multinational Firm and International Regulations."
>
> Ooms is married to the former Theodora J. Parfit of Oxford, England. They live in Bethesda, Maryland, with their three children.

Exercise 12.5   You write for a Minneapolis newspaper. The entertainment editor asks you to write a quick filler using this press release.

News Release

IMMEDIATE RELEASE   8/24/82   LAQ

SUPER SATURDAYS ON WCCO

    Beginning Saturday, September 9, CBS and Channel 4 present the new fall lineup of children's programming. At 7:00 A.M., the one, the only, the original spinach-devouring Popeye the Sailor Man stars in a whole new series of adventures complete with Blutto, Olive Oyl, Wimpy, Swee'pea, The Jeep and Pappy in THE ALL NEW POPEYE HOUR. Then at 8:00 to 9:30 A.M., the further adventures of those classic protagonists of the animated cartoon at the top of its form THE BUGS BUNNY/ROAD RUNNER SHOW with Bugs, Daffy, Sylvester, Tweety, Elmer, the Coyote and the Road Runner.

    At 9:30 a new 90-minute program consisting of five separate, unrelated components will air on TARZAN AND THE SUPER SEVEN. Two of the show's five segments will be either Batman, Tarzan or Web Woman. The other three segments each week will include a live action JASON OF STAR COMMAND who thwarts evil-doers of the universe, ISIS AND THE FANTASTICS including Merlin, Sinbad, Hercules and Toshi the Samurai warrior and THE SUPER COMBOS of Manta and Moray, super heroes of the deep; Super Stretch and Micro Woman; or Starlight and Sunbright who command the limitless powers of the sun and the forces of the night.

    A 4-minute segment of CBS' IN THE NEWS will be shown at 26 and 56 minutes after the hour until noon.

    The new Saturday programs scheduled in the afternoon will not air until later due to sports specials—watch for further news releases.

# # #

WCCO TV 50 South Ninth St. Minneapolis Minnesota 55402 (612) 338-0552

Exercise 12.6

You write for a Los Angeles newspaper. Your editor tells you to call the local sources listed in the release below to find out how soon the new buses will be arriving in each community and what Southern California Association of Governments (SCAG) and San Diego will do with their planning grants. Santa Monica and Montebello expect the new buses to be on the streets within 15 months. Spokespeople explain it takes 10 months to build the buses after orders are placed and orders cannot be placed until the Department of Transportation (DOT) officially releases the money. You are unable to reach the other two sources by press time.

U.S. Department of Transportation

news:

Office of Public Affairs
Washington, D.C. 20590

FOR RELEASE THURSDAY   UMTA 78-50
August 24, 1982   Contact: Linda Teixeira
                     Phone: (202) 426-4043

DOT ANNOUNCES $5 MILLION IN GRANTS
TO SOUTHERN CALIFORNIA COMMUNITIES

　　LOS ANGELES Two California communities will purchase new buses and two others will develop plans for public transportation improvements with the aid of $5 million in federal grants announced today by Secretary of Transportation Brock Adams.
　　Santa Monica will purchase 15 new advance design transit coaches with full accessibility for the handicapped. A federal grant of $1,574,852 assists this project.
　　Montebello will purchase eight new 45-passenger, air-conditioned, advance design buses with the help of a $646,000 grant.
　　The Southern California Association of

Governments, the planning organization for five counties in the Los Angeles area, and the city of San Diego received planning grants of $2,680,000 and $600,000 respectively.

Secretary Adams commended the community of Santa Monica for its effort to improve public transportation for handicapped citizens.

Adams noted that the grants announced today are the first for California cities under a new system aimed at cutting bureaucratic red tape to speed up grant processing.

Mass transit capital assistance grants to communities with populations under 5 million are now approved at the regional level, rather than in Washington. The grants announced today were processed by the Urban Mass Transportation Administration regional office in San Francisco.

Local sources for additional information are J.F. Hutchinson, Director of Transportation, City of Santa Monica, 1620 Sixth Street, Santa Monica, California 90401, (213) 451-5444 (CA-03-0170); Roy R. Peterson, City Administrator, City of Montebello, 1600 W. Beverly Blvd., Montebello, California 90640, (213) 725-1200 (CA-03-0175); W. O. Ackerman, Jr., Director, Transportation Planning, Southern California Association of Governments, 600 S. Commonwealth Avenue, Suite 1000, Los Angeles, California 90005, (213) 385-1000 (CA-09-0069); Lee Haltgren, Director of Transportation, Comprehensive Planning Organization, 1200 Third Avenue, Suite 524, San Diego, California 92101, (714) 236-5300 (CA-09-0071).

170 REWRITES AND PRESS RELEASES

Exercise 12.7 *Rewrite the following two stories, combining the information. Dateline the story San Carlos, California. Keep the rewrite to 400 words.*

A check with your morgue turns up additional information: Patricia Hearst was kidnapped from her Berkeley apartment while a student at the University of California in February 1974. She later joined forces with her kidnappers, the Symbionese Liberation Army. Police forces that had been searching for her captors to rescue her subsequently sought her capture for her role in a May 1975 bank robbery. She was captured in September 1976, and convicted of bank robbery in 1977. In April 1979, after release from prison, she married police officer Bernard Shaw.

WIRE COPY 1

SAN CARLOS—Patricia Hearst, heiress to a newspaper fortune, is training dogs in San Carlos for the regular salary of an intern trainer.

Ms. Hearst works behind the scenes at Prion Animal Institute, a dog-training center, where her work hours are part-time, said Bob Outman, Prion's founder and president.

"She's got a lot of compassion for dogs, and she enjoys working with them," he said.

The affinity between Outman, a former deputy sheriff, and Ms. Hearst began early in 1977 after she was freed on bail while appealing her bank robbery conviction.

Her father, newspaper publisher Randolph Hearst, telephoned Outman and asked him to find and train a dog for Ms. Hearst's security. Outman was not especially interested.

"We can identify with each other, we share terrorist experiences and her love for dogs has made us close friends," Outman said. "But at one time I pursued her as a policeman and hated her."

On the night of Feb. 13, 1976, Outman, then a San Mateo County Sheriff's deputy, was shot twice on a darkened Redwood City hillside while investigating an apparent attempt by terrorists to blow up a power installation.

He later left law enforcement and now runs Prion, one of the largest dog-training centers in the nation.

Outman said Ms. Hearst grew to love dogs through her association with Arrow, a German shepherd that has become her nearly constant companion. She also recently acquired Niki, a young female shepherd and eventually plans to breed the pair.

No special security exists to protect Prion's newest employee, Outman said.

"There are always policemen here training dogs. They come from all over the United States and Arrow comes to work with her, but there's no special security," he explained. (*Source: San Francisco Chronicle,* July 1979)

WIRE COPY 2

Patricia Hearst Shaw, former federal prisoner, has been a beagle trainer for several weeks in San Carlos, working on what her boss called a "secret project" that will "revolutionize" the flop-eared canine's image.

"She has a terrific rapport with the dogs," Bob Outman, owner of the Prion Animal institute, said yesterday.

The institute, he said, is involved in training and selling dogs and studying all aspects of dog life.

Outman said the newspaper heiress started July 1 and works odd hours, receiving the pay of an "intern animal trainer."

Outman refused to say what the secret beagle project is.

"Let me tell you, it's a million-dollar idea I thought of a year and a half ago," he disclosed. "Bigger than guide dogs. Bigger than police dogs. This is a consumer idea, and everyone—including you—will want one of our beagles."

Outman said the current crop of beagles began training as nine-week-old puppies and will graduate fully trained as 6-month-old dogs in about a month.

Hearst is working with dogs now in their third week of training.

Outman said he first met Hearst in 1977, when she was free on bail pending appeal of her conviction for bank robbery. Hearst's father, Randolph, had called Outman and asked him to train a guard dog for his daughter. (*Source: Peninsula Times-Tribune,* July 1979)

Exercise 12.8

Rewrite each of the following news items (A, B, C) into 200-word briefs.

A

MADISON, Wisconsin (AP)—Barbara and Ray Gordon want to adopt a child, but they can't. The state claims they're too fat to become parents, the couple said.

"We started this thing and we're not the type of people to give up on it," said Barbara, who stands 5-foot-9 and weighs 210 pounds.

Gordon, a 6-foot-2, 215-pound shipping clerk at the University of Wisconsin, said they began state adoption proceedings two years ago when doctors said it was unlikely they would ever have children.

When the state Department of Health and Social Services said they would have to wait five or six years for an infant, the Rays said they would rather have a child 5 to 10 years old right away.

Then the couple, both 28, ran into the department's informal guidelines barring adoptions for health reasons.

"They wrote and told us we were obese and could not adopt until we had a substantial weight loss," Gordon said. "Basically, the problem is with my wife, but they told me I should lose, too."

Social workers told Barbara she had to get down to 190 pounds and she did within three months. But then they lowered the weight to 170 pounds, she said.

Jane Thompson, a state social worker who the Rays said had been assigned to their case, refused comment on the case.

Gordon said there were no specific guidelines, and the social workers made the decision according to an insurance company's preferred height-weight chart.

"I think it's just discrimination," he said. "If you were to meet us, you wouldn't say we're obese."

The Rays enlisted state Sen. Peter Bear, who said he is awaiting more information from state officials to determine if the obesity rule is legal.

"It seems ridiculous to me," Bear said. "I don't know how a state agency can deny adoption eligibility on the basis of the prospective parents' weight, especially in the absence of definitions or proof that a health problem exists."

Gordon said he and his wife have been certified in good health by their doctors, and are active in many sports. He said he and his wife, married seven years, own a home and are saving to build a house in the country some day.

"The child is the most important thing in the world to us," said Barbara, a statistics clerk in the Dane County Mental Health agency.

She said her family has a history of being large-boned and overweight, but also of longevity.

"I could lose the weight if I really wanted to, but why do it just until the adoption goes through and then go back to my normal weight?" (*Source: New York Times,* July 1979)

B

LUBBOCK, Texas— A Texas oilman stranded in Nicaragua said in a telephone interview yesterday that panic reminiscent of the fall of Vietnam had swept the city of Managua.

Jack Cox of Abilene, Texas, said National Guardsmen with machine guns were commandeering aircraft at gunpoint to flee the war-torn nation.

Cox, who secretly flew into Nicaragua Sunday with six other Texans to film what he called "the Communist takeover" there, said the group attempted to fly out yesterday but a company of national guardsmen took over the two Red Cross planes at gunpoint.

At the airport he said rioting civilians tried to board planes but were forced back by guardsmen. He said he heard shots fired by the troops but he did not know if anyone was hit.

"We were (first) scheduled to leave Tuesday," Cox said. "But that airplane was taken over by the military and (Nicaraguan) government officials who wanted to get out completely. So our flight was scheduled again this morning for 9 o'clock.

"We were the only people at the airport when the national guard commandeered the two planes which had come in with Red Cross relief supplies.

"We were waiting in line outside. At that point, the troops started moving in and approximately a company of them in armored jeeps and with machine guns came in and sealed off the area.

"They had their own pilots for each plane—they just commandeered them. Then approximately 300 people—just masses—flooded and ran towards the airplanes with men with machine guns standing in all sectors and aiming at us."

Cox said the members of his party had been eating one meal a day "of rice and beans."

He said the country was in total devastation and "there's hunger everywhere. Kids were eating the raw (Red Cross relief) rice right off the pavement." (*Source: New York Times,* July 1979)

C

Special Ambassador Robert S. Strauss will lead a four-day mission to Cairo and Jerusalem beginning next Monday to open up discussions of expanded U.S. trade with the two Middle East countries.

"Our first hope is to show that we can put some economic stability, not just arms, into that area," Strauss said. The plan for the trip came out of Carter's discussions with Israeli Prime Minister Menachem Begin and Egyptian President Anwar Sadat.

A congressional delegation will include Sen. Abraham Ribicoff (D-Conn.), Rep. Ken Holland (D-S. Car.) and Republicans who have been invited but have not yet accepted. The government representatives will include officials of the State, Commerce, and Treasury departments, Export-Import Bank, and the Overseas Private Investment Corp.

Officials stressed the bilateral nature of the talks. Strauss will not get involved in joint Egyptian-Israeli talks, but expects to develop cooperative economic projects between the two former warring states.

Strauss said that his group will "take a look" at agriculture, housing and textiles, among other areas. Included in the mission are key figures from U.S. textile industry and labor, Jerome Gore, chief executive officer of Hart, Schaffner & Marx, and Murray Finely, president of the Amalgamated Clothing and Textile Workers Union.

A Strauss aide said an effort would be made to help the Egyptian textile industry set up some new product lines. (*Source: New York Times,* July 1979)

174 REWRITES AND PRESS RELEASES

Exercise 12.9   *Rewrite the following story, changing the emphasis to Moslem fears in Uganda. Cut the story to 350 words.*

ORABA, Uganda—Tanzanian and Ugandan government forces rolled through Idi Amin's home village over the weekend and reached the Sudanese border, securing the last remaining corner of Uganda for its new rulers.

Tanzanian tanks led an infantry battalion Saturday to within 200 yards of a small bridge marking the frontier. They met no resistance from soldiers loyal to Amin and found no trace of the ousted dictator. The only signs of life in the village, Koboko, were a dog and a chicken.

Amin's house in Koboko, a small, unpainted cement building on a dirt road that forms the border with Zaire, was empty. In Arua, the district capital, the Tanzanians were using another Amin residence as a headquarters and a nearby hut as a radio room.

A commanding officer informally declared the seven-month war at an end. It had began at the end of October, when Amin's throngs invaded a salient of northern Tanzania. The Tanzanians and Ugandan exiles counterattacked, entering Uganda in January and driving 1,000 miles since then to the Sudanese border, where they arrived Saturday.

On the other side of the border Sunday, Sudanese soldiers could be seen in trenches, their weapons ready. The Tanzanians' waves and shouted greetings were not returned.

Sudanese officials have been critical of the Tanzanian role in Uganda. President Jaafar Numeiri said recently that as a result of Amin's overthrow, it was no longer safe to be a Moslem in Uganda.

Moslems made up less than 5% of the population when Amin took power in 1971, but the former dictator took his support largely from those fellow Moslems and from Kakwa tribesmen from northwestern Uganda and from nearby parts of Sudan and Zaire.

In Koboko, the entire population had apparently fled to Sudan or Zaire.

Peasants in nearby villages told Tanzanian forces that Amin's soldiers had warned the population that the Tanzanians were coming to massacre residents of Amin's home area.

Residents of Arua said Amin had not been seen since the middle of April.

As the forces arrived in Oraba, which is situated virtually on the Sudanese border, other units secured Yumbe and Moyo without fighting—thus bringing the last remaining areas of Uganda under the control of the new government.

Senior Tanzanian officers said they expected that their forces would begin returning home in the near future. (*Source: New York Times,* July 1979)

Exercise 12.10 *Rewrite the following morning news story for an afternoon paper, shortening the story to 350 words and changing the emphasis to highlight State Senator Caemmerer's blocking of Governor Hugh Carey's bill that would help meet Environmental Protection Agency (EPA) requirements.*

The Federal Environmental Protection Agency is threatening the New York metropolitan area with the loss of millions of dollars because of the state's failure to put together a program for yearly emission inspections of the region's 3.5 million cars.

And the agency could begin to deny air-quality permits for major new industrial projects if the Governor and the Legislature continue at a stalemate over a plan to meet Federal air-pollution guidelines.

In theory, the state has until July 1 to comply with the Federal clean-air standards. But instituting an emission test for the area's automobiles needs legislative approval, and the Legislature went home last week without acting on a proposal to meet the Federal guidelines put before it by Governor Carey.

Regional E.P.A. officials said yesterday that the sanctions would include an immediate moratorium on Federal highway funds and the gradual elimination of Federal help for sewage treatment and air-pollution control, and other funds.

Plan Blocked by Caemmerer

Last month Mr. Carey sent to the Legislature a plan under which annual pollution inspections would have been required of all autos in the city and in the neighboring counties of Nassau, Suffolk, Westchester and Rockland. The Governor estimated the tests would have cost $8 to $18 each.

But the plan, which Federal officials say would meet their requirements, has been blocked by State Senator John D. Caemmerer, a Republican of Williston Park, L.I., who is chairman of the Senate Transportation Committee. Mr. Caemmerer argues that the Governor's bill would impose too much of a burden on the average driver. And he scoffs at the Federal threats, insisting that President Carter would not dare cut off Federal funds only a year before the 1980 elections.

Instead of the Governor's plan, Mr. Caemmerer would like to see the state embark on a $12 million pilot program that would involve voluntary emission inspections at no cost to consumers, done in conjunction with the state's yearly safety inspection. The program passed in the Senate, but died in the Assembly.

This plan is unacceptable to Federal officials, however, who say it would not cut pollution levels.

"We've known that inspection and maintenance have been needed here since 1973," said Jan Geiselman, acting director of the air and hazardous-materials division of the New York regional office of the

Environmental Protection Agency. "We've seen these programs work in other states, and we don't need more pilot projects."

Miss Geiselman said she hoped the Senate would compromise in time to permit some action by September, when the Legislature plans to take up unfinished business. But she said the Federal Government would need to see "some movement" before July 1 to avoid taking steps toward penalizing the region.

Francis X. McArtle, New York City's Commissioner of Environmental Protection, said yesterday that failure to meet the Federal guidelines could do "incalculable economic harm" to the metropolitan area. (*Source: New York Times,* July 1976)

Exercise 12.11   *To write an award-winning story, you must unscramble the following information phoned into you from a source. Write the story in about 200 words.*

The estimated total cost of the project is about $206 million.

The water will come through 10.3 miles of tunnel and through conduits to a point near Johnson Reservoir in South Anderson County.

From there, a water distribution system within the county will pump the water to other locations.

The San Phillip project has been in planning since 1966, and was authorized by Congress in 1968.

Construction time for the project is estimated at about five years.

The project was delayed, first by federal funding cuts, then by lawsuits, and finally by redesigning.

The actual contract bid by the Russell Company was $49,793,520.

The *Reach 2,* or second construction phase is for 5.3 miles of concrete-lined circular tunnel, with a diameter of 9 feet, 6 inches.

It was the lowest of four bids that ranged as high as $74.3 million for the job. The engineer's estimate was $44.5 million.

The San Phillip project will bring water from the Johnson Reservoir to Homestead, Benito, and Mountain counties.

The award of the contract, totalling more than $49 million, was announced by the Federal Bureau of Reclamation officials.

The contract for the second construction phase of the San Phillip water project has been awarded to the William Russell Company of Jacksonville.

Chapter 13 Crime and Accidents

Occasionally, journalism professors will answer the phone and hear the anguished voice of a recent graduate reporting: "My editor sent me out to cover that air crash on Tuesday. It was terrible. All those bodies . . . and those sobbing relatives I had to talk to. I felt so miserable I almost quit."

Getting accustomed to tragedy and violence is difficult. But it is part of the job for reporters. Crime, air disasters, fires, car crashes, and other calamities always hit the young reporter hard the first time he or she has to cover such a story. When your turn comes, do not let your emotion get in the way of gathering all the facts.

Crime Reports

Many crime stories begin with the formal report filed by the investigating officer. Standard forms are filled in with abbreviations and dry information that the reporter soon learns to interpret. In some communities these reports are routinely available to reporters. In other communities the reports, or police *blotters* as they are called, are doled out at the discretion of the police officer in charge.

Generally, you should gather additional information after reading the report as well as doublecheck all facts. Where possible, original sources should be sought: eyewitnesses, investigating or arresting officers, family, coroner, hospital administrators, morgue, mortuary.

Too often, however, you must file your story quickly to meet approaching deadlines and will need to lean on the report plus information gleaned from police, sheriff, or highway department personnel.

Signed statements attached to the initial police report are just that: statements, *not confessions.* So do not confuse the two and write "he confessed," when you mean "he said in a statement to police. . . ."

Be careful when writing your story not to imply guilt. Until a jury or judge convicts, a person is presumed innocent no matter how damaging the evidence. If you imply otherwise, your paper can be sued for libel.* Therefore, many editors insist that strong statements indicating guilt be attributed to those making the charge—the arresting officer, for instance. However, such attribution can be overdone. Uncontested fact, such as when a crime was committed, can be lifted from the report without writing "according to. . . ."

The terms *suspect* or *alleged* are used to allude to those who have been arrested and charged with crimes but who have not yet been tried and convicted. For example: "Police say the suspect entered the jewelry store from an unlocked back door." Or, "The alleged murderer is John Jones, 29, of 333 Orange Street, White City."

The terms *arrested* and *charged,* incidentally, are not synonymous. A suspect is first arrested and brought to the police station, where the arresting officer must write a formal charge. Sometimes persons are arrested, say for battery, but not formally charged despite spending several hours at the police station. Stories are rarely written about arrests which are not followed by formal charges.

Whether you gather your information only from the police report, or from a combination of the report and personal interviews, make every effort to present the suspect's side, too. For instance, if a person arrested for shooting another is quoted as saying: "I shot him in self-defense because he was coming at me with a baseball bat," get that into the story.

It is an unfortunate commentary on our society that crime and violence are so common that most readers are indifferent to routine occurrences. Reporters, therefore, must write their stories emphasizing unusual aspects. A colleague, formerly a police reporter in Houston, tells the story of the "chili murder" he once reported. A man entered a Houston greasy spoon restaurant, ordered a bowl of chili, and upon being served, threw the bowl back at the waitress shouting: "There's no meat in this chili." Then he whipped out a gun and shot her.

The lead for that story began: "A man shot a waitress last evening, after complaining that the chili she served him did not have enough meat in it."

Abbreviations, acronyms, and other terms used in police reports will vary from community to community, but here are some that you may encounter:

---

*Any false statement, written or broadcast, is libelous if it causes anyone to suffer public hatred, contempt, or ridicule; or if it causes one to be shunned or avoided; or if it injures one in his business or occupation.

179 ACCIDENTS

> *DOA:* dead on arrival *S:* suspect
> *DOB:* date of birth *V:* victim
> *WM:* white male *W:* witness
> *WF:* white female *RP:* reporting party
> *BM:* black male *NA:* not available
> *BF:* black female *TPO:* time and place of
> *complainant:* victim occurrence
> *actor:* suspect *LSW:* last seen wearing
> *AKA:* also known as *NFD:* no further description

When writing your story, remember to identify every person appropriately. Victims, suspects, and other key characters need to be identified by their full names, ages, jobs, and home addresses. Other persons, such as witnesses or family members, do not necessarily need more than full names and jobs or relationship mentioned. Identify police officers by full name and rank.

Gather all pertinent details. If a burglary occurred, cite any stolen property, its value, whether it was insured, the method used to gain entrance, and where the owners were at the time the burglary took place. Time and place of the crime is important. So is the information on whether a gun was found on the suspect, and if a gun was said to have been used during the crime. In homicides, always indicate what weapon police say was used. Quote witnesses, friends, relatives, neighbors, and police from the report, or from personal interviews.

Accidents

Automobile accidents come to a reporter's attention in much the same way as a crime: through a police report or over the police radio that blares away in most newsrooms. Reporters, listening with half an ear as they type other stories, learn to identify major and minor accidents and crimes by the numbers assigned to each. If California reporters hear the police radio operator read: "A 555 at the corner of Newsom and Cypress," they know the accident is minor and can be ignored. A 556, however, may be worth a story.

Both the fact gathering and writing of accident stories is similar to crime reporting. Lead off with the most unusual angle, being sure to include the number of deaths and injuries; cite the official cause of the accident; identify all people fully; list details of injuries, damages, deaths; quote eyewitnesses or survivors; give time and location. In addition, car accident stories usually contain some reference to road conditions and estimated speed of the vehicles.

Weather conditions are important in all accident stories, but particularly so in boat and airplane catastrophes. The airplane crashes are the most difficult to cover under short deadlines because there is so much information to

180   CRIME AND ACCIDENTS

gather, and sources at hospitals, mortuaries, airlines, and public safety departments, as well as eyewitnesses, are themselves under great stress at the time. Work hard to verify all facts before writing.

Cite the precise cause of death and injuries, such as drowning, fire, exposure, or impact, and report where the injured and the dead have been taken. If previous accidents have occurred in the same area, report this.

Comments by such groups as the Coast Guard, air controllers, Federal Aviation Administration, or other official bodies should be included in boat and air accident stories.

Chapter 13 Exercises

Remember:

1. Get as much first-hand information as possible to round out crime or accident reports.

2. Use words precisely. A signed statement is not a confession; a suspect is just that, not a guilty person; not all persons arrested are charged with a crime, and so on.

3. In crime and accident reports, identify all persons correctly.

4. Provide full information in accident reports: cause; current status of victims; monetary losses, and so on.

5. Provide weather information in those accidents where it is an important element.

Exercise 13.1

Write this murder story from the report and statements shown here. Note that police time is given in 24 hours—that is, 1800 is 6 P.M. Sometimes reports and statements contain discrepancies; if no one is available to check with, you will have to decide which version to use when writing your story. Pretend that the murder occurred in your town yesterday.

STATEMENT

My name is Charles Rogers. I am a white male, born October 18, 1936. I live at 1414 Evelyn Drive in San Jose and I work as a truck driver for Mrs. Bartlett's Bread Company. I am giving this statement voluntarily.

Wednesday night, me and a bunch of guys were drinking beer at the Dew Drop Inn on Telephone. I guess I got there about 6 o'clock. I had been putting quarters in the jukebox most of the night. None of the other guys wanted to put money in to play the records. One of the guys at the table, Jake Cobb, I think his name was, had been mouthing off for a little while about how he didn't like the songs I had been playing. I had been playing a bunch of Loretta Lynn and Tammy Wynette songs and he said he was tired of hearing a bunch of women sing.

Well, the jukebox quit playing so I got up to go put some more money in it and Cobb walked over to the jukebox with me and said why didn't I play some Charley Pride or something like that. I told him it was my money and I would play what I damn well pleased. He reached for one of the buttons on the machine and I grabbed his arm and I guess we rassled around a little bit. The bartender, Sam, came over and broke it up and told Jake to leave.

I been drinking at the Dew Drop Inn for a couple of years I guess. This other guy's only been coming in there for about three or four days, but he's got into a couple of arguments before. He pulled a pistol on my friend, Roy Arbuckle, last night after they had been drinking for a while. Well, anyway, after a couple of hours this Jake fellow came busting through the front door hollering something about that guy that don't know nothing about music. He started coming toward my table and he stuck his hand in his pocket like he was going for his gun, so I pulled my pistol and cut loose. I think I shot at him two or three times. I must have hit him because he kind of reeled out the front door and fell in the parking lot. I gave my pistol to Sam and waited in the bar until the police came.

I can read and write the English language and I have read the above statement and it is true and correct to the best of my knowledge.

Charles Rogers
_____
CHARLES ROGERS

WITNESS: *Gail Eng*
WITNESS: *Ed Reinking*

182 CRIME AND ACCIDENTS

POLICE DEPARTMENT FORM #11(63) **CRIME REPORT**

1 CRIME	HOMICIDE
2 CLASSIFICATION	
3 WATCH	2
4 BEAT	S4
5 CASE NUMBER	AM66890
6 DATE AND TIME OCCURRED; DAY OF WEEK	yesterday's date & date
7 LOCATION OF OCCURRENCE	2972 Telephone Rd.
8 INVEST. OFF	L.L. Clebosi
9 DATE AND TIME REPORTED TO DEPARTMENT	yesterday 2300
10 VICTIM'S NAME	Jack Cobb
11 RESIDENCE ADDRESS	2665 Palm
14 PERSON REPORTING OFFENSE	Sam McManus
15 RESIDENCE ADDRESS	240 Cherry St.
16 RESIDENCE PHONE	321 0067
17 BUSINESS PHONE OR ADDRESS	988 7664
18 PERSON WHO DISCOVERED CRIME	above
22 WITNESS (ES): NAME	#1 Sam McManus
23 RESIDENCE ADDRESS	above
24 RESIDENCE PHONE	above
25 BUSINESS PHONE OR ADDRESS	above
26 VICTIM'S OCCUPATION RACE SEX AGE	window washer W M 41
27 TYPE OF PREMISES OR LOCATION	bar
29 WEAPON - FORCE OR MEANS USED	.22-caliber pistol
31 EXACT LOCATION OF VICTIM AT TIME OF OFFENSE	inside bar
33 VICTIM'S ACTIVITY AT TIME OF OFFENSE	standing at suspect's table
35 EXACT WORDS USED BY SUSPECT	"Watch out"

40 REPORT

While on patrol with my partner, G. Blackburn (4887), received a call at 2145 to investigate shooting at Dew Drop Inn, 2802 Telephone Ave. Arrived at location at 2148. No rain. No clouds. Warm. Found complainant lying face up in parking lot about 20 feet from main entrance to Dew Drop Inn. Complainant had three apparent bullet wounds in upper torso. No vital signs. Compl. dressed in blue jeans, khaki shirt, cowboy boots. Compl. identified from information in wallet. No weapon found on compl.
Ascertained from witnesses that compl. had been in bar since approximately 1800 that evening, drinking beer with group of friends. Compl. and actor had been at the same table. About 2000 hours, compl. and actor went to jukebox, stood at jukebox for a few minutes then began hollering at each other. Witnesses said they were arguing over which songs to play. Compl. and actor scuffled in front of juke box and the bartender, Sam McManus, WM 938-7664, came over and told compl. to leave. About 2130, compl. returned to bar, approached actor's table. Actor pulled pistol and shot at compl. four times. Compl. staggered out front door at bar and fell in parking lot.
Actor waited in bar. .22-caliber pistol recovered from bartender and placed in property room (tag # sd54678). Actor placed under arrest, brought to station and statement taken. See attached statements of actor and witness #1.

IF ADDITIONAL SPACE IS REQUIRED USE CONTINUATION REPORT

DATE AND TIME TYPED CLERK	REPORTING OFFICER	SUPERVISOR APPROVING
yesterday's date 2300 MLM	L.L. Clebosi	J. Lewis

STATEMENT

My name is Sam McManus. I am a white male, age 52. I live at 777 Ocawa Circle in San Jose. I am the night bartender at the Dew Drop Inn, 2082 Telephone.

Wednesday night, I was working in the bar. Several customers had been at a corner table since about 6 P.M. The customers included Chuck Rogers, one of my regulars, and a guy by the name of Cobb, who has only been in here a few times.

Chuck had been playing the jukebox most of the evening, or giving me money and telling me what songs to play. He was playing mostly songs by Loretta Lynn and Tammy Wynette.

About 8 P.M., Chuck and Cobb got up and went over to the jukebox. They started scuffling and arguing about something and I went over and broke up the fight. I told Cobb to get out until he could behave himself. He had caused regulars some trouble a couple of times before. He pulled a gun on a guy in here last night. At least that's what some of the regulars said. I was in the back when it happened.

About 9:15, maybe a little later, Cobb came back in. He just blew through the front door, acting real drunk and hollering at Chuck. So then he started heading for Chuck's table and reached into his pocket and that's when Chuck pulled a pistol and shot at him about four times.

The other guy, Cobb, staggered out the front door. Chuck gave me the pistol and I called the police. I guess I had served five or six beers to each of the guys.

I can read and write the English language and I have read this statement and it is true and correct to the best of my knowledge. I have given this statement voluntarily.

signature
SAM MCMANUS

WITNESS: *Jay Smith*

WITNESS: *Mary Kennedy*

184   CRIME AND ACCIDENTS

Exercise 13.2   *Write a brief story from the following crime report.*

POLICE DEPARTMENT   FORM #11(63)   **CRIME REPORT**

1 CRIME	2 CLASSIFICATION	3 WATCH	4 BEAT	5 CASE NUMBER
robbery	commercial	3	L6	79-45671

6 DATE AND TIME OCCURRED; DAY OF WEEK	7 LOCATION OF OCCURRENCE	8 INVEST. OFF.	9 DATE AND TIME REPORTED TO DEPARTMENT
yesterday 2300	2678 Fell St	B. Kline	today 0330

10 VICTIM'S NAME (FIRM NAME IF BUSINESS)	11 RESIDENCE ADDRESS (BUSINESS ADDRESS IF FIRM)	12 RESIDENCE PHONE	13 BUSINESS PHONE OR ADDRESS
Al's Liquor Store	above		444 5555

14 PERSON REPORTING OFFENSE	15 RESIDENCE ADDRESS	16 RESIDENCE PHONE	17 BUSINESS PHONE OR ADDRESS
Joe Lumas	1550 Court St	678 9000	above

18 PERSON WHO DISCOVERED CRIME	19 RESIDENCE ADDRESS	20 RESIDENCE PHONE	21 BUSINESS PHONE OR ADDRESS
above	above	above	above

22 WITNESS (ES): NAME	23 RESIDENCE ADDRESS	24 RESIDENCE PHONE	25 BUSINESS PHONE OR ADDRESS
#1 Mary Smith	3357 King St.	678 1234	
#2 Mark Stevens	3356 King St	678 3345	
#3			

26 VICTIM'S OCCUPATION RACE SEX AGE	27 TYPE OF PREMISES OR LOCATION WHERE OFFENSE WAS COMMITTED
	liquor store

CRIMES AGAINST PROPERTY   **CRIMES AGAINST THE PERSON**

28 POINT WHERE ENTRANCE WAS MADE:	29 WEAPON - FORCE OR MEANS USED:
front door	

30 EXACT LOCATION OF PROPERTY WHEN STOLEN	31 EXACT LOCATION OF VICTIM AT TIME OF OFFENSE
cash register, shelves	

32 INSTRUMENT USED (DESCRIBE)	33 VICTIM'S ACTIVITY AT TIME OF OFFENSE
sword, 5 feet long	

34 METHOD USED TO GAIN ENTRANCE	35 EXACT WORDS USED BY SUSPECT
	"I'll slice your heads off if you make a move."

36 WHERE WERE OCCUPANTS AT TIME OF OFFENSE?
standing at back of store

37 APPARENT MOTIVE - TYPE OF PROPERTY TAKEN OR OBTAINED
money, Ballantine's scotch whiskey

38 TRADEMARK OF SUSPECT(S) - ACTIONS OR CONVERSATION
kept swing sword, saying "Im good at this."   "I drink only the best."

39 VEHICLE USED BY SUSPECT(S) - YEAR, MAKE, BODY TYPE, COLOR, LICENSE NUMBER AND ANY OTHER IDENTIFYING MARKS.
none spotted

40 REPORT

Received call at Station precinct 6 from Al's Liquor Store 2305; responded 231 Mark Stevens, night manager talking with his girlfriend, Mary Smith, at back of store, when suspect ran through front door swinging 5 foot sword,

yelling "I'll slice your heads off if you make a move. I used to throw swords in a circus; I don't miss." S. 6'2" about 210 lbs. w.m., clean shaven, age estimated 40 to 45, grey hair, blue windbreaker, blue satin pants. Demanded all the money in cash register. Stevens reports "about $800 in it."

Then demanded "only Ballantine's scotch; I drink the best." Smith handed him 4 bottles which S. put in net bag. Ran out with scotch and money, warning he would throw sword if they followed. Disappeared in dark. No apparent car or accomplice.

Witness #1: Mary Smith says all she noticed was s. coming through door swinging sword and blue satin pants. Too frightened to note more details.

Says voice was hoarse.

Witness #2: Mark Stevens: provided description of S. Says S. looked like he meant business so did not argue. Cash register has no key. Operated by Cash button. Handed over bills only, no coins. First offered B & W scotch when S. demanded scotch; after S. shouted "Only Ballantine's" W. took bottles from shelf. S. did not ask for more.   Investigation underway.

IF ADDITIONAL SPACE IS REQUIRED USE CONTINUATION REPORT

DATE AND TIME TYPED CLERK	REPORTING OFFICER	SUPERVISOR APPROVING
yesterday's date 2300 MLM	Bob Kline	J. Lewis

Exercise 13.3

Write a news story based on the following traffic collision reports. Additional information: violation charges (VC) 22350 is speeding. 11802A is violating left turn right-of-way.

TRAFFIC COLLISION REPORT

Page: 1 of 2
Number: ND 1621467

Special Conditions: none
No. Injured: 2
No. Killed: 1
Judicial District: yours
County: yours

Location
Collision Occurred On: Webster
At Intersection With: Lincoln
Date: yesterday
Time: 1500
NCIC Number: 1410
Officer I.D.: 684
Injury, Fatal or Tow Away: Yes
State Hwy Related: No

Party 1 (Driver)
- **Name:** Peter A. Sage
- **Street Address:** 1423 Middlefield
- **Driver's License:** BF6017432, yours
- **Birthdate:** 10/21/55
- **Sex:** M, **Race:** W
- **City:** yours
- **Phone:** 456-7890
- **Vehicle:** '75 Ford/Mustang, License 657 MFO
- **Direction of Travel:** East on Lincoln
- **Speed Limit:** 25
- **Disposition of Vehicle:** Gunn Tow, On Orders of Dept.
- **Vehicle Damage:** Major
- **Violation Charged:** 21802A

Party 2 (Driver)
- **Name:** Joe Doakes
- **Street Address:** 1520 Cork Oak Way
- **Driver's License:** PR789023, yours
- **Birthdate:** 6/17/60
- **Sex:** M, **Race:** W
- **City:** yours
- **Phone:** 324-4444
- **Vehicle:** '78 Dodge Dart, License 789 YUI
- **Direction of Travel:** So. on Webster
- **Speed Limit:** 25
- **Disposition of Vehicle:** Gunn Tow, By Driver
- **Vehicle Damage:** Mod.
- **Violation Charged:** 22350

Witness / Injured

Name	Age	Sex	Extent of Injury	Injured Was	Party #
Jane Davis (witness only), 1340 Melville, your city	23	F	Fatal Injury	Pass.	1
Peter A. Sage, as above			Other Visible Injuries	Driver — Taken to Valley Medical Center	1
Joe Doakes, as above			Other Visible Injuries	Driver — Taken to Valley Medical Center	2

Sketch
Webster runs north-south; Lincoln runs east-west.
- Vehicle 1: traveling east on Lincoln, 60' skid, HIT, STOPPED at intersection.
- Vehicle 2: traveling south/west approaching intersection.
- Indicate North: up.

555-01 (REV 8-78) — USE PREVIOUS EDITIONS UNTIL DEPLETED — 64590-456 9-78 OSP 300M

186 CRIME AND ACCIDENTS

DATE OF COLLISION	TIME (2400)	NCIC NUMBER	OFFICER I.D.	NUMBER	PAGE
yesterday MO. DAY YR.	1500	1410	684	ND 1621467	2

COLLISION NARRATIVE

Party 1 traveling E. on Lincoln proceeded to make left turn at intersection of Webster, without slowing or stopping, accdg. 2 witnesses. Party 2 traveling So. on Webster at high speed, same W. report. Party 2 laid down 60 ft skid marks after impact, confirming speed of 55 MPH. Party 1 driven by Peter Sage. ~~VMC ambulance medic diagnosed shock, severe internal injuries, fractured nose, possible broken ribs.~~ Sage could not be interviewed. Party 1 passenger, Jane Davis, thrown from car at initial impact, accdg. W. D.O.A. of investigating officer; taken to Finn Mortuary, 1300 University. Party 2 driver, Joe Doakes, bleeding from head and dazed, but initial ambulance medic diagnosis, no severe injuries. Dr. Don Bunce, VMC ambulance medic. Doakes said he did not realize he was exceeding speed limit; was late for work as janitor at ABC Co., Bayshore at Elm. Said he did not see party 1 car "until too late. I slammed on brakes immediately." ~~Party 1 car heavily damaged left side, motor displaced, roof partially caved in.~~ Party 2 car, moderate damage to grill, hood and radiator. Witnesses: A, Betty Ford, 35, 1345 Webster: just coming out her door when she observed party 1 entering intersection and start left turn without slowing. No view obstruction at NW corner. Observed party 2 traveling "fast" south on ~~Webster hit party 1.~~ W. B, Max Field, 45, walking E. on Lincoln, 20 ft. W. of Webster intersection, saw party 1 pass then enter intersection without stopping, began turning. Observed party 2 "really traveling" come south on Webster and hit party 1   Conclusion: Party 1 at fault for not obeying left turn rights of way; party 2 contributed by unreasonable speed.

PRIMARY COLLISION FACTOR	RIGHT OF WAY CONTROL	1	2	3	4	TYPE OF VEHICLE	1	2	3	4	MOVEMENT PRECEDING COLLISION
A VC SECTION VIOLATION: 21802 A	A CONTROLS FUNCTIONING					A PASSENGER CAR (INCLUDES STATION WAGON)					A STOPPED
B OTHER IMPROPER DRIVING*	B CONTROLS NOT FUNCTIONING	X									B PROCEEDING STRAIGHT
C OTHER THAN DRIVER*	C CONTROLS OBSCURED					B PASSENGER CAR W/TRAILER	X				C RAN OFF ROAD
D UNKNOWN*	D NO CONTROLS PRESENT	X				C MOTORCYCLE/SCOOTER					D MAKING RIGHT TURN
WEATHER	TYPE OF COLLISION					D PICKUP OR PANEL TRUCK					E MAKING LEFT TURN
	A HEAD-ON					E PICKUP OR PANEL TRUCK W/TRAILER	X				F MAKING U TURN
X A CLEAR	B SIDESWIPE					F TRUCK OR TRUCK TRACTOR					G BACKING
B CLOUDY	C REAR END					G TRUCK OR TRUCK TRACTOR W/TRAILER(S)					H SLOWING—STOPPING
C RAINING	D BROADSIDE	X									I PASSING OTHER VEHICLE
D SNOWING	E HIT OBJECT					H SCHOOL BUS					J CHANGING LANES
E FOG	F OVERTURNED					I OTHER BUS					K PARKING MANEUVER
F OTHER:	G AUTO/PEDESTRIAN					J EMERGENCY VEHICLE					L ENTERING TRAFFIC FROM SHOULDER, MEDIAN, PARKING STRIP OR PRIVATE DRIVE
	H OTHER*					K HWY CONST. EQUIPMENT					
LIGHTING	MOTOR VEHICLE INVOLVED WITH					L BICYCLE					M OTHER UNSAFE TURNING
A DAYLIGHT	A NON-COLLISION					M OTHER VEHICLE					N CROSSED INTO OPPOSING LANE
B DUSK—DAWN	B PEDESTRIAN					N PEDESTRIAN					
C DARK—STREET LIGHTS	C OTHER MOTOR VEHICLE	X				O MOPED					O PARKED
D DARK—NO STREET LIGHTS	D MOTOR VEHICLE ON OTHER ROADWAY	1	2	3	4	OTHER ASSOCIATED FACTOR (MARK 1 TO 3 ITEMS)					P MERGING
E DARK—STREET LIGHTS NOT FUNCTIONING*	E PARKED MOTOR VEHICLE					A VC SECTION VIOLATION: 22350					Q TRAVELING WRONG WAY*
ROADWAY SURFACE	F TRAIN										R OTHER:
A DRY	G BICYCLE					B VC SECTION VIOLATION:					
B WET	H ANIMAL:						1	2	3	4	SOBRIETY—DRUG—PHYSICAL (MARK 1 TO 3 ITEMS)
C SNOWY—ICY						C VC SECTION VIOLATION:					
D SLIPPERY (MUDDY, OILY, ETC.)	I FIXED OBJECT:										A HAD NOT BEEN DRINKING
ROADWAY CONDITIONS (MARK 1 TO 3 ITEMS)	J OTHER OBJECT:					D VC SECTION VIOLATION:					B HAD—UNDER INFLUENCE
A HOLES, DEEP RUTS*											C HAD—NOT UNDER INFLUENCE*
B LOOSE MATERIAL ON ROADWAY*	K OTHER:					E VISION OBSCUREMENTS:					D HAD—IMPAIRMENT UNKNOWN*
C OBSTRUCTION ON ROADWAY*	PEDESTRIAN'S ACTION					F INATTENTION					
D CONSTRUCTION-REPAIR ZONE	X A NO PEDESTRIAN INVOLVED					G STOP & GO TRAFFIC					E UNDER DRUG INFLUENCE*
E REDUCED ROADWAY WIDTH	B CROSSING IN CROSSWALK AT INTERSECTION					H ENTERING/LEAVING RAMP					F IMPAIRMENT—PHYSICAL*
F FLOODED*						I PREVIOUS COLLISION	X	X			G IMPAIRMENT NOT KNOWN
G OTHER:	C CROSSING IN CROSSWALK—NOT AT INTERSECTION					J UNFAMILIAR WITH ROAD					H NOT APPLICABLE
H NO UNUSUAL CONDITIONS	D CROSSING—NOT IN CROSSWALK					K DEFECTIVE VEHICLE EQUIPMENT:					I SLEEPY/FATIGUED
	E IN ROAD—INCLUDES SHOULDER					L UNINVOLVED VEHICLE					
	F NOT IN ROAD					M OTHER:					
	G APPROACHING/LEAVING SCHOOL BUS					N NONE APPARENT					

INVESTIGATED BY	I.D. NUMBER	INVESTIGATED BY	I.D. NUMBER	REVIEWED BY
Lane Marcus	684			MLM

EXPLAIN IN NARRATIVE

Exercise 13.4 *Write a story from the following information.*

The Coast Guard station located at Treasure Island, San Francisco Bay, responded to a distress call over the marine radio band at 0130 today. A 25-foot sailboat, *Joy Too*, with four persons aboard, reported at 0120 that it was wallowing out of control about 1 half-mile west of Bonita Point, just outside the entrance to the Golden Gate. Seas were choppy, estimated at 15 feet, winds gusting to 50 knots, visibility clear. Sails were ripped and water was being shipped aboard. Skipper was unconscious after having been hit by boom and no one else aboard able to control the boat.

Coast Guard cutter *Washington Star*, 51 feet, reached *Joy Too* at 0200, by which time boat had hit rocks off Bonita Point and gashed large hole in starboard bow. Three persons were in water near boat, all wearing life jackets. Because of heavy seas, *Washington Star* crew took 40 minutes to rescue three persons in water, using large nets to pull them to boat. Seas too rough to launch dinghy to rescue those in water, or to reach sinking 25-foot Corona class sailboat. Survivors said skipper, James Blaney, 53, Portland Park, was still aboard sailboat. He is presumed drowned. No body has been sighted. The Coast Guard will resume search when weather calms sufficiently.

The survivors are John Brown, 47, of Portland Park, and his son, William Brown, 21, Berkeley; and James Craig, 37, San Francisco. All were taken to Letterman General Hospital, San Francisco, where they are still being treated for exposure. William Brown also suffered broken ribs from being tossed around *Joy Too*.

According to James Craig, Blaney, owner of the boat, had invited the others for an overnight sail to Bolinas Bay, about 30 miles north of San Francisco. They had left the Berkeley Marina, where the boat is docked, at 0700 this morning. When they encountered storm conditions about 4 miles north of the Golden Gate, they turned back to return to Berkeley. "It was awful; I've never seen anything like it," Craig said. "We had no control over that boat and it was too damn rough to go up on deck to try to reduce sails."

Just off the Gate their sails blew out and the outboard motor, soaked by the waves which had swept repeatedly aboard, would not start. Before they could secure the swinging boom, it smashed Blaney on the head. Craig and the younger Brown said they tried to revive Blaney, but he did not come round. They believe he was still alive when last seen.

The three survivors were pitched out of the boat when it hit the rocks. They were unable to climb back aboard to rescue Blaney. William Brown stated: "It all happened so fast, we didn't know what hit us. I'd never been out sailing before. I was sure we were all going to die. I feel terrible about the skipper. I kept trying to climb back aboard, but the boat was pitching and slamming the rocks too hard and my chest hurt. I didn't realize I'd broken

188 CRIME AND ACCIDENTS

some ribs when I was thrown from one side of the boat to another after the sails blew. I'll never go out again."

Blaney and his wife, Joy, live at 33 White Avenue, Portland Place.

Exercise 13.5 *Write a story from the following information.*

The Casper, Wyoming Natrona County International Airport reported a crash of a Twin Otter 15-passenger twin-engine turbojet at 7:15 last night. The plane was on a regularly scheduled flight for Metcalf Commuter Airways between Cheyenne and Casper. It was preparing to land when it suddenly banked vertically and crashed to the ground about 100 yards before the runway. The plane burst into flames. It took 15 minutes for the airport fire team and other rescuers to reach the plane. Twelve passengers and the pilot perished inside the plane. Bodies of two passengers, heavily burned, were found about 100 feet from the wrecked fuselage. The copilot was found wandering near the plane. He was taken to Natrona County Hospital where doctors have listed him as seriously injured, but stable.

A National Transportation Safety Board investigating team flew in at 10:00 A.M. today with an official from the Federal Aviation Administration to check the cause of the accident. By noon today, Jack Smith, head of the NTS team, said that early findings appear to show there were no mechanical failures. A tape recording from the cockpit, in what is believed to be the pilot's voice, shows normal landing exchanges with the air controller until seconds before the tape stopped, when the voice suddenly changed and shouted: "What the hell's happening!" Those were the last words on the tape.

Smith speculated that the small commuter plane may have been caught in "wing-tip vortices," or the wake turbulence of a Boeing 747 that had landed about five minutes earlier. Sometimes a large jet will leave a turbulent wake for as long as five minutes, Smith explained. It was possible the Twin Otter had accumulated ice on its wings because of the sudden snowstorm that had started an hour earlier; the ice would have reduced the aircraft's maneuverability which, coupled with Casper's typical unexpected crosswinds and wake turbulence might have caused the plane to lose control. "The sudden vertical banking which the controller observed would be typical of this kind of problem," Smith said. However, the investigation is continuing.

Bob Winter, one of the first fire fighters on the scene described the crash site as "terrible—there was a horrible burnt smell, and twisted plane parts all over the place."

James Dodson, the copilot, from 1127 Main Street, Cheyenne, has been questioned only once because of his injuries. He reportedly told investigators, "I think we suddenly started bouncing in winds as we were about to touch down."

EXERCISE 13.5

Names of the pilot and passengers killed in the crash will not be released until all next of kin have been notified. There were 14 passengers on the 15-passenger plane. The bodies were removed from the plane and taken to the Elk's Club Lodge awaiting family identification.

Metcalf spokesperson Barbara Spector says the company has no more information than that released by Jack Smith. Spector said regularly scheduled commuter flights are continuing.

Chapter 14 # Reports and Numbers

Reporters wade through considerable jargon every day, both number and word jargon. While converting numbers and incomprehensible words into gripping stories may appear to be the most unappealing part of a reporting job, it is often the most important.

Numbers are language, too, usually representing activities meaningful to readers: food costs, tax rates, employment figures, college admission rates, statistical risks, and the like. These translate into such reader concerns as: How much will I pay for groceries next month? Will I pay more rent because property taxes have increased? Do I stand a good chance for a job when I graduate? If I am a member of a minority, how likely am I to get into graduate school? If I take a job as an X-ray technician, do I increase my risk of cancer?

Hardly a day goes by without news media carrying stories that quote numbers, percentages, or statistics. Election results, political statistics, budget figures, tax reports, cost of living increases, census statistics, automobile sales, freeway accidents, and crime rates typically make news.

Just as numbers may strike you as dry and uninteresting, yet contain information vital to reader interest, so will many lengthy jargon-filled reports.

An 1100-page report from the Health, Education, and Welfare Department in the 1960s, for example, changed the school busing habits of our nation for the next decade, though the original document, according to most reporters at the time, was virtually unreadable. The report described research on learning among black and white children when in integrated schools.

Similarly, planning reports from local school districts, city councils, architectural review boards, and many other governmental bodies may presage important changes in a reader's community, changes that will cost money and alter living habits. Yet these reports and others may be so obtusely worded that the average citizen would be confused after reading them.

Your task as a reporter is to translate complicated numbers and impenetrable communications into everyday language that will provide meaningful information to the reader. Whether you are coping with voluminous statistics or words, here are several helpful hints:

highlight significance:	How will the reader be affected?
compare past and future:	What changes will take place?
condense information:	Do not report every detail.
use simple language:	Omit technical jargon or unnecessary numbers.

Dealing with Numbers and Statistics

Reporters would be surprised to be told they are walking statisticians since most hate math. They have, however, been trained to gather observations and process and reduce them to readable articles.

Observations analyzed and reduced to quantitative terms are called data. Data organized in summary forms are called statistics. So, in a sense, a reporter is a statistician who summarizes data in a way the general public can understand.

Keep public understanding in mind when you write articles making use of numbers or statistics. Are you writing about a state or federal budget dealing in billions of dollars? Billions are difficult to comprehend. After citing such a figure, for example, tell what percentage of total expenditure that figure represents. This tactic reduces the numbers to comprehensible terms. Thus: "The Defense Department budget submitted yesterday asked Congress for $100 billion, nearly 40 percent of next year's projected total federal expenses."

Are you describing the cost of an airport expansion? Consider personalizing the figures by relating costs to purchase of an airline ticket. A local weekly handled a nearby expansion this way:

"If you fly from San Jose to Burbank today, the standard coach ticket will cost you $21.50. Five dollars represents the airline's rent payments to the San Jose Airport. If the airport completes its expansion plans to accommodate wide-bodied jet planes, rental costs will increase to $6.50 on that $21.50 ticket to pay for new construction costs."

Unit comparisons are often helpful to a reader when you are describing governmental expenses. Frederick O'Reilly Hayes, former budget director of New York City, suggested some useful themes in a *Columbia Journalism Review* article in February 1976: For example, we can examine school systems in unit cost per child, or per pupil-teacher ratio, or average class size.

Readers can relate to these concepts, just as they can relate to your writing that the fire department in New Orleans costs twice as much per person as it does in San Antonio where there are 60,000 more people.

When writing a story based on statistical analysis, break up long lists with narrative information. Explain what the statistics say, highlighting important points.

For example a Census Bureau report a few years ago gave the following information:

> People living in husband/wife household: (numbers in millions)
> Husbands, 47.5; wives 47.5; children under 18, 50.3; older children and other older relatives (aunts, uncles, grandparents), 17.2. The total, 162.5.

Total population that year was 211 million, which meant that 77 percent of the population at that time lived in husband/wife households.

Here is part of a story from the *Washington Post* on those statistics:

> The "nuclear family" is still doing quite well in the United States, despite recent news from the Census Bureau these days.
>
> Americans still love families with a mom and a pop and perhaps some kids and maybe some aunts and uncles all living together—and that's where most of them still live, census expert Dr. Paul C. Glick said Tuesday.
>
> Divorce may be up and so may the number of couples living together without benefit of a marriage certificate.
>
> But about 77 percent of the people in the United States still live in husband-wife households.
>
> According to figures compiled by Glick, there were 47.5 million husbands and 47.5 million wives in such households, plus 50.3 million children under 18 and about 1.7 million older children or other, older relatives like uncles, aunts and grandparents.
>
> Thus, husband-wife households totaled 162.5 million people or 77 percent of the total population.
>
> In 1949, 82 percent of the population lived in such families. (*Source: Washington Post,* July 1979)

When quoting statistics, always put them in context. For example, in the census statistics on husband/wife households, information was provided which showed that households with unmarried men and women living together had gone from 1.1 million in 1967 to 2.3 million in 1977. This means such households had doubled in the preceding decade. Many news stories led off with that "doubled" information without stating in the body of the story that the numbers were small in relation to the married population. The *Washington Post*'s story quoted above handled the information thusly:

> Census experts said there are some trends tending to undermine the status of the nuclear family and they could be quite marked if they persist far into the future.
>
> For example, divorce rates are high, and while the number of young men and women living together unmarried is really small (2.3 million people), it has more than doubled over the last decade. (*Source: Washington Post,* July 1979)

Check the significance of rankings, too. A common habit is to accept at face value information that "we ranked third in such and such a rating"—without checking what the total number ranked was. It is one thing, for example, if a university states: "Our business school ranked third in the nation," when only 5 business schools were ranked—and quite another thing if 20 business schools were ranked.

Learn, also, to correctly use such terms as "doubling" and "jumped 200 percent." Many students believe "doubling" is the same as increasing 200 percent. It is not. For example, if your tuition is $311 this year and is scheduled to go up to $622 next year, the correct phrases would be: Tuition costs will go up 100 percent; or, tuition costs will double.

Here is how to figure percentages:

$$\frac{\text{new number minus base number}}{\text{base number}} \times 100$$

The new number on the above example would be $622; the base number $311. So, $622 minus $311 equals $311, divided by $311 which equals 1. Multiply 1 by 100, and you get 100 percent.

Here's another one: if tuition is $100 and will go up to $150, what's the percentage increase?

The new number is $150. Minus the base number, $100, it equals $50, divided by $100, which equals .5. Multiplied by 100, that equals 50 percent.

Reporters often round off figures to make such calculations to provide readers with quick generalities about numbers and statistics.

One final caution: whenever you are reading charts or statistical tables, be sure to note whether the numbers have been reduced to hundreds, thousands, or millions. Normally, this information will be noted at the top or bottom of the chart or table.

Reports

Most lengthy documents are broken into sections. Frequently these sections will either begin or end with a summary that highlights the contents. Reporters, writing under deadline pressure, use these summaries to gather key facts.

Here, for example, is the airport summary section of a 300-page county budget report:

    The Airport Division is recommended for a funding at a gross appropriation of $452,200 at no net county cost. This is a gross appropriation increase of $85,200, (23.2%) fully offset by revenue. One new position, Assistant Airport Manager, for Half Moon Bay Airport is recommended.
    This level of funding will permit the Airport Division to maintain its current level of service as well as plan for a 5-year capital project/land acquisition. Airport revenues historically exceed operations and maintenance costs. The balance of revenue is to be reinvested in airport related planning, engineering, or acquisitions. For 1981–82, $17,600 is expected to be available for these purposes. (*Source:* Santa Clara County Budget Proposal, 1980, p. 208)

Reducing jargon to simple English will present you with one of your major challenges as a reporter. Following is a copy of a human relations report presented a few years ago at a school district meeting:

    In human needs identification it is useful to build a classification of needs which shows their relatedness. This is most readily and validly done on a local basis—at the city level, for instance—because of the knowledge born of proximity that data gatherers have of their community. There are two generic approaches to the development of a needs classification. One approach is to develop an a priori classification of needs and then to assess their existence in the community. The difficulty with this approach is the same as that described above: The danger of overlooking existing needs due to need definition in terms of service. However, there is work going on now in some geographic areas toward the development of systems of need classification for general application. These would still require modification and expansion for local use, but would provide a helpful beginning framework for needs assessment. The other approach to needs classification is to research real needs relationships in the community through the use of cluster-analysis techniques.
    An integral phase of the needs identification process is the definition of qualitative and quantitative criteria of human needs.[1] (*Source:* Working Draft, Project Redesign, Palo Alto Unified School District, 1976–1981, Long Range Plan)

---

    [1]A useful theoretical framework for the consideration of needs criteria is Bradshaw's four-fold classification of need, based on the derivation of the criteria adopted for determining need. *Normative need* is what the expert or professional perceives to be need in a given situation. *Felt need* is need perceived by the subjects themselves. *Expressed need* (demand) is felt need turned into action in the form of a request for service. *Comparative need* is need deduced in circumstances where individuals not in receipt of a particular service have similar characteristics to others who receive it. It's apparent that all four categories of need have elements of

normative criteria. Even felt need, the most subjective of the four, is determined to some degree by the individual's experience with available ameliorated services.

Pity the poor reporter who had to write the story!

See how well you can do at rewriting the following excerpt from a savings plan booklet:

> There is no tax upon cash withdrawal of all or part of a participant's allotment if the withdrawal does not exceed the allotments not previously offset against distributions and withdrawals. Ordinarily there will be no tax upon such a withdrawal, inasmuch as the withdrawal will not exceed the participant's own allotments adjusted for previous withdrawals. In certain situations, the Internal Revenue Service can be expected to assert a tax upon such a withdrawal on the ground that an allotment previously offset against such distributions or withdrawals may not be offset against distributions or withdrawals in a subsequent year.

Here's that same information in plainer English: If you take out more money than you put in, the IRS may tax you.

Chapter 14 Exercises

Remember:

1. Give readers information that affects their lives: Tell them what changes will take place, how much something will cost, how the new plan will be enforced, and so on.
2. Interpret numbers and technical jargon in simple language that highlights points significant to the reader.
3. Put statistics in context.
4. Learn how to figure percentages so you can help readers understand changes involving numbers.

Exercise 14.1

Do not be confused by the mathematics in exercises presented below. This is a reporting workbook! However, you will find reporters must do a lot of arithmetic to reduce incomprehensible numbers to percentages or fractions that readers can understand more readily. Answer the questions below to practice doing this.

1. Class enrollment jumped from 50 to 150. What percentage increase was this? If you wanted to express the increase in doubled, tripled, or quadrupled terms, what would you write?

2. Robert bicycles at 7 miles per hour, and Mary bikes at 19 miles

196 REPORTS AND NUMBERS

per hour. About how much faster does Mary bike than Robert? (Express in "times faster.")

3. The Agriculture Department reports that beef costing $1.09 per pound in June and $1.20 per pound in July is likely to cost $1.32 per pound in August. What is the approximate rate in percentages that beef has gone up each month? If beef reaches $1.32 per pound in August, what will be its percentage increase since June?

Exercise 14.2

Following is the new Moldavia city budget. Write a story in 300 or less words, interpreting significant aspects of the budget.

City Budget

Item of Expense	Next Year	This Year
Public Health and Safety (police, fire, food inspection, health department, etc.)	$2,138,654	$1,986,725
Administration (salaries of mayor, city manager, commissioners; election expense, printing, advertising, postage, insurance, municipal court, legal services, etc.)	707,369	631,924*
Public Services (garbage collection, streets, bridges, engineering, weights and measures, sanitation)	2,161,392	2,096,241
General Welfare and Relief	369,024	128,568
Recreation and Parks (zoo, library, art museum, youth centers, playgrounds, golf courses, etc.)	607,926	599,859
Rental and Building Maintenance	231,715	226,472
Water Works and Gas Plant	1,582,274	1,402,196
Miscellaneous	1,392,883	1,091,892
Total Operating Expenses	$9,191,237	$8,163,877
Anticipated Income		
Water Department	$1,834,213	$1,665,855
Gas Plant	2,891,581**	2,375,288
Occupational Licenses	217,897	231,947
Police Court Fines	463,225	447,832
Property Taxes	3,417,549***	3,112,990
Inspection Fees	70,619	65,544
Garbage Service Fees	132,874	118,635
Rentals and Concessions	101,695	92,461
Golf Fees, Park Concessions	61,584	53,325
Total Income	$9,191,237	$8,163,877

*No election last year
**Rates to increase 15 percent
***Taxes to increase from $2.40 to $2.50 per $100 of assessed valuation.

Exercise 14.3

Here are statistics from a survey of freshman entering Podunk State College, in Navato, Arizona. Table A shows academic fields the freshman intend to study during their four years at PSC. Table B shows the home states of the freshman class. Write a news story for the Podunk student newspaper, approximately 350 words, from these statistics.

Table A

Field	Women #	Women %	Men #	Men %	Total #	Total %
Social sciences	219	30.6	208	24.2	427	27.1
Natural sciences, math, technology	149	20.8	169	19.6	318	20.2
Premed, predental, allied health	118	16.5	158	18.4	276	17.5
Engineering	65	9.1	179	20.8	244	15.5
Humanities	112	15.7	63	7.3	175	11.1
General education	36	5.0	50	5.8	86	5.5
Not available	16	2.2	34	3.9	50	3.2
Total	715		816		1,576	

Table B Geographical distribution of the freshman class entering in 1979 (as of June 13)*

Area	Women	%	Men	%	Total	%
Northern California	220	30.78	175	20.32	395	25.06
Southern California	162	22.66	169	19.63	331	21.00
Western region	119	16.64	153	17.77	272	17.26
Eastern region	65	9.09	107	12.43	172	10.91
Lakes region	55	7.69	96	11.15	151	9.58
Southern region	35	4.89	60	6.97	95	6.03
Midwest region	29	4.06	38	4.41	67	4.25
Foreign	11	1.54	27	3.14	38	2.41
Not available	19	2.66	36	4.18	55	3.49
Total	715		861		1,576	

*West: Alaska, Hawaii, Washington, Oregon, Idaho, Montana, Wyoming, Nevada, Utah, Colorado, Arizona, and New Mexico.

East: New York, Vermont, New Hampshire, Maine, Massachusetts, Connecticut, Rhode Island, New Jersey, Pennsylvania, Maryland, and West Virginia.

Lakes: Minnesota, Wisconsin, Michigan, Illinois, Indiana, and Ohio.

South: Texas, Louisiana, Mississippi, Alabama, Georgia, Florida, Tennessee, Kentucky, Virginia, North Carolina, and South Carolina.

Midwest: North Dakota, South Dakota, Nebraska, Iowa, Kansas, Missouri, Oklahoma, and Arkansas.

Foreign: Anything outside the 50 states, including U.S. citizens living overseas.

Exercise 14.4

You are writing a story on the change in food costs from last year to this year. Use the following table to generalize on food costs as well as to mention specific foods. You are writing for a Detroit paper.

The Market Basket

Shopping Date: June 14

Item	Last Year's Average Price	This Year's Average Price	Percentage difference	Tampa Price	San Diego Price	New York Price	Des Moines Price	Memphis Price	Detroit Price	Philadelphia Price	San Francisco Price	Dallas Price	Atlanta Price
MILK, homogenized, ½ gallon	$ .85	$ .94	+10.6%	$1.03	$ .85	$ .91	$1.00	$1.11	$ .99	$ .88	$ .80	$1.04	$1.16
EGGS, 1 dozen, Grade A, large	.60	.72	+20.0%	.59	.75	.59S	.74D	.71	.63	.89	.79D	.78	.50S
CHEESE, 10 ounces, sharp, Cracker Barrel	1.52	1.65	+8.6%	1.74	1.73	1.65	1.49	1.39	1.44	1.65	1.79	1.73	1.69
MARGARINE, 1 pound, 4 sticks, Blue Bonnet or Parkay	.60	.63	+5.0%	.53S	.66	.79	.59	.49	.59	.79	.57	.67	.45
BREAD, white, sliced, 24-ounce loaf	.48	.49	+2.1%	.40A	.49	.39A	.63	.29S	.53	.43A	.50	.39S	.40
FLOUR, 5 pounds, all-purpose, Gold Medal or Pillsbury	.86	.94	+9.3%	.94	.83	.85	.49S	.85	.77	.93	.87	.88	.75
SPECIAL K, 11-ounce package	.93	1.03	+10.8%	1.04	1.01	.93	1.04	.87S	.98	.96	1.05	1.05	.93
SUGAR, 5 pounds, white, granulated	1.07	1.14	+6.5%	.98	1.15	.98S	1.05	.99	1.04	1.09	1.17	1.23	.99
INSTANT COFFEE, 10 ounces, Maxwell House or Nescafe	4.54	4.13	−9.0%	3.89	3.96	4.19	3.59	3.94	4.18	4.89	3.89	3.79	3.99
GREAT NORTHERN BEANS, dry, 1 pound	.45	.44	−2.2%	.44A	.40	.45	.42A	.39	.49	.36	.41	.43	.39
RICE, 2 pounds, Uncle Ben's converted	1.23	1.24	+0.8%	1.16	1.21	1.19	1.29	1.23	1.24	1.19	1.29	1.19	1.29
MAYONNAISE, 1 quart, Best Foods, Hellman's or Kraft	1.36	1.43	+5.1%	1.19S	1.22	1.29	1.29S	1.39	1.19	1.25	1.45	1.49S	1.28
PEANUT BUTTER, 18-ounce jar, smooth, Jif, Peter Pan, Planters or Skippy	1.08	1.18	+9.3%	1.14	1.11	1.19	1.07S	1.09	1.17	1.09	1.29	1.27	1.09
TUNA, 6½-ounce can, light chunk meat in oil, Chicken of the Sea or Starkist	.72	.74	+2.8%	.59	.69	.69	.69S	.73	.76	.69	.77	.59S	.75
EVAPORATED MILK, 13 fluid ounces, Carnation, Gold Key or Pet	.37	.42	+13.5%	.39	.40	.39	.43	.35S	.41	.44	.43	.42	.39
CLING PEACH HALVES, 29-ounce can, heavy syrup, Del Monte, Hunt, Libby or Stokley	.60	.71	+18.3%	.68	.61	.65	.66	.57	.73	.75	.69	.68	.78
PINEAPPLE, 20-ounce can, sliced, heavy syrup or own juice, Del Monte or Dole	.62	.68	+9.7%	.68	.65	.67	.70	.68	.61	.59	.67	.67	.59
ICE CREAM, ½ gallon, any brand	1.22	1.26	+3.3%	.99	1.09	.99S	1.09	1.15	.99	.99	1.59	1.35	.89S
FROZEN ORANGE JUICE CONCENTRATE, Grade A, least expensive brand	.40	.39	−2.5%	.34	.41	.39	.43	.32	.40	.43	.39S	.34S	.42
BROCCOLI SPEARS, frozen, 10-ounce package, Grade A or Fancy	.47	.47	0	.50	.47	.39	.59	.45	.59	.39	.49	.39S	.45
RUMP ROAST, boneless, Choice, 1 pound	1.99	2.34	+17.6%	1.99S	1.98	1.97	2.19	2.19	2.28	2.39	1.98	2.98	2.47
SIRLOIN STEAK, bone-in, Choice, 1 pound	2.41	2.69	+11.6%	2.88	2.59B	2.69	2.83	2.38	2.68	2.59	2.74B	1.97	2.88
GROUND BEEF, 75% lean, 1 pound	1.21	1.59	+31.4%	1.58	1.39	1.69	1.49E	1.58E	1.59	1.79	1.88	1.58G	1.38
PORK LOIN CHOPS with tenderloin, 1 pound, ½ to ¾-inch thick	1.98	1.86	−6.1%	1.99S	1.97	1.89	1.69	1.48	2.09	1.79	2.14	1.75	1.69
TOMATOES, 1 pound, vine-ripened, 3-inches in diameter	.48	.76	+58.3%	.58	.79	.69	.59	.79	.77	.79	.79	.89	.79
ORANGES, 5 pounds, juice fruit	1.37	1.62	+18.2%	1.28	1.45	1.74A	1.79	1.29	1.35	1.50A	1.45S	1.87A	1.29
SUB-TOTAL	36.47	38.30	+5.0%	35.53	35.76	36.62	36.63	34.88	37.55	38.18	38.21	38.22	36.77
Percentage tax on food	—	—	—	0	0	0	0	6.0%	0	0	0	0	4.0%
Amount of tax on market basket	—	—	—	0	0	0	0	2.10	0	0	0	0	1.47
TOTAL	$36.96	$38.98	+5.5%	$35.53	$35.76	$36.62	$36.63	$36.98	$37.55	$38.18	$38.21	$38.22	$38.24
Percentage different from average	—	—	—	−8.9%	−8.3%	−6.1%	−6.0%	−5.1%	−3.7%	−2.1%	−1.97%	−1.95%	−1.89%

A — Price adjusted
B — Price of boneless steak adjusted downward 20 cents a pound
C — With coupon
D — Grade AA eggs
E — Ground beef 70% lean
F — Pound price for whole ham
G — Ground beef 73% lean
H — Special price of bread adjusted from 22.5-ounce loaf
J — Special price adjusted from 39 cents a pound
K — Special price; with coupon and $15 order at very special price of 1c
S — Special

Exercise 14.5 Write a short filler for your daily paper on sales of radio, television, and videotape recorder sets for the month of June and year to date. Pretend you are writing this July 15, 1982.

Total U.S. Market Statistics
Sales to Dealers June 1982 versus June 1981

	June 1982	June 1981	Percent Change	Year to Date 1982	Year to Date 1981	Percent Change
Television						
Monochrome	563,555	515,944	+ 9.6	2,756,558	2,587,134	+ 6.5
Color	995,931	918,622	+ 8.4	4,628,344	4,578,312	+ 1.1
Total Television	1,559,486	1,434,566	+ 8.7	7,384,902	7,165,446	+ 3.1
Radio						
AM	516,270	684,516	−24.6	3,002,205	3,882,266	−22.7
AM/FM or FM	3,571,524	4,314,570	−17.2	10,086,140	11,995,263	−15.9
Total	4,087,794	4,999,086	−18.2	13,088,345	15,877,529	−17.6
Automobile	1,213,893	1,146,983	+ 5.8	6,937,769	6,525,781	+ 6.3
Total Radio	5,301,687	6,146,069	−13.7	20,026,114	22,403,310	−10.6
Home VTR	33,500	31,339	+ 6.9	180,444	142,490	+26.6

Source: EIA Marketing Services Department
Information contained in this report reflects total market statistics for products produced and/or sold in the United States regardless of the brand name or country of origin.

Exercise 14.6 Rewrite each of the following, in simple language understandable to your classmates. Whenever possible, use short sentences and words with three or fewer syllables.

FROM AN ALUMNI PUBLICATION

To this purpose a Center for the Study of the Future is presently being established to provide a focal point, catalyst, and assistor in establishing curricula studies and cross disciplinary activities dealing with the future. The Center, in coordination with the Department of Institutional Planning and Development, provides the necessary machinery for reexamination, evaluation, and implementation of new directions in higher education.

Just as genetic diversity favors the survival of the species, the variety of educational opportunities and programming at the University enables us to meet the many needs of the many people we serve.

FROM PUBLICITY ON A PHILANTHROPIC ORGANIZATION

The voluntary sector, as represented by one of its largest components—the United Way—is mobilizing its resources of money, time, and talent in response to the call to arms issued by President Nixon in his inaugural address. New programs are being established, sources of federal funds are being tapped to finance citizen-planned projects, streamlined techniques are being adopted and funds are being reallocated to spread available money more widely, and campaign goals are being set substantially higher. To single out only a few examples. . . .

FROM A COMMITTEE CHAIR'S LETTER ABOUT A PLANT OPEN HOUSE

The number of persons to attend any one of the various functions planned for June 10 cannot, of course, be reliably estimated until shortly before that date. It is therefore desirable that detailed planning be based, and that tentative but noncommitting preparatory measures be initiated, on the assumption that there will be capacity attendance at all functions and there there may be overflows at some. In other words, planning and prearranging are to be done so that all last-minute adjustments will be downward adjustments, and therefore feasible with minimum difficulty on short notice. This principle will apply particularly to such matters as the following, regarding which further word may issue from time to time as found desirable. . . .

Chapter 15
The Newspaper-Magazine of the Future

Television journalism has changed the nature of newspaper writing in recent years. Metropolitan and suburban newspapers alike, in efforts to compete with the inroads made on readership by television viewing, are publishing more and more magazine-like articles. Sometimes these are outright features, sometimes hard news written in magazine styles.

Not only is the writing done in magazine style; the page layout is as well. More photos are used, prettier graphics are designed, and wider spacing for copy is provided. A slicker appearance is created.

Though some magazine articles tend to be longer than newspaper articles, others can be quite short if intended for special sections. All, however, are written in story-telling format with a beginning, middle, and end. Otherwise, magazines emphasize the same basics as newspapers: thoroughness, accuracy, and bright writing. But magazine writers usually have more time to develop these characteristics.

Because magazines are published monthly—or weekly, in the case of newsmagazines or Sunday magazine sections of newspapers—writers can be more leisurely in gathering and checking information. Magazine readers, therefore, expect stories to supply background information with facts that have been checked and rechecked for accuracy.

Influence of the Newsmagazine on the Newspaper-Magazine of the Future

Some magazines, especially newsmagazines, have separate research staffs that double back over each number, name, and fact to ensure that each is accurate. This is not to say that errors do not slip through. They do. But the likelihood of error is considerably reduced.

Newspaper writers rarely have separate staffs to recheck their facts, so they must bear the burden themselves, making certain that their articles are flawless.

Newspaper writers also have to gather most of their own information, without depending on correspondents or other reporters to add depth and breadth. Newsmagazines, for example, have time and personnel to query a broad spectrum of sources spread throughout the world. Other magazines also sometimes use separate reporters to supply major portions of a story. You can note this in such magazines as *Discover,* a national science magazine, where the top of the story carries the writer's name, and the bottom, the name of the reporter.

As newspapers become more magazine-like, they take on some of the same techniques. For example, several reporters may pool information to write a long news-feature that is more akin to a magazine article than an old-fashioned newspaper article. Commonly, in such instances, all reporter names will appear together at the top or bottom of the article.

But, one reporter or editor must do the writing. This means that person has to synthesize the information provided by all the others.

When this occurs, the newspaper writer is acting in the same fashion as many modern magazine writers, especially those on newsmagazines. This integration of information from different reporters and editors has been called "group journalism" and it is a growing phenomenon on newspapers.

The technique calls for considerable ability to select and condense mounds of data, anecdotes, and background information to extract both substance and mood. Sometimes 40,000 words may have to be condensed accurately to 1000 in a newsmagazine. Newspapers, however, seldom cope with quite that amount of input. Still, a writer may have to take 3 or 4 individual stories of 2000 words each and create a satisfactory amalgam of, say, 3000 words. In the process, nuances may get lost as a writer under time pressure feverishly searches for quick transitions from one element of a story to another.

Of course, synthesizing information from diverse sources is typical of most magazine writing, whether the information has been gathered by a single person or many. The mark of a magazine article, in fact, is the in-depth research that precedes its writing.

Once a writer has researched information thoroughly, the problem is to select out the essentials, then organize them so that the story will flow smoothly. As we have mentioned previously, magazine style calls for stories with a beginning, middle, and end. They also usually call for wider perspectives, as they look into the past and toward the future.

Outlining the key ideas before you start writing helps greatly. The most important first step, however, is to settle on a central theme. The second step is to toss aside all material that does not stick closely to that central theme, no matter how fascinating the information or appealing the anecdote. It is a rule that seems simple and obvious, but one that is very difficult to follow.

This rule becomes even more important when a newspaper decides to publish a page of short magazine-like briefs, with attractive layout and photos, as a enticement to lazy readers. Newspapers are devoting their third pages to this format more and more often, and each brief must catch the eye. Newspapers also run short, magazine-like stories as weekend roundups on the week's news. These, too, are grouped together. Such stories are written as *wrap-ups*—including both historical information and future action, if known.

Here again, newsmagazines have something to teach reporters for newspapers of the future. Newsmagazine writers have learned to pack a wallop into brief items through careful selection of key elements, twists on cliches, colorful imagery, and amusing endings. An example from the "People" section of *Time* follows:

> In 1969 **Elizabeth Taylor**'s fifth husband wowed her with the gift of a rare and incredible gem: a $1.2 million, 69.42-carat diamond. Now that **Richard Burton** has gone his way and Taylor is married to **John Warner,** the apricot-size gem has, for Burton at least, become love's labor's cost. Taylor, taking advantage of changing markets as well as men, quietly sold the stone for nearly $3 million to New York City jeweler **Henry Lambert.** Two bidders, neither of them American, are dealing with Lambert for the clear white, 58-facet stone. Both want the diamond as an investment; for them, unlike Burton, love is never having to say you were starry.

Notice how, despite what some may consider gimmickry, the writer stayed with the central theme: the diamond.

Here is a similar example, but this time from a newspaper that uses the third-page magazine-brief format, the *San Jose Mercury:*

> Our favorite business person this week is Karisa Rothey. She is 6 years old and . . . ah, but you are wondering why she's holding that chicken. Does she sell eggs? you ask. Perhaps, but that's not why photographer Peter Gillens posed her with a clucker. Karisa lives in Sandy, Utah, where grasshoppers abound. Mostly they abound into the gardens of Karisa's neighbors, where they eat the leaves off anything that grows above that level known as knee-high to a grasshopper. So Karisa makes a little extra money by renting her pet chickens, on weekly contracts, to the local gardeners.
>
> The report is that chickens are more effective than insecticides and, as a bonus, there isn't a chance in the world that you'll be poisoned by accidentally inhaling one during application.

Again, despite diverse elements, the writer stayed with a central theme: Chickens make good insecticides.

Writing in Newspaper-Magazine Style

Magazine writing is generally more sprightly than standard newspaper writing. Colorful descriptions of background scenes, personal mannerisms, appearances, the color of the sky, clothes, food, or references to an historical incident often are included in magazine-like pieces written for newspapers.

When you are writing magazine-style articles, you must learn to observe and ask about the most minute details, as we mentioned in our feature writing section. Once again, the training newsmagazine reporters get is useful: their editors may query them—"What color socks was the candidate wearing?" Or, "What did the ambassador eat for breakfast?"

Here are a few examples of how details have been put to work in newsmagazines:

> Presidential Press Secretary Jody Powell, setting forth on his lunch hour to pick up a pin-stripe suit for a diplomatic mission one day last week, discovered that the gas gauge on his battered yellow Volkswagen read empty. From the top of a hill he just coasted down the slope—and into a gas line, in which he waited for more than an hour. (*Source: Time,* from a gas-shortage story)

> The monsoon-laden clouds were hanging low over Hanoi and the temperature was reaching into the 90's. Even so, the streets were filled with thousands of cyclists, pedaling aimlessly about. The Vietnamese, a family-oriented people, do not like to go home these days. One recent night, police raided Hanoi's Thong Nhat (Unification) park and arrested 300 couples who were making love in a public place. Most were married adults. They were in the park because their allotment of 16 square feet of living space per person did not allow them enough room at home to sleep together. (*Source: Newsweek,* from a story on postwar Vietnam)

> In the early-morning gloom of Saigon's muggy pre-monsoon season, an alarm clock shrills in the stillness of a second-floor bedroom at 5:30 on Phung Khack Khoan Street. The Brahmin from Boston arises, breakfasts on mango or papaya, sticks a snub-nosed .38-cal. Smith & Wesson revolver into a shoulder holster, and leaves for the office. (*Source: Time,* from a Vietnam war era story on then Ambassador Henry Cabot Lodge)

Magazine writers, even newsmagazine writers, have more freedom for creativity than newspaper writers. They can take more liberties with word use and juxtaposition of ideas, often because their readers are better educated than newspaper readers.

One device commonly used is characterizing scenes, particularly in leads, to give readers an instant sense of atmosphere. For example, if two men had robbed the Twin City Bank, ordering 50 customers to lie on the floor while they made off with $1 million in cash, here is how a newspaper might start the story as opposed to a newsmagazine:

> Two masked gunmen robbed the downtown branch of the Twin City Bank of $1 million cash today, after ordering 50 customers to lie face down on the floor.

A newsmagazine might run the lead:

> It was like a scene out of the movie *Bonnie and Clyde*.

Here, from an energy story, is a "characterizing" example from *Newsweek*:

> Like some Biblical plague, the nation's energy problems just keep on multiplying. . . .

Unexpected juxtaposition of visual images works well in magazine writing. This technique is especially common in newsmagazines, whose style is being borrowed by newspapers. Following is a passage from an article about the *New York Times* columnist William Safire, from *Newsweek*:

> Although syndicate executives report a steady growth of subscribers for their columnists, many regional editors insist that readers find them boring.
> Bill Safire bores, too—but like a dentist drilling for hidden decay. To this crusade Safire brings unique weapons: a sense of outrage over the "double standard applied to Nixon," and an ex-insider's optic on how power really works, and a pre-White House career in public relations that taught him to know flimflam and duplicity the way a mugger knows Central Park. The pale blue eyes narrow to laser beams and Safire's soft voice lilts with delight when he talks of that rare education. "I used to write government reports," he explains.

Magazine writing often considers creative impact. A writer, knowing the general rules full well, may deliberately break them to call up emotion or imagery in the reader. Newspaper writers seeking to emulate magazine writing must proceed more cautiously because their audience may be less well educated. Nonetheless, occasional unorthodoxy works well when handled skillfully.

Newsmagazines, yet again, offer examples of creative writing adaptable to newspapers of the future. Several years ago *Time* writer John Skow wrote a memorable cover story on another *New York Times* columnist, Russell Baker. Baker, a humorist, frequently uses interior monologue devices. Skow, in his profile, evoked Baker's style by imitating him. The story began:

> A man is getting ready for bed. He takes off his shoes, then his socks. He looks idly at his feet. Hmmm. They are feetlike, ordinary. They do not look interesting, but they look tired, and it is time to wedge them down between the sheets to the bed's own foot, where they will wiggle a bit and then fall dormant. The man lifts his feet into bed, but as he does he feels the tingle of a half-framed thought. Oddly, it is about umbrellas. . . .

The article continues in this fashion throughout the first graf. Second graf:

> Next day the man goes to his office, hangs up his coat and sits at a typewriter. Time passes. No typing occurs. The man's natural optimism wilts. He is vacant of ideas, except for one that grows progressively more attractive: this, finally, is the day for throwing himself out of the office window.

Several more grafs follow; the man recalls his feet-and-umbrella connection the night before. Then: "By now the man is typing at great speed. . . ."

Finally, the long, interior vignette, or scene setter, concludes with a new graf:

> It is 6 P.M., and once again the office window has been cheated of its prey. . . .

Thereafter, the story launches into a description of Russell Wayne Baker, 53, for the previous 17 years a humor columnist. He is dissected, put back together, biographed, mused about, and awed over for 6 pages. The story ends:

> He hustles to his typewriter and strums a slightly self-pitying ode to his own death by vegetable. In this column, he imagines an Associated Press report—POTATO MASHES MAN—and broods about his friends saying 'Poor devil, he never knew what hit him.' 'What did hit him?' 'Haven't you heard?' Baker's high-wire act has never been snappier. He finishes typing and thinks about making himself a drink.

Obviously, such a story resulted from lengthy and provocative questions asked by the interviewer. And, no doubt, considerable time spent observing. These are the techniques future newspaper writing will demand more often.

Chapter 15 Exercises

Because many aspects of newsmagazine writing foretells newspaper-magazine style, our exercises are drawn from newsmagazine experience.

Remember:

1. Condense, selecting key information from each source and meld into a new story. Do not become frustrated because you cannot fit everything into the shortened version.

2. Write in narrative fashion, with beginning, middle, and end, using transitions carefully to move from element to element.

3. Write leads that tease the reader or characterize the action.

4. Use colorful language and visual images, as well as anecdotes and quotations.

5. Keep in mind that magazine articles have a longer perspective than newspaper articles. Therefore you may wish to project farther into the future, or dip farther into the past.

Exercise 15.1

Reduce the following item, or file, to 250 words for a brief that could be used on a newspaper-magazine page. The brief would be similar to Time's *"Americana" or* Newsweek's *"Newsmakers" sections. These items highlight unusual people or events, and are treated lightheartedly. The following situation is taken from real life.*

Patricia Carol Blair's life became complicated when Patricia Carol Blaire applied for a Social Security card. A clerk decided they were the same person. The mistake led to 12 years of confusion and frustration, all complicated by government computers that could not tell Blair from Blaire.

The women shared one Social Security number, which meant when one got married, the Social Security computer assigned her new name to the other. And one's earnings were credited to the other's Internal Revenue Service records, causing a threat of legal action when fhe IRS failed to get the money it expected from the other.

"We were one and the same," said Blaire.

Blair and Blaire were both born on September 3, the former in 1961 in New York City and latter the next year in Boston. All was fine until Blaire applied for a Social Security number and was given a duplicate of Blair's number.

For a long time, Blair did not know someone shared her number. She just knew the IRS was asking for taxes on income she hadn't earned.

"I first sent them a letter, and then I called them," she said. "I stated I had never worked at these jobs. I wouldn't get any answer. Then I'd get another letter." One of the letters eventually demanded that she pay $2567 in back taxes.

Blaire, however, had known of the duplication for several years. It didn't help. She asked for a new number, but a Social Security worker in New York told her to keep using the one she had.

Eventually, the Social Security Administration realized the problem and issued Blaire a new number. But no one told her. Then Blaire discovered from a Social Security computer printout that Blair had moved to Brookline, Mass., not far from Blaire's home in Framingham.

Blaire renewed her efforts to untangle the mess—and finally, after more telephone calls, met with apparent success. Now the Social Security office and the IRS seem to believe Blair and Blaire are two people. Blair, who declines to reveal the troublesome number, said the Social Security office had assured her "they would send me a letter about how they straightened it out."

"And they told me not to bother going to court," she said yesterday. But the women, who have met, aren't convinced the troubles are over.

"I'll believe it when it happens," said Blair.

And Blaire?

"Someone told me, 'You gotta be careful, Pat. If she dies, they're going to come and bury you.'"

Exercise 15.2 *Reduce the following file to 250 words for a brief similar to Exercise 15.1. The following file is real, though names and places have been changed.*

Peter Principle, 18, valedictorian of his Marble, Minnesota, high school class, robbed a bank of $78,000 in August. Last week, an Itasca County Superior Court jury found him innocent, though he had been caught just outside the bank door with the money, an unloaded pistol, a fake bomb, and three hostages from the bank.

This week he enters the University of Minnesota, St. Paul, as a freshman. He has won a Regent's Scholarship there, Minnesota's highest honor award, though it carries only a nominal stipend, $100 per year.

Though Principle's secondary plea of not guilty was by reason of insanity, the jury appeared to place more stress on his defense "that he did not intend to deprive the bank of the money permanently." He had planned to invest the money in the stock market until "he had raised billions," testimony disclosed, then he would fund a foundation to colonize the stars. The purpose of this colonization was to relieve the earth of overpopulation and pollution.

Once the "forced loan" from the bank had been used as seed money to achieve this purpose, he had every intent of paying the bank back, his attorney, John Austin of Grand Rapids, successfully argued. Some testimony implied return of the loan could take 20 years.

Under Minnesota law, prosecutors must show that a defendant

had the specific intent to "steal permanently." Austin remarked in his closing arguments: "To me, that means forever."

Jurors, who initially deadlocked on a 6–6 count, eventually agreed with Austin. After the verdict, several said they were persuaded by the permanency issue, along with Principle's honor student status, lack of a prior record, and the substantial characterization of him as honest, sincere, idealistic, concerned with helping mankind. Perhaps, too, the "diminished capacity" testimony of defense psychiatrists played a role.

Principle's Calumet High School counselor testified that Principle was "the most mature student" he had had in 30 years.

"There's no question in my mind that when the jurors walked into the courtroom and saw this exemplary-looking young man, with his ruddy cheeks and pleasant face, they were looking for a way to exonerate him," remarked a member of the District Attorney's office when discussing the case with reporters.

Principle, bespectacled, 5"10', 150 pounds, with dark hair and hazel eyes, was also praised by his accomplice in the bank robbery, Dan Wayne, 22, Coleraine. The two had met while both worked at a local McDonald's restaurant, about 3 years ago.

Wayne, sentenced to 5 years probation and 400 hours of community volunteer work after he pleaded guilty September 15, praised Principle's sincerity in court testimony. "I had faith in him," testified the accomplice who acquired the gun and drove the car for Principle. Wayne's own record is "positive," according to a probation report.

"I asked Dan for his help," Principle said from his St. Paul campus residence. "I did most of the talking during the year or so we talked about world problems and space travel as a way of solving them."

Principle said his plan for raising money for an interstellar space travel foundation "jelled" about three or four months before the robbery in August. The active phase of the planning began about three weeks before the robbery. He picked Bovey First Trust Bank.

Once sufficient money was raised to fund a foundation, Principle expected scientists to overcome the need for spaceships to travel faster than the speed of light if they were to reach stars carrying men and machines.

Psychiatric testimony during the trial alluded to the possibility that Principle was suffering from "diminished capacity" to commit a crime. Defense psychologists and psychiatrists asserted he was operating under a delusion that controlled his reason, and that he had been so operating for over a year. However, jurors indicated the permanency issue had been the key to their decision.

The jury may have made legal history in acquitting an admitted bank robbery on that point. No one locally is familiar with a similar case. Deputy District Attorney Philip Conklin, who prosecuted the case, tried to show that the bank robbery was marked by "careful planning, then a step-by-step carrying out of the scheme." He said taking the money from the bank with the intention of investing it in outer space is "permanently depriving someone of their money, in common horse sense."

The jury was divided 6–6 on guilt or acquittal on the first ballot, according to foreman Justin Rhoades, a Calumet attorney. Later, jurors asked the court for a definition of "permanent." They were instructed to figure out the definition for themselves, from their own experience and as it applied to this case. The jurors favoring conviction were persuaded to shift to a unanimous verdict of innocent on grounds of reasonable doubt.

William Leeds, chief criminal deputy district attorney for Itasca County, said afterwards that he feared the decision might cause a rash of "Robin Hood" bank robberies. "This was a flukish decision. Normally the interpretation of 'intent to steal permanently' is considered to be 'subject to substantial risk of loss' to the owner. Future would be robbers may discover that commonly accepted legal definition is more forcefully presented next time."

One of the jurors, Martha Brooke of Marble, once robbed while working as a grocery clerk, said she was concerned with the possibility that anyone could go into a bank and demand money on the excuse that he intended to pay it back some time later. But Austin said Principle's incident was a special case because of his exemplary background. Brooke, and two reserve police officers also on the jury, apparently agreed.

Testimony at the trial indicated Principle had once thought of training as a minister; later his interests switched to physics, which probably will be his major in college. During high school he was also interested in theatre and photography.

While his trial was pending, he served as a research assistant in the psychiatric lab at Itasca General Hospital. His work involved regulation of enzymes found in the adrenal gland.

His father, Ralph, is a pharmacist and his mother, Ruth, an elementary school teacher.

Because he was acquitted, Principle is under no compulsion from the court to seek psychiatric counseling. However, he said that he is voluntarily seeking such counsel on a regular basis and plans to continue for as long as is necessary.

Though he is still concerned with problems of pollution and overpopulation, Principle indicated he no longer believes that he can solve them by himself.

211   EXERCISE 15.3

Exercise 15.3

Reduce the following 2 files to 350 words, as they would be for the "Medicine" section of Newsweek *or* Time, *or "Latest in Health" section of* U.S. News and World Report.

FILE 1

WASHINGTON, D.C.—A man made of spare human parts, a race of supermen and women, maybe even near immortality might not be all that remote.

A Georgetown University cryobiologist is working on the problems of freezing the cells of mammals and then bringing them "back to life." Dr. David Robinson is figuring out what it takes to keep the mammalian cells from being damaged by freezing and thawing and how some cells can completely repair themselves.

"Low-temperature biology is a young science," explains Robinson. "It hasn't gotten far yet, however. It can provide freeze preservation of single cells such as red blood cells, sperm and ova.

"In addition, freezing can be used for certain grafts such as skin and cornea where there is not the concern about keeping every single cell alive."

Attempts made at freeze preserving organs have so far proved unsuccessful because of the size and the difficulty of providing uniform cooling and warming for items that are large.

One way Robinson and other researchers have found to begin getting around the problem with heart cells is to add a protective agent. Ethylene glycol, which we use as anti-freeze for our autos, is one of these cryoprotective devices.

Using antifreeze to replace the water (which freezes and ruptures the cells), Robinson has frozen the cells with liquid nitrogen and later unfrozen them. These pacemaker cells, after being unfrozen, and rewarmed, spontaneously began beating rhythmically.

He feels that in the future preservation of whole mammalian hearts could be attempted using such compounds.

Robinson's work at Georgetown is basically involved in two areas. First, seeking an answer to the question of "what happens in heart cells when they are cooled to about 30 degrees Centigrade?" This temperature is sometimes used in certain types of heart surgery.

"Often the cells will stop beating normally and will jerk spasmodically," Robinson said. "This also happens in the intact organ and causes heart failure.

"In this research we've been able to come up with the idea that water on the cell's surface (in a two or three molecule layer) changes its structure radically, causing a severe reaction when the cell reaches the fibrillation temperature."

The second endeavor of the Georgetown research is dealing with cells in concentrations that approach the thickness of tissue.

"Some cells in these large groups become damaged and release their contents which include enzymes that are normally used to digest their food," Robinson said.

"These chemicals attack neighboring cells that survive the freezing. We feel if the enzymes can be inactivated there will be a higher survival rate of cells and we will have made an important step toward whole organ preservation."

The ramifications of being able to freeze whole organs or organisms are interesting.

"In regard to frozen sperm and ova and the first test tube baby, the road is now open to implant fertilized eggs, say from an Albert Einstein and a Gloria Steinem, in foster mothers . . . and thereby create a super race," he points out. "The area is very open to abuse and we must begin to think about the extent to which activities of this sort should be regulated."

He also noted that frozen sperm is already a great boon to the cattle industry where the frozen sperm of a prized bull can be used for many years after the death of the bull.

"As progress is made toward organ preservation, there is the chance, with proper typing, that a person could have multiple organ transplants—for instance, a heart, lungs, liver," Robinson explains. He feels this could be done successfully if organs could be typed, frozen and stored in large banks. A then near-perfect match could be made to the person needing the organ, thereby avoiding much of the rejection problems experienced today.

"The nervous system is the most complicated part of man and will therefore probably be the last to be successfully preserved," he continued. "However, when that is accomplished, science will be close to the preservation of a whole human.

"Then we have to ask some questions like, Why would we want to extend personal immortality? Is this the most sensible way to use our human resources? Earth's present problems certainly won't be helped if everyone can avoid death."

FILE 2

SAN FRANCISCO—Cryogenic specialist John Marks, a University of California Medical Center physician who has been conducting low-temperature medical research, confirms the optimism expressed by Dr. David Robinson of Georgetown University that freezing may be the answer to some medical problems.

Marks and others at UC Med Center have successfully used low-temperature techniques to increase patient survival rates in long, complicated procedures such as heart bypass surgery and kidney transplants. Operations of this sort have sometimes taken up to 12 hours.

Normally, patients have poor survival rates when surgery lasts for such lengthy periods. But about 8 years ago, research demonstrated that reducing body temperatures to 30 or 35 degrees C. for up to 6 hours could slow body function sufficiently to allow surgeons extra operating time, thus increasing the likelihood of patient survival.

To reduce temperature, ice packs are placed around the patient until the desired body temperature is reached. The patient then lies in a special tub, surrounded with cooled water that maintains the desired body temperature. Though not technically "frozen," the term "freezing the body," is often used in referring to this cryogenic surgical method.

Heart beat, respiratory action, blood flow, and other functions are dramatically slowed when the body is in this low-temperature state. This reduces the body's need for oxygen. After surgery, the patient's temperature is slowly brought back to 37 degrees C. and normal functions are resumed.

"If Dr. Robinson's group can learn to control cell reaction to these low temperatures, obviously, survival rates would be increased even more. As it is now, reducing body temperature does carry risks. The surgeon has to decide which is better for the patient: the risk of lengthy surgery at normal temperature, or low temperature," Marks explained.

He said that reducing cryogenic surgery risks would mean that more complicated surgical procedures could be undertaken in the future, opening the way for saving many lives now lost because such surgery is impractical today.

Exercise 15.4 *Reduce the following stories, plus reporter information, to 400 words for the weekend "Nation" section of a newspaper-magazine.*

STORY 1:

SAN CLEMENTE, California—Richard Nixon will be moving from what had formerly been the Western White House because he can no longer afford the upkeep. Inflation has pushed the maintenance of the twelve-room Spanish-style villa beyond the pocketbook of the former president.

However, after he leaves La Casa Pacific, the idyllic 26-acre retreat he purchased in 1969 for $1.5 million, no one need feel sorry for him. He will be moving just one mile down the road from San Clemente to Cypress Shores, a private compound, where he will be buying a $650,000 five-bedroom home.

As with La Casa Pacific, Nixon will have help from one of his long-time buddies, Charles ("Bebe") Rebozo in purchasing his new home. Rebozo has already purchased the house in Cypress Shores and plans to sell it soon to his friend, just as he did an earlier estate in the Florida Keys. Another pal, Robert Abplanalp, helped purchase the Western White House by going into partnership with Nixon.

La Casa Pacific has been sold to a group of Orange County businessmen for an undisclosed sum.

Nixon should have no trouble with his new house payments. He gets $80,000 in federal pension, plus royalties from memoirs and television appearances. (*Source: Los Angeles Times*)

REPORTER INFORMATION

After Nixon purchased the San Clemente property, $6.1 million worth of improvements were made to the estate at taxpayer expense. Much of this was used to install the communications links and elaborate security facilities required by a president and to provide working and sleeping accommodations for the large staff that accompanied Nixon whenever he left Washington. Among those expenditures were guard posts ($56,903), bulletproof glass windowscreens ($12,894), and the office complex ($1.7 million).

In addition, there were outlays for brightening up the estate for the Nixons and making life more comfortable: A flagpole, for example, cost $2,329; golf carts ran to $15,929; and a bill for decorative pillows came to $86.

The Nixons never did reimburse the government for these nonsecurity improvements. Whether they should, now that the estate is being sold, is under study. Peter Hickman, a spokesperson for the General Services Administration, said that "if anything there is government property, it remains government property." By that, Hickman meant that the government would remove what it could, including security equipment that might be used to protect Nixon at his new residence.

STORY 2:

Nearly all property surrounding the home in which Richard Nixon secluded himself after resigning the presidency will be used for single-family homes, say the three men who bought the 28-acre estate.

Donald Koll, George Argyros and Gavin Herbert said, however, that "La Casa Pacifica," known as the Western White House during Nixon's 5½ years as president, would be kept intact and "available for private residency" on its lushly landscaped 5.9 acres.

The three said Wednesday that single-family dwellings would be built on the remaining land if the city council and the California Coastal Commission approve.

The three men did not disclose the price they paid for the estate, which was owned by the Nixons and Robert Abplanalp, a close friend.

It was announced May 25 that the property had been sold and that the

Nixons would move into a $650,000 home in the closely guarded community next door, Cypress Shores.

In announcing the sale last month, Nixon spokesman Jack Brennan said the government was apparently no longer interested in having the place. Nixon had said in 1973 that he would eventually donate it to the public.

Nixon bought La Casa Pacifica, known also as the Cotton estate, in 1969 during his first year as president. Questions were raised thereafter as to the ownership of the land and the fairness of the assessed valuation assigned to it for tax purposes.

In addition, controversy arose over millions of dollars worth of improvements to the estate, which the Secret Service and the General Services Administration said were necessary for security.

Herbert is president of Allergan Pharmaceuticals in Irvine. He and Argyros, president of Arnel Development Co. in Santa Ana, are members of the United Republican Finance Committee, which sponsored a fund-raising event at the Nixons' home last Aug. 27. (*Source: Los Angeles Times*)

Exercise 15.5

Reduce the following three files, to 500 words. Treat as a weekend wrap-up.

FILE 1

TOLEDO, Ohio—Saying he never "completely gave up hope," a gaunt and disheveled William Nielson came home to a tearful reunion with his family yesterday after nearly 3.5 years as a captive of leftist guerrillas in Venezuela.

Nielson, more than 40 pounds under his normal weight of 190 pounds and with shoulder-length gray hair, met briefly with reporters at the Toledo airport after being flown from Venezuela.

"I'd like to go with my family to my house," he said, breaking into tears. Nielson had been a vice-president of ABC Box Company, Toledo, living in Caracas, Venezuela, at the time he was abducted in February 1979.

During the news conference, the 48-year-old Nielson said that sometimes he thought he would never be released by his captors.

"There were times when I lost hope, but I never completely gave up all hope," he said.

Nielson said he was moved 10 or 12 times during his captivity. He spent much of the time in the Venezuelan jungle, covered only by a plastic sheet strung among the trees. His last home was a 13-foot by 16.5-foot shack with walls of mud, a zinc roof and no windows.

"From the first day of the kidnaping until the last, they (the kidnapers) said that I would never be shot, never be killed. They would always release me alive. It was a political act and they were not assassins or murderers," he said.

Dressed in blue jeans that were too short and a blue short-sleeve sport shirt that was a little large for him, Nielson described his captivity.

"I had a table of about 3 feet by 1.5 foot to eat off of." He slept in a hammock and also had a metal chair.

The box company executive said he was not tortured and not mistreated but his legs were chained every night by his captors.

Nielson, who was manager of the box manufacturer's Venezuelan operations, was in good physical condition following the ordeal.

While in captivity, Nielson received only one letter written by his wife, Jane. It was in June, 1980. Otherwise, he said, he saw letters from her that had been reprinted in newspapers.

Nielson and his wife will observe their twenty-fifth wedding anniversary this month. They have three children.

The Venezuelan police, who were in the jungle apparently looking for a cattle rustler, rescued Nielson late Friday after a shootout. While taking Nielson to a nearby city, the police escort was ambushed by leftist guerillas and Nielson spent another day in the jungle before being rescued a second time Saturday.

He was abducted on February 27, 1979, when seven armed men broke into his Caracas home.

A previously unknown group calling itself the Argimiro Gabaldon Revolutionary Command claimed to have kidnaped Nielson.

The group had issued ransom demands in a series of messages.

The demands included payment of a $3.5 million ransom, payment of a $116 bonus to each of 2000 Venezuelan employees, donations to the poor, and publication of a political manifesto.

But the government prohibited negotiations with the kidnapers or compliance with their demands.

FILE 2

TOLEDO, Ohio—Executive William Nielson said Monday he doubts he would be able to recognize any of the South American guerrillas who held him captive for more than three years in Venezuela.

"I never saw a face uncovered. I never saw anyone without a mask," the 48-year-old Nielson said at a news conference Monday in the living room of his home in a Toledo suburb.

Nielson had returned home two days ago, after more than three years in the jungles as a captive of leftist guerrillas. He had been a vice-president of ABC Box Company, headquartering in Caracas, Venezuela, at the time he was abducted.

Shorn of the shoulder-length hair he came back with, the executive was dressed casually as he answered reporters' questions.

Nielson said he maintained his sanity by having faith in God and keeping up to date with current events. His captors supplied him with newspapers and magazines and discussed politics with him.

He said that during his captivity he was moved from place to place in the thick jungle. He said he was not surprised that he was not found sooner. "There are groups that have been in the jungle for 10, 12 years," he said.

Nielson said that although he talked politics with his captors, he never agreed with them. "They are of the ultraleftist Marxist revolutionary group," he said.

"They gave me the opportunity to express my opinion. They expressed their opinion. I can honestly say we never agreed," he said, adding that his captors "do not believe in anything except the dictatorship of the proletariat."

Nielson, former director of box manufacturing operations in Venezuela, was kidnapped from his home February 27, 1979 as he and his wife prepared to go to a party.

Rescued Saturday by Venezuelan police who were looking for cattle rustlers, he was whisked away from the country and flown to Toledo where he met his family at Toledo Express Airport early Sunday.

In the more than three years he was a prisoner, he said he wore the same pair of boots and only changed clothes when his garments wore out.

He said he never was seriously ill during his captivity. But at one point he did have a slight skin infection that resisted healing, he said. Nielson said his kidnappers brought him medicine and gave him injections. After a time, the infection went away, he said.

But despite this attention, he said, "I don't believe I have any real affection for any of them."

Nielson spoke nothing but Spanish during his ordeal because none of his captors spoke English. He apologized during the news conference for what he thought was a slowness to express himself. He said he still thinks in Spanish and must translate in his mind back to English before speaking.

FILE 3

CARACAS—Two men and a woman have been arrested in the kidnaping of Ohio executive William F. Nielson, Venezuelan police said yesterday.

The suspects were arrested Sunday near the small shack in southeast Venezuela where Nielson, a vice-president of ABC Box

Company, was found Friday. He had been kidnaped 40 months ago by leftist guerrillas who held him for $3.5 million ransom.

Jorge Sosa Chacin, head of the Technical Judicial Police—Venezuela's equivalent of the FBI—told reporters "Police also found a large quantity of arms . . . near the place where Nielson was found.

"Based on the investigation, two months ago I knew that Nielson was alive," Sosa Chacin said. "But I had absolutely no idea where he was."

Appendix A AP Stylebook (abbreviated)

Use The Associated Press Stylebook. The following is a beginning. This is reprinted, courtesy of Associated Press.

abbreviations and acronyms A few universally recognized abbreviations are sometimes required. Others are acceptable but, in general, avoid alphabet soup.

Apply the same guidelines to acronyms—pronounceable words formed from the letters in a series of words: *ALCOA, NATO, radar, scuba,* etc.

Guidelines:

1. Use *Dr., Gov., Lt. Gov., Mr., Mrs., Rep., the Rev., Sen.,* and abbreviate certain military titles before a name outside direct quotations. Spell out all except Mr., Mrs. and Dr. before a name in direct quotations. See titles.

2. Abbreviate junior or senior after a person's name. Abbreviate company, corporation, incorporated and limited after a company name.

3. Use *A.D., B.C., a.m., p.m., No.* and abbreviate certain months with the day of the month. See months.
   Right: In 450 *B.C.;* at 9:30 *a.m.;* in room *No.* 6; on *Sept.* 16.

219

Wrong: Early this *a.m.* he asked for the *No.* of your room. The abbreviations are correct only with the figures.

Right: Early this *morning* he asked for the *number* of your room.

4. Abbreviate avenue, boulevard and street in numbered addresses: He lives on Pennsylvania *Avenue.* He lives at 1600 Pennsylvania *Ave.* See addresses.

5. Certain states, the United States and the Union of Soviet Socialist Republics (but not other nations) are sometimes abbreviated. See state(s).

6. Some organizations are widely recognized by their initials: *CIA, FBI, GOP, TVA,* which are acceptable. Even then, an abbreviation is not always necessary. If it fits the occasion, use *Federal Bureau of Investigation,* for example, rather than *FBI.*

    Do not use an abbreviation or acronym in parentheses after a full name. If the abbreviation would not be clear without this arrangement, do not use it. Do not reduce names to unfamiliar acronyms solely to save a few words.

7. Follow the listings in this book for capital letters and periods. For words not in this book, use the first-listed abbreviation in Webster's New World Dictionary.

academic degrees If it is necessary to establish credentials, avoid an abbreviation. Make it: a *bachelor's* degree, a *master's* (note the apostrophe), a *doctorate* in psychology.

Use *B.A., M.A., LL.D., Ph.D.,* etc., only when many listings would make the preferred form cumbersome. Use the abbreviation only after a full name—never after just a last name.

Set an abbreviation off by commas: *Mary Smith, Ph.D., spoke.* But don't use both *Dr.* and an abbreviation in the same reference. See doctor.

Wrong: *Dr.* Jane Jones, *Ph.D.*

Right: *Dr.* Jane Jones, *a chemist.*

For spelling and abbreviations, follow the first listing in Webster's New World Dictionary.

academic departments Lowercase except for proper nouns or adjectives: *the department of history, the history department, the department of English, the English department.*

academic titles Capitalize and spell out such formal titles as professor, dean, president, chancellor, chairman, etc., before a name. Lowercase elsewhere.

Lowercase such modifiers as history in *history* Professor Oscar Handlin or department in *department* Chairman Jerome Wiesner.

addresses Use *Ave., Blvd.* and *St.* with a numbered address: 1600 Pennsylvania *Ave.* Spell out without a number: Pennsylvania *Avenue.*

Lowercase standing alone or in plural uses: the *avenue,* Massachusetts and Pennsylvania *avenues.*

Do not abbreviate similar words, such as alley, drive, road and terrace. Capitalize as part of a formal name: Printers *Alley.* Lowercase standing alone or in plural uses: the *alley,* Broadway and Tin Pan *alleys.*

Use figures for an address number: *9* Morningside Circle.

Spell out and capitalize First through Ninth as street names; use figures with two letters for 10th and above: 7 *Fifth* Ave., 100 *21st* St.

Abbreviate compass points that indicate directional ends of a street or quadrants of a city in a numbered address: 220 *E.* 42nd St., 600 K St. *N.W.* Do not abbreviate if the number is omitted: *East* 42nd Street, K Street *Northwest.*

AFL-CIO Preferred in all references for the American Federation of Labor and Congress of Industrial Organizations. Headquarters is in Washington.

ages Always use figures. When the context does not require *years* or *years old,* the figure is presumed to be years.

Hyphenate as a compound modifier before a noun or as a noun substitute. Ages in apposition are set off by commas.

A 5-year-old boy. The boy is 5 years old. The boy, 7, has a sister, 10. The woman, 26, has a daughter 2 months old. The law is 8 years old. The race is for 3-year-olds. The woman is in her 30s (no apostrophe).

air base Two words. Use *air force base* in the United States and *air base* abroad: *Lackland Air Force Base, Texas. Clark Air Base, Philippines.*

On second reference: *the Air Force base, the air base* or *the base.* Do not abbreviate even in datelines:
LACKLAND AIR FORCE BASE, Texas (UPI)—
CLARK AIR BASE, Philippines (UPI)—

aircraft Use a hyphen to add figures to letters; no hyphen to add a letter to figures: *B-1, BAC-111, C-5A, DC-10, FH-227, F-4, F-86 Sabre, L-1011, MiG-21, Tu-144, 727-100C, 747, 747B, VC-10.*

For other elements of a name, follow the terminology adopted by the manufacturer or user. If in doubt, consult Jane's All the World's Aircraft.

Do not use quotation marks for aircraft names: *Air Force One, the Spirit of St. Louis, Concorde.* For plurals: *DC-10s, 727s.* But: *747B's.* For sequence of aircraft, spacecraft and missiles, use Arabic numerals, but no hyphens: *Apollo 10.*

Use *engine,* not *motor,* for the units that propel aircraft: a *twin-engine* plane (not twin-engined). Use *jet plane* or *jetliner* to describe only those aircraft driven solely by jet engines. Use *turboprop* to describe an aircraft on which the jet engine is geared to a propeller. Turboprops are sometimes called *propjets.*

air force Capitalize references to U.S. forces: *the U.S. Air Force, the Air Force, Air Force regulations.* Do not use *USAF.*

Many nations do not use *air force* as a proper name. For consistency, lowercase all others: the Canadian *air force.*

airport Capitalize as part of a proper name: *La Guardia Airport, Newark International Airport.*

The first name of a person and *international* may be deleted while the remainder is capitalized: *John F. Kennedy International Airport, Kennedy International Airport* or *Kennedy Airport,* as appropriate.

Do not make up proper names such as Boston *Airport.* The proper name is Logan International Airport. The Boston *airport* is acceptable.

a.m., p.m. Lowercase, with periods. Note: *10 a.m. this morning* is redundant.

Anglo- Always capitalized. Hyphenate with a capitalized suffix: *Anglomania, Anglophile, Anglo-American, Anglo-Catholic, Anglo-Indian, Anglo-Saxon.*

ante- Hyphenate with a capitalized word or to avoid a double e: *ante-Victorian.* Elsewhere, follow Webster's New World, hyphenating words not listed there.

anti- Hyphenate all except the following words:

antibiotic	antigen	antipasto	antiserum
antibody	antihistamine	antipathy	antithesis
anticlimax	antiknock	antiperspirant	antitoxin
antidote	antimatter	antiphon	antitrust
antifreeze	antiparticle	antiseptic	antitussive

Hyphenated words, many of them exceptions to Webster's New World, include: anti-aircraft, anti-bias, anti-inflation, anti-intellectual, anti-labor, anti-slavery, anti-social, anti-war.

capitalization Avoid unnecessary capitals. Use a capital letter only if you can justify it by one of these guidelines:

1. Capitalize proper names of a specific person, place or thing: *John, Mary, America, Boston, England.*

2. Capitalize common nouns such as party, river, street and west as an integral part of a proper name: Democratic *Party,* Mississippi *River,* Fleet *Street, West* Virginia. Lowercase common nouns that stand alone: *the party, the river, the street.* Lowercase common noun elements in all plural uses: the Democratic and Republican *parties,* the Hudson and Mississippi *rivers;* Main and State *streets.*
   Capitalize popular, unofficial names that serve as a proper name: *the Combat Zone* (a section of Boston), *the Badlands* (of South Dakota).

3. Capitalize words derived from a proper noun and still dependent on it for their meaning: *American, Christianity, English, French, Marxism, Shakespearean.*
   Lowercase words derived from a proper noun but no longer dependent on it for their meaning: *french fries, herculean, manhattan* (cocktail), *malapropism, pasteurize, quixotic, venetian blind.*

4. Capitalize the first word in every sentence.
   In poetry, capital letters are used for the first words of some phrases that would not be capitalized in prose. See poetry.

5. Capitalize the principal words in the names of books, movies, plays, poems, etc. See composition titles.

6. Capitalize formal titles before a name: Lowercase mere job descriptions and formal titles standing alone or set off by commas. See titles.

7. Capitalize some abbreviations and acronyms. See abbreviations and acronyms.

8. Capitalize the interjection *O* and the pronoun *I.*

China When used alone, it refers to the mainland nation. Use *People's Republic of China, Communist China* or *mainland China* only when needed to distinguish the mainland and its government from Taiwan. Restrict *Red China* to quoted matter. Peking stands alone in datelines. Others:

SHANGHAI, China (UPI)—

For datelines on stories from the island of Taiwan:

TAIPEI, Taiwan (UPI)—

In the body of a story, use *Taiwan.* Use *Nationalist China* only when needed to distinguish the island from the mainland. Use the formal name of the government, *Republic of China,* only when required for legal precision.

composition titles In titles of books, movies, plays, poems, programs, songs, works of art, etc., capitalize the first word and all succeeding words except articles and short (four letters or less) conjunctions or prepositions. Use quotation marks for most:

"The Star-Spangled Banner," "The Rise and Fall of the Third Reich," "Gone with the Wind," "Of Mice and Men," "For Whom the Bell Tolls," "Time After Time," the NBC-TV "Today" show, the "CBS Evening News," "The Mary Tyler Moore Show."

Use no quotation marks for the titles of a sacred book or its parts: *the Bible, the New Testament, the Koran, the Apocrypha, the Torah, the Talmud;* or reference works: *Jane's All the World's Aircraft, Encyclopaedia Britannica, Webster's New World Dictionary, the World Almanac, the UPI Stylebook.*

Translate a foreign title into English unless it is known to Americans by its foreign name: *Rousseau's "War."* Not: *Rousseau's "La Guerre."* Also: *Leonardo da Vinci's "Mona Lisa." Mozart's "The Marriage of Figaro" and "The Magic Flute."* But: *"Die Walkuro" and "Gotterdammerung" from Wagner's "The Ring of the Nibelungen."*

dates Use figures without letters: *April 1.* Not: *April 1st.*

When a month is used with a specific date, use the abbreviations Jan., Feb., Aug., Sept., Oct., Nov. and Dec. Spell out other months.

When a phrase lists only a month and a year, do not separate with commas. When a phrase refers to a month, day and year, set off the year with commas.

January 1972 was a cold month. Jan. 2 was the coldest day of the month. Feb. 14, 1976, was the target date. His birthday is May 15.

daylight-saving time Not *savings.* Note the hyphen. When linking the term with a time zone: *Eastern Daylight Time, Pacific Daylight Time,* etc.

Lowercase daylight-saving time in all uses and daylight time standing alone.

A federal law specifies that daylight time applies from 2 A.M. on the last Sunday of April until 2 A.M. on the last Sunday of October in areas that do not specifically exempt themselves. See **time**.

days Capitalize them: Monday, Tuesday, etc. Other guidelines:

1. Spell out days of the week in stories for morning newspapers. Use *today, tonight,* etc. but not *yesterday* or *tomorrow,* for afternoon editions. Avoid an awkward placement: *The police jailed Tuesday,* etc.

2. Avoid an unnecessary use of *last* or *next.* Past, present or future tense are an adequate indication of which day is meant.
   Wordy: It happened *last* Tuesday.
   Better: It happened Tuesday.

3. Do not abbreviate, except in tabular format (three letters, without periods): *Sun, Mon, Tue, Wed, Thu, Fri, Sat.*

See **time**.

decimal units Use a period and figures to indicate decimal amounts. Carry decimals to two places. See fractions.

dimensions Use figures and spell out inches, feet, yards, etc. to indicate depth, height, length and width. Hyphenate adjectival forms before nouns.
He is 5 feet 6 inches tall, the 5-foot-6-inch man, the 5-foot-6 man, the 5-foot man, the basketball team signed a 7-footer. The car is 17 feet long, 6 feet wide and 5 feet high. The rug is 9 feet by 12 feet, the 9-by-12 rug. The storm left 5 inches of snow.
Use an apostrophe to indicate feet and quotation marks to indicate inches (5'6") only in very technical contexts.

diocese The district under a bishop's jurisdiction. Lowercase unless part of a proper name: the *diocese* of Rochester, the Rochester *diocese, the diocese.* But: the Eastern *Diocese* of the Armenian Church of America. See Episcopal Church and Roman Catholic Church.

directions Always lowercase compass points (north, south, northeast, northern, etc.) that indicate direction: He drove *west.* The cold front is moving *east.* Elsewhere:

1. Capitalize compass points that designate regions of the world or United States: The *North* was victorious. The *South* will rise again. Settlers from the *East* went *west* in search of new lives.

Also: *the Far East, the Eastern establishment, the Eastern Hemisphere, the Middle East, the Mideast, the Midwest, the Northeast, a Northerner, the North Woods, a Northern liberal, Southeast Asia, a Southern strategy, the South Pacific, the West, a Western businessman, Western Europe, the Western Hemisphere, the Western United States, the West Coast* (the region; lowercase west coast for the physical coastline itself.)

2. Capitalize compass points as part of a proper name: *North America, the South Pole, North Dakota, Northern Ireland, West Virginia, the Eastern Shore* (see separate entry).

3. Lowercase compass points with other nations except to designate a politically divided nation: *northern France, eastern Canada*. But: *East Germany, South Korea*.

4. In general, lowercase compass points to describe a section of a state or city; *western Texas, southern Atlanta*. But they may be capitalized if a particular section has a widely known popular name: *Southern California, South Side* (Chicago), *Lower East Side* (New York). If in doubt, use lowercase.

director Capitalize as a formal title before a name: *FBI Director J. Edgar Hoover*. Lowercase as a job description: *company director Joseph Warren*.

district Do not abbreviate. Use a figure and capitalize to form a proper name: *District 3, the 2nd District, the 1st Congressional District*. Lowercase standing alone: *the district, the congressional district*.

district attorney Do not abbreviate. Capitalize as a formal title before a name: *District Attorney Hamilton Burger*. Use *DA* (no periods) only in quoted matter.

District of Columbia If used with Washington, abbreviate as D.C. Spell out when used alone. Use *the district*, not *D.C.*, on second reference.

doctor Spell out if not a title: An apple a day keeps the *doctor* away.
Use *Dr.* (or *Drs.* in plural) as a title before the name of a physician, including direct quotations: *Dr. Jonas Salk*. Drop the title after first reference.
Dr. may also be used with *the Rev.* in first reference to Protestant clergy who have doctor of divinity degrees: *the Rev. Dr. Norman Vincent Peale*.
Do not use *Dr.* for those who hold only honorary doctorates. With

other doctorate degrees, use *Dr.* with care; the public often identifies *Dr.* only with physicians.
See **academic degrees.**

dollars Always lowercase. Use figures and the *$* sign in all except casual references or amounts without a figure: *The book cost $4. Dad, please give me a dollar. Dollars are flowing overseas.*

For specified amounts, it takes a singular verb: *He said $500,000 is what they want.*

For amounts of more than $1 million, use the *$* and figures up to two decimal places. Do not use hyphens: *He is worth $4.35 million. He is worth exactly $4,351,242. He proposed a $300 billion budget.*

The form for amounts less than $1 million: *$4, $6.35, $25, $500, $1,000, $650,000.*

eve Capitalize a holiday: *Christmas Eve.* But: *the eve of Christmas.*

Fahrenheit The temperature scale commonly used in the United States, after Gabriel Daniel Fahrenheit, a German physicist who designed it. In it, the freezing point of water is 32 degrees and the boiling point is 212 degrees at sea level.

The forms, if needed: *86 degrees Fahrenheit* or *86 F* (note the space and no period after the F).

To convert to Celsius, subtract 32 from the Fahrenheit figure, multiply by 5 and divide by 9 (77 minus 32 equals 45 × 5 equals 225 divided by 9 equals 25).

FBI Acceptable in all references for Federal Bureau of Investigation.

federal Lowercase unless part of a proper name: *federal assistance, federal court, the federal government, a federal judge, federal Judge John Sirica.* But: *the Federal Trade Commission* (the name of a federal agency), *the Federal Express* (a private company).

felony, misdemeanor A *felony* is a serious crime. A *misdemeanor* is a minor offense. Further distinctions vary from jurisdiction to jurisdiction.

At the federal level a misdemeanor carries a potential penalty of no more than a year in jail. A felony carries a potential penalty of more than a year in prison. Anyone convicted of a felony is a felon even if no time is actually spent in confinement. See the prison, jail entry.

fiberglass The trademark is *Fiberglas* (single s).

filibuster   To *filibuster* is to make long speeches to obstruct legislation. A legislator who uses such methods is also a filibuster, not a filibusterer.

Filipinos   The people of the Philippines.

fiscal year   A 12-month period used for bookkeeping purposes. The federal government's fiscal year starts three months ahead of the calendar year. Fiscal 1978, for example, runs from Oct 1, 1977, to Sept. 30, 1978.

flash   An emergency signal to editors that outstanding news is breaking. No more than 10 words, a flash has priority to break any other wire story. The slugword on a flash is *bc-flash.* Use no date or logotype in sending a flash. A flash is sent without capital letters in copy.

A flash stands alone. It does not relead an existing story and it is not itself reled. It must not include a *more* slug.

A flash must be followed immediately with a bulletin—releading if an existing story is affected; establishing a new story if no existing story is affected.

Example of a flash:

a315
   f w
      bc-flash
         washington—nixon resigns.

food   Most food names are lowercase: apples, cheese, peanut butter.

But capitalize brand names and trademarks: Roquefort cheese, Tabasco sauce, Smithfield ham.

Many words derived from proper names are capitalized: eggs Benedict, Bloody Mary, Salisbury steak. Many are lowercase: french fries, graham crackers.

foot   The basic unit of length commonly used in the United States. A foot is exactly 30.48 centimeters, usually rounded to 30 centimeters. For most conversions, multiply by 30 (5 feet $\times$ 30 equals 150 centimeters). To be more exact, multiply by 30.48 (5 $\times$ 30.48 equals 152.4 centimeters). To convert to meters, multiply by 0.3 (5 feet $\times$ 0.3 equals about 1.5 meters). To be more exact, multiply by 0.3048.

foreign governmental bodies   Capitalize the name of a specific foreign government agency: *the French Foreign Ministry.* Or simply: *the Foreign Ministry.* But: *the ministry.*

foreign legislative bodies Capitalize the name of a foreign legislative body: Diet (in Japan), Supreme Soviet (in the Soviet Union), Knesset (in Israel), Parliament (in Britain), etc.

Capitalize also if an English equivalent is used in a clear and specific reference.

foreign particles Lowercase particles (de, la, von, etc.) as part of a given name: *Charles de Gaulle, General de Gaulle, Baron Manfred von Richthofen.* Capitalize only at the start of a sentence: *De Gaulle spoke to von Richthofen.*

foreign words Many words and abbreviations with foreign origins, such as *bon voyage* and *etc.,* are widely accepted in English and may be used without explanation if they are clear in the context.

Words and phrases not widely accepted in English—they are marked in Webster's New World with a double dagger (‡)—may be used if they are placed in quotation marks and an explanation is provided: *"ad astra per aspera,"* a Latin phrase meaning *"to the stars through difficulties."*

former Always lowercase: *former* President Nixon. Do not use former before a title to denote the action of a person who previously held the title.

> *Wrong:* In 1968 former Gov. Nelson Rockefeller ran for president. (He was not a former governor at that time.)
> *Right:* In 1968 Gov. Nelson Rockefeller ran for president.

fort Do not abbreviate for cities or for military installations:

> FORT LAUDERDALE, Fla. (UPI)—City fathers met today.
> FORT BRAGG, N.C. (UPI)—Military leaders met today.

forty, forty-niner *'49er* is also acceptable.

Fourth of July, July Fourth The federal legal holiday is observed on Friday if July 4 falls on a Saturday, on Monday if it falls on a Sunday.

fractions Whenever practical, convert fractions to decimals. See decimals. Fractions are preferred, however, in stories about stocks and in recipes.

When using fractional characters, remember that most newspaper type fonts can set only ⅛, ¼, ⅜, ½, ⅝, ¾ and ⅞ as one unit. For mixed numbers, use 1½, 2⅝, etc., with a space between the whole number and the fraction. Other fractions require a hyphen and individual figures, with a space between the whole number and the fraction: *1 3-16, 2 1-3, 5 9-10.*

If fractions must be spelled out, hyphenate them: *two-thirds, three-fourths, twenty-seven-hundredths.*

geographic names The authority for spelling place names in the U.S. states and territories is the U.S. Postal Service Directory of Post Offices. But do not use the postal abbreviations for state names (see separate entries), and abbreviate saint as St. and sainte as Ste. in U.S. names.

The first source for the spelling of all foreign place names is Webster's New World Dictionary. Use the first-listed spelling if an entry gives more than one. If the dictionary provides different spellings in separate entries, use the spelling that is followed by a full description of the location. Also:

1. Use West Germany, East Germany, etc. for divided nations.
2. Use Cameroon, not Cameroons or Cameroun.
3. Use Maldives, not Maldive Islands.
4. Use Sri Lanka, not Ceylon.

The last three exceptions conform with the practices of the United Nations and the U.S. Board of Geographic Names.

If the dictionary does not have an entry, use the first-listed spelling in the Columbia Lippincott Gazetteer of the World.

Follow the styles adopted by the United Nations and the U.S. Board of Geographic Names on new cities, new independent nations and nations that change their names. If the two do not agree, the news services will announce a common policy.

Capitalize common nouns as an integral part of a proper name, but lowercase them standing alone: *Pennsylvania Avenue, the avenue; the Philippine Islands, the islands; the Mississippi River, the river; the Gulf of Mexico, the gulf.*

Lowercase all common nouns that are not part of a specific proper name: *the Pacific islands, the Swiss mountains, Chekiang province.*

girl Applicable until 18th birthday is reached. Use woman or young women afterward.

GOP See **Grand Old Party.**

gospel Lowercase unless referring to the first four books of the New Testament: a famous *gospel* singer, the *Gospel of St. John*, the *Gospels.*

government Always lowercase. Never abbreviate. A *government* is an established system of political administration: *the U.S. government.*

A *junta* is a group or council that often rules after a coup: A military *junta* controls the country. A junta becomes a government after it establishes a system of political administration.

Regime is a synonym for political system: *a democratic regime, an authoritarian regime.* Do not use it to mean government or junta. For example, use Franco *government* in referring to the government of Spain under Francisco Franco. Not: Franco *regime.* But: The Franco *government* was an authoritarian *regime.*

governmental bodies Capitalize the full proper names of governmental agencies, departments and offices: *the U.S. Department of State, the Georgia Department of Human Resources, the Boston City Council, the Chicago Fire Department.* Retain capitals if the specific meaning is clear without the jurisdiction: *the Department of State, the Department of Human Resources, the state Department of Human Resources, the City Council, the Fire Department, the city Fire Department.* Elsewhere:

1. Capitalize names flip-flopped to delete *of*: *the State Department, the Human Resources Department.*

2. Capitalize widely used popular names: *Walpole State Prison* (the proper name is Massachusetts Correctional Institution-Walpole).

3. Lowercase when the reference is not specific: *Nebraska has no state senate.*

4. Lowercase generic terms standing alone or in plural uses: *the Boston and Chicago city councils, the department.* See foreign governmental bodies and foreign legislative bodies.

governor Use *Gov.* (plural: *Govs.*) as a formal title before a name on first reference in regular text. Drop the title on second reference. Capitalize and spell out as a formal title before a name in direct quotations. Lowercase and spell out in all other uses.

graduate *(v.)* A person may *graduate* from a school. It is correct, but unnecessary, to say he *was graduated.* But, do not drop *from* in: John Adams graduated *from* Harvard.

granddad, granddaughter, grandfather, grandmother, grandson

grand jury   Always lowercase: *a Los Angeles County grand jury, the grand jury.*

gray   Not grey. But: *greyhound, Greyhound bus.*

Hanukkah   The Jewish Feast of Lights, an eight-day commemoration of the rededication of the Temple by the Maccabees after their victory over the Syrians. It usually occurs in December, but sometimes falls in late November. This spelling is an exception to Webster's New World Dictionary.

heavenly bodies   Capitalize the proper names of planets, stars, etc.: *Mars, Arcturus, the Big Dipper, Aries, Halley's comet.*
   Lowercase sun and moon, but if their Greek names are used, capitalize them: *Helios and Luna.* Lowercase nouns and adjectives derived from the proper names of planets and other heavenly bodies: earthling, jovian, lunar, martian, solar, venusian.

homicide   The killing of one human by another.
   Murder is malicious or premeditated homicide. Do not say a victim was murdered until someone is convicted of murder. Instead, use *killed* or *slain.* Do not describe someone as a *murderer* until convicted of the charge in court.
   Manslaughter is homicide without malice or premeditation.
   A *killer* is anyone who kills with a motive of any kind.
   An *assassin* is a killer of a politically important person.
   To *execute* is to kill in accordance with a legally imposed sentence.

house   Lowercase most nongovernmental uses: a fraternity *house,* a *house* of worship, the *house* of Tudor, bring down the *house,* like a *house* on fire.
   Capitalize proper names of organizations and institutions: *the House of Delegates of the American Medical Association, the House of Bishops of the Episcopal Church.*
   Capitalize a reference to a specific legislative body: *the U.S. House of Representatives, the Massachusetts House, the Virginia House of Delegates, the House of Commons, the House of Lords, the House of Burgesses.* Or:

   BOSTON (UPI)—The House adjourned for the year.

   Lowercase plural uses: the Massachusetts and Rhode Island *houses.*

lawyer   A general term for a person trained in the law. Do not use *lawyer* as a formal title.

An *attorney* is a person legally appointed or empowered to act for another, usually, but not always, a lawyer. An *attorney at law* (no hyphens) is a lawyer.

A *barrister* is an English lawyer especially trained, who appears exclusively as a trial lawyer in higher courts. He is retained by a solicitor, not directly by the client. There is no equivalent in the United States.

A *counselor* is one who conducts a case in court, usually, but not always, a lawyer. A *counselor-at-law* (hyphenated) is a lawyer. *Counsel* is frequently used collectively for a group of counselors.

A *solicitor* in England is a lawyer who performs legal services for the public and appears in lower courts but does not have the right to appear in higher courts, which is reserved to barristers.

A *solicitor* in the United States is a lawyer employed by a governmental body. It is generally a job description, but in some agencies it may be a formal title.

Solicitor general is the formal title for a chief law officer (where there is no attorney general) or for the chief assistant to the law officer (when there is an attorney general). Capitalize when used before a name.

legislative titles Capitalize formal titles before names; lowercase elsewhere. Use Rep., Reps., Sen. and Sens. before names in regular text, but spell them out in direct quotations. See **party affiliation.**

Spell out other legislative titles (assemblyman, assemblywoman, city councilor, delegate, etc.) in all uses. Other guidelines:

1. Use *U.S.* or *state* before a title only if necessary to avoid confusion: *U.S. Sen. Herman Talmadge spoke with state Sen. Hugh Carter.*

2. The use of a title such as Rep. or Sen. in first reference is normal in most stories. It is not mandatory, however, provided the title is given later in the story: *Barry Goldwater endorsed President Ford today. The Arizona senator said he believes the president deserves another term.*

3. Do not use legislative titles before a name on second reference unless they are part of a direct quotation.

4. Use *congressman* and *congresswoman* as capitalized formal titles before a name only in direct quotation.

5. Capitalize formal, organizational titles before a name: *Speaker Thomas P. O'Neill, Majority Leader Robert Byrd, Minority Leader John Rhodes, Democratic Whip James Wright, Chairman John Sparkman of the Senate Foreign Relations Committee, President Pro Tem John Stennis.*

legislature   Capitalize with or without a state name if a specific reference is clear: *the Kansas Legislature.* Or:

TOPEKA, Kan. (UPI)—The state Legislature adjourned today.

Legislature is not part of the proper name in many states, but it is acceptable in any: *the Virginia Legislature* (the proper name is General Assembly). Lowercase legislature in all generic and plural references: *No legislature has approved the amendment, the Arkansas and Colorado legislatures.*

In 49 states, the legislature consists of two bodies, a Senate and another body, such as House or Assembly. The Nebraska Legislature is a unicameral body.

magazine names   Capitalize, without quotation marks. Lowercase magazine unless it is part of the publication's formal title: *Harper's Magazine, Newsweek magazine, Time magazine.* Check the masthead if in doubt.

mass   It is celebrated, said or sung. Lowercase in all uses: *high mass, low mass, requiem mass.* In Eastern Orthodox churches, the term is *liturgy* or *divine liturgy.*

M.D.   *Physician* or *surgeon* is preferred. See doctor.

Medicare   The federal health care insurance program for people aged 65 and over, and for the disabled. In Canada, Medicare refers to the national health insurance program.

military academies   Capitalize Air Force Academy, Coast Guard Academy, Military Academy, Naval Academy. Lowercase standing alone or in plural uses: the *academy,* the Army, Navy and Air Force *academies.*

Cadet is the proper title on first reference for men and women enrolled at the Army and Air Force academies. *Midshipman* is the proper title for men and women enrolled at the Navy and Coast Guard academies.

Drop the title on second reference, using Miss, or Ms. if she prefers it, for a woman.

military titles   Capitalize a military rank as a formal title before a name on first reference. Lowercase elsewhere. Drop the title on subsequent references.

Do not abbreviate any title standing alone or in a direct quotation.

In some cases it is pertinent to explain a title: Army Sgt. Maj. John Jones, *who holds the Army's highest rank for enlisted men,* said the attack was unprovoked.

Do not capitalize or abbreviate job descriptions, such as machinist, radarman, torpedoman, etc.

To form plurals of the abbreviations, add s to the principal element in the title: *Majs., Maj. Gens., Sgts. Maj., Specs. 4, Pfcs., Pvts.*

military units Use figures and capitalize the key words when linked with the figures: *1st Infantry Division* (or the 1st Division), *5th Battalion, 395th Field Artillery, 7th Fleet.* But: *the division, the battalion, the artillery, the fleet.*

months Capitalize the names of months in all uses. Use the abbreviations *Jan., Feb., Aug., Sept., Oct., Nov.* and *Dec.* with a specific date. Do not abbreviate any month standing alone or with a year alone.

In tabular material, use three letters without a period: *Jan, Feb, Mar, Apr, May, Jun, Jul, Aug, Sep, Oct, Nov, Dec.*

See dates for punctuation guidelines.

Moslems The preferred term to describe adherents of Islam. But use Muslim for certain U.S. organizations, such as the Black Muslims, and their members.

mph Acceptable in all references for miles per hour or miles an hour.

NAACP Acceptable in all references for National Association for the Advancement of Colored People. Headquarters is in New York.

nationalities Capitalize the proper names of nationalities, peoples, races, tribes, etc: *Arab, Arabic, African, Afro-American, American, Caucasian, Cherokee, Chinese, Eskimo, French Canadian, Gypsy, Japanese, Jew, Jewish, Latin, Negro, Nordic, Oriental, Sioux, Swede,* etc.

Lowercase descriptive words: *black, white, yellow,* etc.

Lowercase such derogatory terms as *honky, nigger,* etc. Use them only in direct quotations when essential to the story. See race.

No. Use this abbreviation for number with a figure to indicate position or rank: *No. 1 man, No. 3 choice.*

Do not use in street addresses, with this exception: *No. 10 Downing St.,* the office and residence of Britain's prime minister.

Do not use *No.* In the names of schools: *Public School 19.*

numerals A numeral is a figure, letter, word or group of words expressing a number.

Roman numerals use the letters *I, V, X, L, C, D* and *M.* Use Roman numerals for wars and to show personal sequence for animals and people: *World War II, Native Dancer II, King George VI, Pope John XXIII.*

Arabic numerals use the figures *1, 2, 3, 4, 5, 6, 7, 8, 9* and *0.* Use Arabic forms unless Roman numerals are specifically required.

people, persons Use *people* when speaking of a large or uncounted number of individuals: Thousands of *people* attended the fair. Some rich *people* pay no taxes. What will *people* say? Do not use *persons* in this sense.

Persons is usually used for a relatively small number of people who can be counted, but *people* often can be substituted.

Right: There were 20 *persons* in the room.
Right: There were 20 *people* in the room.

People is also a collective noun that requires a plural verb and is used to refer to a single race or nation: The American *people* are united. In this sense, the plural form is *peoples:* The *peoples* of Africa speak many languages and dialects.

percent One word. It takes a singular verb when standing alone or when a singular word follows an "of" construction: The teachers said 60 percent was a failing grade. He said 50 percent of the membership *was* there.

It takes a plural verb when a plural word follows an "of" construction: He said 50 percent of the members *were* there.

percentages Use figures and decimals rather than fractions: *1 percent, 2.5 percent, 10 percent.* For amounts less than 1 percent, use a zero and decimals: *0.5 percent, 0.03 percent.*

Repeat percent with each individual figure: *He said 10 percent to 30 percent of the electorate may not vote.*

president Capitalize as a formal title before names: *President Kennedy, Presidents Kennedy and Johnson, President John Smith of Acme Corp.*

Drop the title after the first reference.

Lowercase in all other uses: The *president* left today. He is running for *president.* Lincoln was *president* during the Civil War.

The first name of a present or former U.S. president usually is not needed, but may be used in feature or personality stories. Use a first name if needed to avoid confusing one with another: *President Andrew Johnson, President Lyndon Johnson.*

Use a full name on first reference to others: *President Josip Broz Tito of Yugoslavia.* Not: President Tito.

prison, jail In general, a *prison* is any place of confinement: His back yard was his *prison.* As a place where criminals are confined:

> A *prison* or *penitentiary* is for those convicted of serious crimes carrying a penalty of more than a year.
>
> A *jail* is for those convicted of relatively minor offenses carrying a penalty of less than a year, for civil offenses such as non-payment of alimony, and for those awaiting trial or sentencing.
>
> A *reformatory* or *reform school* is for young offenders convicted of lesser crimes, sent for training and discipline intended to reform rather than punish.

Several euphemisms—*correctional institution, correctional center, detention center*—are widely used in proper names.

Capitalize a proper name or a widely used popular name: *Massachusetts Correctional Institution-Walpole* (the proper name), *Walpole State Prison* (a widely used popular name).

Lowercase plural or generic uses: *the Colorado and Kansas state penitentiaries, the federal prison, the state prison, the prison, the county jail, a federal detention center.*

prisoner of war *POW* is acceptable on second reference. Hyphenate as a compound modifier before a noun: *a prisoner-of-war trial.*

race Use a racial identification only if it is clearly pertinent, such as:

> In biographical and announcement stories, particularly when they involve a feat or appointment that has not been routinely associated with members of a particular race.
>
> When it provides the reader with a substantial insight into conflicting emotions known or likely to be involved in a demonstration or similar event.
>
> When describing a person sought in a manhunt.

In some stories that involve a conflict, it is equally important to specify that an issue cuts across racial lines. If, for example, a demonstration by supporters of busing to achieve racial balance in schools includes a substantial number of whites, that fact should be noted.

Do not use racially derogatory terms unless they are part of a quotation that is essential to the story. See nationalities.

royal titles As with all other titles, capitalize royal titles before a name; lowercase standing alone or set off by commas. See titles.
Some examples:

Queen Elizabeth II of England; Queen Elizabeth; Elizabeth, queen of England; the queen of England; the queen.

Prince Rainier of Monaco; Prince Rainier; Rainier, prince of Monaco; the prince of Monaco; the prince; a prince rules Monaco.

the duke of Windsor; the duchess of Windsor.

Prince Charles; Charles, prince of Wales; the prince of Wales; the prince; Charles, heir apparent to the British throne.

Princess Caroline of Monaco; Princess Caroline; the princess.

Russia, Soviet Union Russia is only one, but the largest, of 15 republics of the Soviet Union. Each republic has its own language, culture and history, although the Russian language is becoming more common throughout.
The distinction is often not observed. Most dictionaries, including Webster's New World, recognize *Russia* as the popular name of the Soviet Union.
As long as the meaning is clear, either name is acceptable. If needed, specify a particular republic, Russia, Georgia, Armenia, Lithuania, etc., in the text. The Ukrainian and Byelorussian republics are separate members of the United Nations.
Moscow stands alone in datelines. The form for others:

LENINGRAD, U.S.S.R. (UPI)

scores Use numerals exclusively, placing a hyphen between the totals of the winning and losing teams: *The Reds defeated the Red Sox 4-3. The Giants scored a 12-6 football victory over the Cardinals. The golfer had a 5 on the first hole but finished with a 2-under-par score.*
Use a comma in this format: *Boston 6, Baltimore 5.*
See separate listings for each sport.

sex changes Follow these guidelines in using proper names or personal pronouns when referring to an individual who has undergone a sex-change operation:

If the reference is to an action before the operation, use the proper name and gender of the individual at that time.

If the reference is to an action after the operation, use the new proper name and gender.

For example:
Dr. Richard Raskind was a first-rate amateur tennis player. *He* won several tournaments. Ten years later, when *Dr. Renee Richards* applied to play in tournaments, many women players objected on the grounds that *she* was the former Richard Raskind, who had undergone a sex-change operation. *Miss Richards* said *she* was entitled to compete as a woman.

slang Slang terms are not generally regarded as conventional. They are used, however, even by the best speakers, in highly informal contexts.
Examples: *short snort* for a drink of liquor or *bash* for a party.
Use slang terms with caution; they often pass into disuse in time. If slang is used, do not self-consciously enclose it in quotation marks unless it is a direct quotation. Provide a definition for any unfamiliar term.

state(s) Usually lowercase: *New York state, the state of Washington.* Also: *state Rep. William Smith, the state Transportation Department, state funds, state church, state bank, state of mind, state of the art.*
Capitalize as part of a proper name: *the U.S. Department of State, Washington State University.*
Four states—Kentucky, Massachusetts, Pennsylvania and Virginia—are legally known as commonwealths rather than states. Make the distinction only in formal uses: The *commonwealth of Kentucky* filed a suit. Elsewhere: Tobacco is grown in the *state of Kentucky.*
Always spell out the names of the 50 U.S. states standing alone.
With the name of a community, some states are abbreviated in stories, datelines or with party affiliation. See party affiliations.
Rule of thumb: Spell out Alaska and Hawaii. Abbreviate any of the 48 contiguous states with six or more letters; spell out those with five or fewer. The list:

Ala.	Conn.	Ill.	Md.	Mo.	N.M.	Ore.	Texas	Wis.
Alaska	Del.	Ind.	Maine	Mont.	N.Y.	Pa.	Utah	Wyo.
Ariz.	Fla.	Iowa	Mass.	Neb.	N.C.	R.I.	Va.	
Ark.	Ga.	Kan.	Mich.	Nev.	N.D.	S.C.	Vt.	
Calif.	Hawaii	Ky.	Minn.	N.H.	Ohio	S.D.	Wash.	
Colo.	Idaho	La.	Miss.	N.J.	Okla.	Tenn.	W.Va.	

time Specify the time in a story if it is pertinent: *a wreck at 3 a.m. Tuesday* gives a clearer picture than simply *a wreck Tuesday.*
Time zones usually are not needed: *a wreck at 3 a.m.* provides a clear picture without the time zone.

For planning purposes, provide times in a note above the body of the story:

Editors: The meeting begins at 10 a.m. PST.

In the continental United States use the time in the dateline community.

Outside the continental United States provide a conversion to Eastern time, if pertinent: *The kidnappers set a 9 a.m. (3 a.m. EDT) deadline.*

The forms:

1. Use figures except for noon and midnight. Use a colon to separate hours from minutes: *11 a.m. EST, 1 p.m.* today, *3:30 p.m.* Monday. Avoid redundancies such as *10 a.m.* this morning. Also, if clear: *4 o'clock.*

2. For sequences, use figures, colons and periods: *2:30:21.6* (hours, minutes, seconds, tenths).

3. The time zones in the United States and Greenwich Mean Time may be abbreviated as *EST, PDT, GMT* etc., if linked with a clock reading: *noon EDT, 9 a.m. MST, 3 p.m. GMT.* Do not abbreviate if there is no clock reading. Do not abbreviate other time zones outside the United States.

4. Capitalize each word of the proper name: Chicago observes *Central Daylight Time* in the summer. But: Denver is in the *Mountain time zone.*

titles Capitalize only formal titles when used before a name. Some specifics:

1. Lowercase and spell out all titles not used with a name: The *president* spoke. The *pope* gave his blessing. The *duchess of Windsor* smiled.

2. Lowercase and spell out all titles set off from a name by commas: The *vice president,* Nelson Rockefeller, declined to run again. Paul VI, the current *pope,* does not plan to retire.

3. Capitalize Mr., Mrs., Miss, Ms., etc., when used. See courtesy titles.

4. Capitalize formal titles with names: *Pope Paul, President Washington, Vice Presidents John Jones and William Smith.*

5. Lowercase titles that are primarily job descriptions: *astronaut John Glenn, movie star John Wayne, peanut farmer Jimmy*

Carter. If in doubt about whether a title is formal or merely a job description, set it off by commas and use lowercase.

6. Capitalize duke, king, queen, shah, etc., only when used directly before a name.

7. Set long titles off with a comma and use lowercase: *Charles Robinson, undersecretary for economic affairs.* Or: *the undersecretary for economic affairs, Charles Robinson.*

8. If a title applies to only one person in an organization, insert *the:* John Jones, *the* deputy vice president, spoke.

See **composition titles, honorary titles, legislative titles, military titles and religion.**

women   Women should receive the same treatment as men in all areas of coverage. Physical descriptions, sexist references, demeaning stereotypes and condescending phrases should not be used.
   To cite some examples, this means that:

Copy should not assume maleness when both sexes are involved, as in: *Jackson told newsmen . . . or in the taxpayer . . . he* when it can easily be said *taxpayers . . . they,* etc.

Copy should not express surprise that an attractive woman can also be professionally accomplished, as in: *Mary Smith doesn't look the part but she's an authority on . . .*

Copy should not gratuitously mention family relationships when there is no relevance to the subject, as in: *Golda Meir, a doughty grandmother, told the Egyptians today . . .*

Use the same standards for men as for women in deciding whether to include specific mention of personal appearance or marital and family situation.

In other words, treatment of the sexes should be evenhanded and free of assumptions and stereotypes. This does not mean that valid and acceptable words such as *mankind* or *humanity* cannot be used. They are appropriate if they fit the occasion.

Appendix B: Glossary of Newspaper Terms

A
Ad: any advertisement.
Ad alley: part of the production department that composes advertising.
Add: copy to be added to a story that is already written.
Agate: the type that is 5.5 points in depth.
Alive: type or copy that is still usable.
All up: all copy is in type.
AM: morning newspaper.
A-matter: copy to be set before the main body of the story.
Angle: a slant or the special aspect of a story.
AP: associated press.
Art: a general term for all newspaper illustrations, including photographs.
Astonisher: slang word for an exclamation point.

B
Backroom or Backshop: the mechanical section of a newspaper.
Bad break: makeup editors or printers use this term for difficulties in breaking a story from one column to another or when the first line in a column is short.
Bank: a part of a headline that is ordinarily used to designate the secondary part of a headline.
Banner: a headline stretching all or almost all the way across a page; also known as streamer, ribbon, or line.
Beat: an exclusive news story; also, a reporter's regular run, as *city hall beat*.
Ben Day: an engraving process to obtain shading effects in newspaper line illustrations.
B.F.   an abbreviation for boldface or black face type.
Bit: an elementary unit of digital information.

GLOSSARY OF NEWSPAPER TERMS

Bite off: to remove a paragraph(s) at the end of a story in making up a page.
Bleed: a cut bleeds when it runs to the edge of a page.
Blow up: an enlargement of any printed or engraved matter.
Body type: small type, usually 8-point, in which most news stories are printed.
Boil: to cut the length of a story, ordinarily by excising excess wordage.
Boiler plate: this is usually time copy in stereotype form.
Boldface: type that is darker and heavier than roman.
Book: a page of copy that has attached carbons.
Box: rules that are used to give a story or the headline alone prominent display on Page 1 or inside.
Break: when a story goes from one column to another or when a story goes from one page to another this term is used.
Bright or brightener: an amusing feature story.
Budget: a newspaper's or wire service's list of stories that are to come.
Bull dog: the earliest edition of a newspaper.
Bulletin: an urgent, last-minute news brief.
Bureau: a news-gathering force set in one city by a newspaper or wire service.
Byline: a signature of a reporter preceding a story.
Byte: a string of bits.

C

California case: an arrangement of letters in a font of type.
Camera-ready copy: the kind of copy ready for a platemaking system.
Canned copy: copy sent to newspapers by a public relations agency or another kind of business or organization.
Caps: capital letters.
Caption: the type appearing below or beside a cut.
Center: a short line of type that is set so that an equal amount of space is at the right and left of it.
Chase: a metal frame in which type and engravings are fitted to make a page.
Circus makeup: this kind of makeup uses display type, multiple-column heads, and much art in an unorthodox manner.
Clip: a newspaper clipping.
Cold type: characters set through a photographic or other process without the use of a Linotype machine or metal type.
Column: vertical area in a page. The work of a columnist is also known as a column.
Column rule: a thin line that runs from the top to the bottom of a page between two columns. Few newspapers use this today.
Command and command keys: a VDT operator directs the computer by pressing command keys.
Compiling: combining the text into a story from more than one source.
Control keys: the VDT keyboards have all the letters and figures. Control keys usually are marked in red to warn the operator that these keys will wipe out what is on the screen when used.
Copy: all news and feature typescript.
Copy desk: the desk where copy is edited and the headlines written.
Copy fitting: determining the size of type that will make an amount of copy fit a predetermined space.
Copyreader: a man or a woman who edits stories and writes headlines before they are sent to the composing room.
Core or core memory: a computer with the amount of memory available.

244 GLOSSARY OF NEWSPAPER TERMS

Correspondent: an out-of-town reporter.
Cover: to obtain all the available news about an event.
CPU: the part of a computer system that "thinks." The Central Processing Unit is the primary component of a computer.
CQ: anything marked with this is correct.
Credit line: a phrase that acknowledges the source of a cut or story.
Crop: cutting away sections of a picture.
Crossline: a one-line headline that is one of the decks. Few newspapers use this kind of headline today.
CRT: cathode ray tube. A TV-like screen; part of a terminal where a reporter works.
Cursor: a spot or line of light which may be moved from line to line and letter to letter on VDT screens to show the point where a correction must be made.
Cut: any art used in a newspaper (noun). To reduce the length of a story (verb).
Cutline: the type appearing below or beside a cut.
Cutoff rule: a line placed horizontally across one or several columns to separate units such as cuts, multicolumn heads, and the like.

D

DataNews: the high-speed news wire used by UPI.
DataSpeed: the high-speed news wire used by AP.
Dateline: the line at the top of Page 1 giving the date and place where the newspaper is published. Also, the line preceding an out-of-town story giving the date and place of origin.
Dead: material that has been killed. Used both in type and in copy.
Deadline: the last moment to have copy in for an edition.
Deck: a section of a headline.
Dingbat: any typographical ornament.
Directory: a listing of files contained in a computer's memory.
Display type: this is type larger than body type.
Dope story: this is an interpretive story beyond a straight news story.
Dot matrix: a pattern of dots representing each character on a VDT screen. This is illuminated by beams aimed at each dot.
Double truck: two pages of advertising or editorial matter made up as one page.
Down style: a style of writing that specifies little capitalization.
Drop head or Dropline head: a kind of headline where line is stepped at the right.
Dummy: a diagram or layout of a newspaper page.

E

Ears: small boxes or type on either side of the newspaper nameplate (flag) on Page 1.
Edition: all copies of a newspaper printed during one run of the presses.
Editorialize: to inject the writer's opinion into a news story or headline.
Electronic text processing: systems for processing text electronically in a computer.
Electronic typesetting: typesetting systems that are controlled electronically.
Em: the square of any size of type.
En: half an em.
Exclusive: a story printed by only one newspaper.
Extra: an edition other than those regularly published.

F

Face: a design of a family of type.
Family: all type of any one design.
Feature: to give special prominence to a story; also, the most important or interesting fact in a story; also, human interest or magazine-type of story.
File: send story by wire; also, a collection of back issues of a newspaper.
Filler: a short, minor story to fill space where needed.
Flag: front page title of a newspaper; also known as nameplate.
Flash: the wire services use this term to identify the first information of an important story.
Flimsy: the kind of thin paper used to make carbon copies or the carbon copy itself.
Fold: the point at which the front page is folded in half.
Follow-up: a story presenting new developments of a story previously printed; also known as a second-day story.
Font: an assortment of type of design, style, and size.
Form: a page of type within a chase.
Format keys: the VDT keys that give typesetting commands.
FORTRAN: a much used computer language.
Front-end system: everything that precedes platemaking in automated production.
Function keys: on VDT keyboards, the function keys carry out functions such as moving the cursor.
FYI: for Your Information.

G

Galley: a shallow metal tray for holding type as it comes from a composing machine.
Galley proof: a proof of a galley of type.
Glossy: this is short for *glossy print.*
Gothic type: a race of type.
Graph or graf: a paragraph.
Guideline: a slug or title given each story as a guide to both copy editor and printer.
Gutter: the margin between facing pages.

H

Halftone: a reproduction of a continuous-tone original.
Handout: a piece of publicity material.
Hard copy: a printout from a computer or the output of a high-speed machine that can print any text stored in a computer.
Head: headline.
Head schedule: a list of the typefaces used in a newspaper that specifies the unit count for each.
Hold for release **(HFR):** news not to be printed until a specified time or under specified circumstances.
Hole or newshole: the space available for news, features, columns, and the like.
HTK: head to come; endorsed on copy indicating that the headline will follow.
Human interest stories: an emotional appeal in stories; stories with emotional appeal as contrasted with straight news.
Hyphenation: systems on a computer that divide words between lines.

I

Index: a guide to the news run usually on the front page.
Input-output: a computer system uses the name "input" as unprocessed information; "output" is the same information after processing.
Insert: new material inserted in the body of a story already written.
Inverted pyramid: the standard straight news story with the facts in descending order of importance.
Issue: one day's newspaper, which may consist of several editions.
Italics: type in which letters and characters slant to the right.
ITU: International Typographical Union.

J

Jump: to continue a story from one page to another.
Jump head: a headline carried over a continued portion of a jumped story.
Justification: filling lines of letters and spaces or columns of lines. Also, for line justification in computer-based composition systems.

K

K: a measure of the size of the memory of a computer.
Kerning: fitting letters together closely.
Kicker: a small, short overline, often underlined, over the headline.
Kill: to strike out or discard part or all of a story.

L

Label head: a headline that lacks a verb.
LC: abbreviation for lower case.
Laser technology: a scanning device to transmit photographs. Also, a device that scans entire pages to produce page plates.
Layout: a diagram or a dummy of a newspaper page.
Lead (pronounced "led"): a strip of metal used for additional space between lines of type.
Lead (pronounced "leed"): the first paragraph (or several paragraphs) of a news or feature story.
Lead to come (pronounced "leed"): a copy mark is made to show that the lead will be sent to the composing room later. This is often used on a running story.
Letterpress printing: a process in which ink is given to paper from a raised surface.
Letterspace: inserting spaces between letters in a line of type.
Library: the same as a morgue. A place where the newspaper has clippings, photographs, and the like, as well as reference material.
Linage: this is the number of agate lines of advertising printed.
Line: the same as banner, streamer, or ribbon.
Linecasting machine: a usual term for machines that cast lines of type.
Line cut: an engraving that prints only black and white.
Live type: the type that may still be used.
Localize: to stress the local angle of a wire service story.

M

Makeover: this means making up a revised version of a page.
Makeup: arrangement of news, feature, art, and the like on a newspaper page.

247 GLOSSARY OF NEWSPAPER TERMS

Masthead: an editorial page box giving information about the paper. Does not refer to the flag or nameplate.
ME: managing editor.
Megabyte: 1000 bytes.
Memory: the storage of a computer.
Merge: to combine two or more sets of items into one.
Minion: seven-point type.
More: a word placed at the bottom of a page meaning that more is to come.
Morgue: the same as the library.
Must: a designation used on copy ordering that it be used without fail.

N

Nameplate: the newspaper's name at the top of Page 1.
New lead: a new or rewritten item replacing a lead already prepared; new lead usually contains new developments.
Nonpareil: six-point type.

O

Obituary: a death story or a biography of a dead person.
OCR: optical character recognition or reader; a device which interprets typewritten copy for a computer or typesetting machine.
Offset: because of the nature of the process, this is called photolithography printing.
On-line: ready to go. This is linked to the other hardware in a system.
Overline: the same as a kicker.
Overset: the type that has been set but cannot be used because of the lack of space.

P

Pad: to make a story or a headline longer by padding it with words.
Page proof: makeup errors are usually found in scanning the proof of an entire page.
Pagination: assigning page numbers to pages. Also, using large VDT screens to assemble entire pages.
Pagination terminal: a VDT designed to lay out pages.
Pasteup: this is process of making up a page for the camera.
Personal: brief news about one or more persons.
Photolithography: a process where ink is placed on paper from a rubber roller that has taken the impression from a plate.
Pi: jumbled type.
Pica: twelve-point type.
Pica em: twelve points by 12 points.
Pick up: add material already set.
Pi line: a line set by a machine that has been filled out with random letters.
Pix: pictures.
Plate: a piece of metal or plastic from which a page is printed.
Play up: to give prominence to.
PM: an afternoon newspaper.
Point: approximately 1/72 of an inch.
Policy: a story written to reflect the publisher's point of view.
PR: public relations.
Precede: a story that has new developments from a different kind of origin.

Privilege: a right granted to the press by the Constitution to print information with immunity that might otherwise be libelous.
Proof: an impression of type made on paper to make corrections.
Proof press: the press used to make proofs.
Proofreader: anyone who reads proofs for corrections.
Puff: a publicity item.

Q

Q and A: copy in question-and-answer form.
Queue: a memory segment of a computer that is reserved for particular use.
Quote: quotation.

R

Race: type in a set of similar families.
Ragged right: type that is not justified at the right.
Railroad: rushing copy to the composing room without editing.
Readout: a bank or a deck of headline type that is followed by a story.
Release: permitting publication of a story on a date and/or an hour.
Replate: recasting a page of type to insert more or later information or corrections.
Revise: after the first proof has been corrected, a second proof will be made to check for errors in the corrections.
Rewrite person: a staff member who rewrites but does not cover news.
Ribbon: the same as banner, streamer, and line.
Rim: outer edge of a copy desk where copyreaders work.
Ring: circling a copy correction.
Roman type: one of the basic races of type.
Rotogravure: a process of printing in which copy is etched on a copper roller.
Roundup: a comprehensive story from several sources.
Routing: cutting metal from blank areas in a casting or cut.
Rule: a metal strip that prints as a line.
Run: a term for a reporter's beat. Also, a press run.
Running story: a fast-breaking story written in sections or takes.

S

Scanner: an optical character reading (OCR) machine.
Schedule: a city editor's record of assignments.
Scoop: an exclusive story.
Script: a kind of typeface designed to imitate handwriting.
Scrolling: a user of a VDT can roll back and forward the lines on a screen to see what has already been input.
Second-day story: new developments in a story printed in a previous edition.
Set and hold: a copy mark that means "Set in type and hold for release."
Shoulder: a space on any piece of type between the bottom of a character and the edge of the slug.
Slant: to emphasize a phase of a story.
Slot: the inside of a copy desk where the chief sits.
Slug: a guideline set in type. Also, a notation placed on a story to identify it or specify disposal.
Software-hardware: software refers to the computer programming that operates any computer based system. Hardware means the computer, terminals, and other electronic machinery.

Stereotype: converting the newspaper page into a semicylindrical metal plate to fit a rotary press.
Stet: a copy mark meaning "Let it stand"; used to correct a mistake in editing.
Straight news: a plain recital of new facts written in a standard style and form.
Streamer: the same as banner and line.
String: the stringer's newspaper clippings. Also, a reporter's output during a period.
Stringer: a part-time reporter who works for a newspaper and who is paid by the amount of space his or her reports take.
Style sheet: a list of spellings, capitalizations, and the like to insure that the editors and reporters know the style of a newspaper or wire service.
Subhead: a small head inserted in the body of a newspaper story to break up long stretches of type.
Summary lead: a lead summarizing high points, usually including all five Ws.
Suspended interest: a news story with the climax at the end.
Syndicate: an organization that sells many kinds of feature materials.
System: computer capabilities including a central processing unit (CPU).

T

Tabular subroutines: word processing systems can be programmed to fit keyboarded information into tabular formats.
Take: a portion of copy in a running story, often one page.
Telegraph editor: an editor (also known as "wires editor") in charge of handling telegraph or wire news.
Teletypesetter (TTS): a trademark applied to a machine that transmits and sets news into type automatically.
Think piece: a background story or an opinion story.
Thirty (30): the end of a story; placed on the last page to signify the end.
Throughput: in a unit of time, the amount of information processed by a system.
Tie-back or tie-in: information previously printed and included in a story to refresh the reader's memory.
Time copy: stories that are relatively timeless. They can be used at any time.
Tip: information that may lead to a story.
Tombstone: placing side by side two or more headlines that are similar in typeface.
Top deck: the first and most important part of a headline.
tr: a mark meaning *transpose.*
Trim: the same as boil.
Typeface: the same as face.
Type-high: the height of type—.918 inches—in hot metal systems.
Typo: short for typographical error.

U

Universal desk: on large newspapers, this is a copy desk where all copy is handled, except for specialized copy.
UPI: United Press International.
Uppercase: capital letters.
Up style: a style of writing that calls for much capitalization.
Urgent: this is the third designation by wire services (*flash* is first, *bulletin* is second) that signals an important story or the beginning of a story.

V

VDT: video display terminal. Synonymous with CRT.

W

White space: blank space.
Widow: a word or part of a word that stands alone as the last line of a paragraph of body type. When a widow appears at the top of a column, it is called a bad break.
Wild: a story that may run on any inside page.
Word: a string of bits that is treated as a unit.
Wrap: continuing a story from a column to the next column.
Wrap up: this means finishing a story when all the facts are in. Also, an edition is finished when all copy has gone to the composing room.
Wrong font: type of one size or style appearing with type of another size or style.

X

Xerography: electrostatic printing.

Z

Zinc: a photoengraving.